Natural Born!

Circus, Sideshow, and the Art of Being Human

Aaron Smith

Published by Outside Talker Press (an imprint of Vaudevisuals Press)

in partnership with Shocked and Amazed! Imprints (a subsidiary of

Dolphin-Moon Press)

Copyright © 2025 by Aaron Smith

All rights reserved. No portion of this book may be reproduced in any form without written permission from the publisher or author, except as permitted by U.S. copyright law.

Layout by Nathan Wakefield
Edited by James Taylor
Cover design by Lisa Marie Pompilio
Front cover photography by Laure Leber

PER002000   PERFORMING ARTS / Circus
DRA032000   DRAMA / Disability Theater *
BIO033000   BIOGRAPHY & AUTOBIOGRAPHY / Disability

ISBN: 978-1-790585816

Library of Congress Control Number: 2023910643

Published by Outside Talker Press (an imprint of Vaudevisuals Press) in partnership with Shocked and Amazed! Imprints (A Subsidiary of Dolphin-Moon Press).

www.outsidetalkerpress.com
www.shockedandamazed.com

For Sam and Winona

Contents

Foreword	1
Introduction: Why I Wrote Natural Born!	3
1. Shorty the Half-Man	7
2. The Lobster Girl	14
3. The Seal Boy	24
4. The Poison Pill	30
5. American Horror Story	34
6. Black Scorpion	41
7. The Bendable Girl	49
8. Life After Freak Show	58
9. Tyler West	65
10. Coney Island	70
11. Freak Finder	81
12. The Patchwork Girl	84
13. The Mayor of Coney Island	94
14. Woman With a Beard	102
15. Illustrated Penguin	112
16. Modified Marvel	120
17. Sarah the Bird Girl	126
18. Jackie the Human Tripod	130
19. Lil Miss Firefly	139

20. World of Wonders	147
21. Alan Silva	155
22. Xander Lovecraft	161
23. John T. Rex	172
24. Dakota the Bearded Lady	181
25. Being Human	186
26. Shorty's Last Tour	191
27. Nik Sin	196
28. Nati Returns to Coney	202
29. Rik Daniels and the Omnium Circus	206
30. Cottonmouth Clown	213
31. Florida Man	216
Additional Photos	224
Photo Credits	225
Bibliography	230
About the Author	244
About the Foreword Author	245

Foreword

> Lisa B. Lewis,
> founder of
> Omnium
> Circus

It is a great gift in this world to be able to live life on your own terms. To love and respect the body you inhabit and the skin you are in. To define yourself as you choose to be perceived, and to make that statement loud and proud- living your life to its fullest and making the world a better place for you having done so. In my humble experience, this simple goal is fraught with a variety of challenges for each of us: financial, societal, physical, and emotional. 25% of the people in the world have a disability, 90% of us will experience one at some point in our lives. This human desire is too often additionally hindered by a world that is only in its infancy of understanding that we are all human and capable of greatness, each in our own way.

I am the founder of Omnium Circus. Our mission is to create world-class entertainment that celebrates diversity, accessibility, and inclusion. We are loud and proud of who we are and the incredible skills we have worked so hard to achieve, and we want to share this with the world.

Toward that goal, we consciously remove as many barriers as possible for performers and audiences so everyone can have equitable access to incredible entertainment in every show. Accessibility benefits everyone!

Those who are "natural born", those who have learned new ways of using bodies whose usage has changed, and those who have faced entirely different challenges along their journeys.

Driven by the voices which had filled my ears for many years... families begging for a place to bring their entire family, the sibling with autism and the sibling without, the parent who is blind and the cousin who is deaf.

They never saw themselves represented in the arts, they couldn't even enjoy it together because the bridges of access did not exist for them with any consistency. It was time to make it happen.

The word "Omnium" means "of all and belonging to all." We strive to present award-winning artistry by people with and without disabilities from a mosaic of cultures and communities, just like our world. We provide additional access for our audiences through a bilingual production in ASL and English, captioning, audio description for the blind and low vision, tactile experiences and sensory supports and a relaxed environment so everyone can feel welcome. The result is a magical experience for performers and audiences alike.

At almost every single Omnium Circus show, there is at least one individual for whom the achievements by those with situations similar to their own have given them hope and motivated them to try harder. While I have not attended every single performance of every artist featured here, I imagine a similar experience is often true for them as well. They share their artistry, their frustration, their joy, and their passion so that we, the audience, are better for the experience.

Each "natural born" artist featured in this book faces challenges and opportunities in their own way, making their own choices and together creating a community of genuinely gifted performing artists. To quote Rik Daniels, "This is the body I was born with. If you have an issue with it, that is your problem, not mine."

Perhaps there is more potential inside each of us than a passing glance will uncover? Perhaps it is worth the effort to dig deeper. Perhaps when we share laughs, screams, ooohs, and aaaahhs, we connect on a deeper level—a more purely human one. Maybe we can take that connection back to our home communities, workplaces, and houses of worship and maybe... change the way we perceive others. Possibly, we will be more mindful of creating access and genuine welcome so people with disabilities can spend less time figuring out how to open the door and more time actually "in the room where it happens" (quote from *Hamilton*, the musical).

I am honored to write the foreword for these stories. I hope that each of you reading this book, with or without a disability, will respect and honor the achievements of these talented performers, deeply consider your choices to live your own life to its fullest, and take responsibility for making sure others can do the same.

Introduction: Why I Wrote Natural Born!

Aaron Smith

Natural Born! Circus, Sideshow, and the Art of Being Human is a non-fiction book about disabled performers in sideshows and circuses. This is not a history book. It's a living, breathing, 21st-century story about performers who call themselves "natural born," or "naturals," because they were born with their disabilities, which places them at the top of the sideshow hierarchy, above the non-disabled. My book features interviews with 20 naturals who explain in their own words why they choose to exhibit themselves in sideshows, like Coney Island, and circuses, like Omnium Circus.

Sideshows originated in the circus, and both platforms have a mixed history that includes exploitation. For example, Millie and Christine McCoy were Black American conjoined twins who were enslaved in the 19th century. Daisy and Violet Hilton were conjoined twins who were practically enslaved even though they were living in the 20th century. They were sideshow naturals forced to perform in freak shows and vaudeville.

But to my knowledge, no one is being forced to exhibit themselves in sideshows or circuses anymore. The people I interviewed for this book – including Mat Fraser, Kim Kelly, Aaron Wollin, Black Scorpion, Alan Silva and Rik Daniels – insisted it's a voluntary occupation. So why do they do it?

I'm a journalist and a former circus worker. I started to write *Natural Born!* during the COVID pandemic in 2021. I had already written *Circus Jerks* about my teenage adventures with Ringling Brothers and Barnum & Bailey and the Big Apple Circus. I wanted to write another book that was exciting and unique.

In May 2021, I saw the term "natural born" on the website for the Sideshow Hootenanny, an organization of sideshow performers and producers. The Hoot, as they call it, was offering membership discounts to anyone natural born. I was familiar with the term "natural born" from the Constitution, but the Hoot was using it in a different context, to refer to physically disabled performers. I was amazed to learn that there were still natural born performers in sideshows in the U.S. and that there enough of them to warrant a membership discount. I decided to write a book about them.

I contacted Aaron "Shorty" Wollin, a self-proclaimed "half-man" with sacral agenesis who was touring with a Florida-based circus sideshow called Hellzapoppin. I watched Shorty's masochistic act in New Jersey where he leapt onto broken flaming glass with his bare hands, even though he walks on those hands because he has no feet. Shorty, a former race driver, has toured the world as a sideshow stuntman. "This is the life I've chosen, and if anybody is exploiting anybody, I'm exploiting myself," he said. He had a unique and customized performance that no one else could do.

I interviewed Mat Fraser, a sideshow celebrity and TV actor with Thalidomide-induced phocomelia, Black Scorpion, a sideshow performance artist with ectrodactyly, and Kim Kelly, a journalist with ectrodactyly who wrote about her sideshow experiences. They had all performed at Coney Island's Sideshows by the Seashore and they introduced me to other people in the business. Mat is a disability activist and TV actor who co-starred in the *Freak Show* season of *American Horror Story*. Mat told me that a "born freak" gets top billing at a freak show, compared to firebreathers and glass walkers who aren't disabled. "Some poor guy who's got half his face burned off, and his lungs burned up, and he's been fire breathing for 20 years, he's got to take second place to me," said Mat.

Mat wrote a panto musical called *Dick Rivington & The Cat*, directed by his wife Julie Atlas Muz in 2022 and co-starring Tyler West, a little person, as a costumed cat clown with a penchant for acrobatics and wisecracks with double entendre. Tyler was already a circus veteran when I spoke to him at age 27 in the fall of 2024. He had just moved to Las Vegas to perform in the risqué Western-style Atomic Saloon Show at Spiegelworld. He'd been in four circuses, often as a clown. "When I work in circuses, I try really hard not to be the butt of the joke," said Tyler. He said that in *Dick Rivington*, Mat and Julie cast him as the most powerful character in the show, the only one who can connect with the audience as well as the cast.

Natural borns still perform in modern-day circuses, though the roles have changed. Alan Silva, a little person, was the ringmaster of the Big Apple Circus when I saw him perform as an aerialist in the winter of 2022-2023. That was at Lincoln Center in Manhattan, the traditional wintering spot of the Big Apple circus. When I was in the circus, in the 1980s, the little people were clowns. Alan, a sixth-generation circus performer from

Brazil, said that other children threw rocks at him when he was a kid. They said he could only be a clown. Alan, who is rippling with muscle, did become a clown, and also an aerialist who performed on *America's Got Talent*. He's married, with two kids.

The fundamental reality of *Natural Born!* is that I am a non-disabled person writing a book about disabled people. I did my best to present the perspectives of sideshow naturals in their own words, whenever possible and to show respect for whom they are and what they're doing.

There are some good books about sideshow and circus naturals including *Freak Show* by Robert Bogdan, *Very Special People* by Frederick Drimmer and *The Wonders* by John Woolf. But those are history books about naturals who died a long time ago. This book showcases live circus naturals in the 2020s, like a modern version of *Freaks*, the classic movie that serves as a 1932 time capsule of natural borns.

The point of *Natural Born!* is to bring attention to sideshows and circuses as a modern artform for disabled performers who choose to exhibit themselves on the bally platform, the stage and in the center ring. Sideshow has an offensive reputation for exploiting disabled people and is therefore shunned by upstanding citizens who won't pay to gawk at exhibitionists with physical disabilities. Fair enough. But this perception is a hangover from the 19th and 20th centuries which ignores the fact that many naturals, including Tom Thumb and Prince Randian, prospered as sideshow stars.

Rik Daniels, born with arthrogryposis, is an acrobatic dancer at the Omnium Circus, his third circus. He uses a wheelchair and his muscular torso contrasts with his diminutive legs. He learned to break-dance while growing up in the Bronx and competed in high school gymnastics as an NCAA All-American seven-time champion, placing on pommel horse, parallel bars and still rings. He wheels onto the stage at Omnium for a dance performance that blends break-dancing with gymnastics. He does handstands on the wheelchair, his child-like legs pointing to the ceiling. "I think that people with disability have as much right as anybody else to objectify themselves," he explained.

Sideshows and circuses have evolved since the days of the Elephant Man and the Lobster Boy. The 21st-century performers are independent and autonomous, with sophisticated self-awareness and a punk rock attitude. They know what they're doing and they know what people think. They know that the reality of sideshows and the popular perception of them are different things. Many people, especially disabled people, don't like sideshows. Jackie "The Human Tripod" Molen performed as a natural in various sideshows and said the protesters never actually saw the performances. If the critics haven't seen a modern sideshow, then they're basing their criticism on what they used to be.

In writing this book, I had the honor of meeting Prof. Jennifer Miller of Pratt Institute, AKA Woman with a Beard. She used to perform at the Coney Island Circus Sideshow, but she also has her own show, Circus Amok. I saw her perform on the Coney Island boardwalk in the summer of 2024. She was juggling with her LGBTQ-friendly partners and changing through a dizzying array of outfits at the foot of the iconic Parachute Jump. She told me that attitudes about sideshow naturals have changed. "Now, it's with a wink," she said. "It's part of a post-modern reconstruction deconstruction."

Disabled people have chosen sideshows and circuses as their platform for customized artistic expression, where their disability serves as the centerpiece. They feel empowered rather than exploited, especially since they're acting on their own volition.

I'm a Florida native, and I grew up across Tampa Bay from Gibsonton, home of the World of Wonders, the oldest still-operating sideshow in America, and quite possibly the world. Tommy Breen, the owner of World of Wonders, said that most of his audience members are seeing sideshow for the first time, so for them it's completely new. This means that modern performers are free to reinvent sideshow as they see fit while adhering to enough of the old traditions to keep it real, recognizable, and authentic.

Natural Born! invites you to consider the modern role of sideshows in America as a positive force for disabled artists. They are the stars of an art form that they have claimed and reinvented as their own. The sideshow belongs to the natural born.

Nov. 15, 2024
Brooklyn, NY

Chapter 1

Shorty the Half-Man

"Born to lose. Live to win."
- Motörhead frontman Lemmy Kilmister's tattoo

This was not an ordinary night in New Jersey, and this was not an ordinary nightclub act. Aaron Wollin is a sideshow half-man daredevil who goes by the stage name Short E. Dangerously. He's a human trunk, with a head and arms and some tattoos, but no legs. Clad in a cowboy hat and leather biker vest, Shorty — as his friends call him — hopped bodily from his circus bucket stool and landed hands-first on a flaming pile of broken glass. He grimaced as the shards, splinters, and bottlenecks popped, tinkled and stabbed under the impact of his fingers and palms. He howled, his face transfixed with what must have been pain. But then he started kneading the glass shards with his long and sinewy hands, and he smiled and nodded to the audience, as if he were *enjoying* it. He pounded and ground his fingertips into the glass, bouncing from one hand to the next. While laughing at us! Everyone in the audience knew we were going to watch a legless man jump onto broken glass. It seemed like an open-minded crowd, receptive to nontraditional thrills. ("I'm transgender," said the audience member next to me. "I know what it's like to feel like a freak.") But it was still shocking to see Shorty up close. "This is not fake glass," he announced to the crowd. "Not sugar glass. This is *real fucking glass*." He warned the audience that he was wearing "no protection" and they should be ready to dial 911.

Walking on broken glass on either your hands or feet isn't easy, but a lot of performers do it. Over the years, it's become a risky and classic sideshow act, like sword swallowing, fire breathing, pushing skewers through live flesh, and inserting power tools into the cranial cavities of living people.

Shorty's hips and legs were amputated when he was two and a half years old. He only has his arms and his hands, which is what makes his stunt unique. When he jumps onto broken glass doused in lighter fluid, he sacrifices his precious hands, which he uses for walking and most everything else.

"I wanted to risk it all," he told me after his show, displaying his scarred hands as proof that the stunt was real. "And what bigger risk could I take than by using my hands?"

Shorty, as he prefers to be called, is a Mötorhead-loving masochist who breathes fire. He does a one-armed handstand, balancing on one hand while raising his free fingers in the infamous devil horn salute. He stage-dives into mosh pits at punk and heavy metal shows. He's been to 22 countries, four continents, and all over the U.S. He was a sponsored drag racer in a car specially outfitted with hand controls.

I hesitated to call him by a nickname that seemed to mock his condition, but he insisted that I call him Shorty. He didn't want to be called by his first name. His mother was the one who called him Aaron, he explained. He credits his mother for raising him as a single parent from age 5 after his parents split up. She died in 2005. He thinks about her when people call him Aaron, and it makes him sad.

As a half-man, Shorty is the most unreal of any living natural I've met, in the sense that he almost seems impossible, as if his lower half is invisible. But it's not invisible. It just simply isn't there. Shorty has a rare birth defect called sacral agenesis where the lower part of the spine, the sacrum, is contorted during the development of the fetus. One baby out of tens of thousands is born this way. No one seems to know why. There are different types of SA and several names for it, like SA/CRS, which stands for sacral agenesis/caudal regression syndrome, a blanket acronym for the condition. There's another form called lumbosacral agenesis, where vertebrae are missing. There are different levels of severity. Some people with SA/CRS have legs, and some do not.

People with SA/CRS have done amazing things. On Sept. 23, 2021, 19-year-old Zion Clark, who has a muscular torso but no legs or hips, ran using only his arms and set a Guinness World Record for the fastest man on hands: 20 meters in 4.78 seconds.

Shorty, who calls himself the shortest daredevil in the world, is a so-called natural born, which puts him in a unique class of disabled sideshow performers. These are the human oddities, as they were once called — the people have been known throughout history by the offensive term "freaks." Shorty refers to them as naturals, though he's less sensitive when describing himself.

"I don't care; I'm a freak," said Shorty, when I asked if there's a correct label for disabled sideshow performers. "A freak of nature is somebody who does not look normal and who doesn't do normal things. A natural-born freak is someone like myself."

Sideshow naturals are rare, but they do exist. The Coney Island Circus Sideshow in Brooklyn, New York, is the epicenter of the modern freak show, located in an antique building off the boardwalk that has hosted sideshows since the old days. Coney Island has staged shows by Mat Fraser of *American Horror Story: Freak Show*, a British actor whose arms were shortened by thalidomide; Kim Kelly, a journalist with ectrodactyly who has performed as Greta the Lobster Girl; and a paralympic swimmer from Australia named Sarah Houbolt who performs as KooKoo the Bird Girl. She named herself after the original KooKoo, who appeared in the 1932 movie *Freaks* with a half-man named Johnny Eck.

Shorty wasn't always a sideshow star. He smoked weed to get through his teenage years, ditched his wheelchair for a skateboard, and eventually found his way. His career as a sideshow stuntman and entertainer has been circuitous. He started as an emcee in strip clubs, where only the novelty of a natural entertainer, a half-man with corny self-deprecating wisecracks, could distract the horny clients from the dancers. It was possible, said Shorty, to make $1,000 or even more on an exceptional night in the strip clubs.

Shorty, who lives in Daytona, Florida, has worked as a DJ and emcee in nightclubs and strip clubs for 16 years. In 2012, he joined a sideshow called World of Wonders, and he found himself traveling the world as a professional half-man. Later that year, he joined the Hellzapoppin Circus Sideshow Revue, a fire-breathing, sword-swallowing, razor-blade-eating troupe that's a blend of punk rock, sickening stunts, burlesque, tattoos, heavy metal and old-school carnival. He was with them in the summer of 2021, touring America during the dark days of the coronavirus pandemic.

Shorty is an admirer of his predecessor Johnny Eck, a suit-wearing half-man who starred in the legendary *Freaks*, a creepy but ultimately sympathetic portrayal of sideshow naturals that got banned in some places — which made people want to see it more. Johnny walked on his hands, just like Shorty. Johnny used to do his signature one-armed handstand, just like Shorty, but without the devil horns. Johnny and Shorty were both race car drivers, using vehicles with hand controls. Shorty and Johnny would both wear heavy gloves when hand-walking outside.

In other ways, Johnny was different from Shorty. Johnny was born in 1911 with no legs, along with an identical twin brother who was not disabled. He began performing as a tween and developed a wide range of skills. According to the book *Very Special People*, he could swim, dive, play the clarinet and saxophone, walk the tightrope, juggle, dance and compose music. He was the conductor of his 12-piece orchestra in Baltimore.

A coffee table book by Ripley's Believe It Or Not! called *Sideshow and Other Carnival Curiosities* features impressive photo spreads of Shorty balancing on bowling balls and Johnny (real name John Eckhardt Jr.) driving a 1930s race car called the "Special." It explains how Johnny was walking on his hands before his brother Robert learned to walk on his feet. They would perform in the sideshow together, playing off their identical appearance to shock the rubes.

"Johnny is a personal hero of mine," said Shorty. The Ripley's profile features side-by-side photos of Shorty and Johnny doing handstands.

"He paved the way for guys like me," he said. "I hope to live up to his legacy and surpass it at the same time. I know that he never did fire breathing or glass walking or any of that stuff." By turning up his act, by making it more dangerous, Shorty plans to get his adrenaline fix and surpass his hero at the same time. "My goal? In 40 years, I want people to talk about me, like they talk about him now," he said. Shorty is making his mark on the world. He appeared in a *National Geographic* profile and AMC's reality TV series *Freak Show*. He's the lone natural among a cast of heavily tattooed and body-modified entertainers known in the trade as "self-made," or "self-inflicted," because they weren't born that way. They did it to themselves. Shorty has also performed at live events for Ripley's, and he said they made wax statues in his likeness, displayed around the world. He has appeared in numerous publications including *High Times*, which is how I met him.

In the summer of 2021, Shorty performed at a nightclub in Clifton, N.J., with the Hellzapoppin Circus Sideshow Revue, and I went there to see him.

When I first saw Shorty, I was in the audience and he was on stage, doing his one-armed handstand and flashing his signature devil horns. As he built up to his glass act, he talked a bit about his condition. He said that he overhears people say, "I thought *I* had problems," when they catch sight of him. He figured he'd become a professional performer. "Now, they've got to *pay* to stare at me," he said.

Crew members dumped the glass onto the stage and invited the audience to grind a wine bottle into the shards. Bryce "The Govna" Graves, founder and frontman of Hellzapoppin, then doused the glass with lighter fluid and set it all on fire, and Shorty did his thing. I was close enough to hear the glass pop as he ground his fingers into it.

Later in the show, the sword swallower Auzzy Blood swung Shorty from a pair of logging chains that were hooked onto the lower bone ridges of Auzzy's eye sockets. Since Shorty weighed 80 pounds, Hellzapoppin claimed this as a world record.

After the show, I introduced myself, and Shorty was standing on his hands on the stage. We talked briefly, and he paused to fist-bump a colleague, which he did effortlessly while balancing on his other hand. He scarcely moved his torso while doing this, as if he were standing on two legs. After chatting with him for a few minutes, I realized that since he was on stage and I was offstage, we were the same height, and I had forgotten, for part of that time, that he had no legs or hips.

Later, in Hellzapoppin's RV after the show, he seemed to sink into the couch, like a man whose legs and waist had been swallowed up by the furniture. He was holding a bong that was taller than he was. Then he went back outside to guard the gear while his colleagues were loading it in the truck. He donned protective gloves and hand-walked along the sidewalk outside the nightclub. It was strange to see him take this precaution with his hands, an hour after he used them to break his fall on a pile of broken bottles — but he needed to give his brutalized hands a break. A couple of weeks later, as Hellzapoppin toured Michigan, Shorty told me by phone that his hands were "beat the fuck up – they look like hamburger."

We strolled over to the trailer. The night was warm and dry. A few people were walking around, even though it was late. When he's out in public, Shorty's height becomes more noticeable to onlookers, though it's not so noticeable to him. He's insouciant about getting stared at.

"I feel the eyes on me, but I'm numb to it," he said.

Shorty rested on a cushion that he brought with him to the sidewalk next to the trailer. The back door was slid open, revealing stacks of lighting structures. His co-workers Bryce and Auzzy showed up with more equipment to load into the trailer. They were wearing orange safety helmets required by OSHA, which was ironic. Just an hour before, Auzzy was doing pushups while swallowing swords, twisting a gigantic corkscrew through his nose, and swinging Shorty from his orbitals. Bryce had been putting a power drill up his nose and also a screwdriver and a condom, which he flicked into the audience. "Don't be a fool, wrap your tool!" he advised.

I wrote a story about Shorty and his love of cannabis sativa for *High Times* called "Shorty: Weed-Smoking Sideshow 'Half-Man' Lives on Bong Hits and Broken Glass."

Shorty has a Florida medical marijuana card and uses it to treat pain. He pulled off his gloves, revealing the scars and cuts and chafing on his hands, with many shows yet to go on the tour, and many more sessions of bouncing on glass.

Shorty told me that he quit drinking several years ago. The cannabis helped him to stay off the booze. But he briefly fell off the wagon to do "half a shot" with the Lizardman to celebrate his birthday because, as he explained, "The Lizardman is my boy."

After midnight, we wrapped it up. It was hard to leave Shorty and his friends. I told them that I used to be in Ringling Brothers and the Big Apple Circus, as a talker, a vendor and a roustabout. While Bryce acknowledged that my circus credentials were legit, I still felt like an interloper in this elite troupe as it was tearing down and packing up to head somewhere new, to breathe fire and swallow swords and jump on glass.

It seemed to me like Shorty wasn't missing out on anything, though he'd picked a rough way to make a living, slicing up his precious hands most every night.

Some sideshows had a history of exploitation, but modern sideshows allow naturals to enjoy autonomy and make a living. I asked Shorty if he was being exploited.

"This is the life I've chosen, and if anybody is exploiting anybody, I'm exploiting myself," he said.

I also asked Bryce about it. I'd heard that people had accused him of exploiting Shorty, though it didn't seem to me that he was. He vehemently denied the accusations.

"Just because someone like Shorty is a half-man doesn't mean he can't also be a performing artist!" said Bryce. "Shorty has lived the life of 10 men and has experienced things most can't even dream of."

Chapter 2

The Lobster Girl

"Over the past century and a half, the museum's collection has grown to include tumors cut from presidents, the jarred brains of madmen and geniuses, deformed skeletons displayed in delicate glass cases, Civil War surgical tools still caked in dried blood, and even the death cast of Chang and Eng Bunker, the famous sideshow act, a pair of conjoined brothers who inspired the term Siamese twins."
– from *Dr. Mutter's Marvels* by Christin O'Keefe Aptowicz

Kim Kelly is a natural born sideshow performer with ectrodactyly. She's a rare and elite prodigy, a fire-breather, born with eight fingers, who walks on broken glass.

She's also a journalist and an author. She has written about her experience training in Coney Island as a sideshow performer named Greta the Lobster Girl. Kim lives in Philadelphia, home of the Mütter Museum, a sprawling Wunderkammer of medical and pathological remains. The museum is a macabre presence in downtown Philly, a stone mansion that stands out like Dracula's Castle. There are skeletons in glass cases, rows and rows of human skulls, and collections of "wet specimens," which are fleshy body parts suspended in liquid, in glass jars with hand-written labels from the 1800s.

I asked Kim to accompany me to the Mütter Museum, which houses the collection of the ground-breaking 19th-century surgeon Dr. Thomas Dent Mütter. I figured that as a journalist, she would be intrigued. But I was worried that she would take offense at my audacious invitation to a medical museum filled with human body parts presented as specimens.

Thankfully, she said yes. She *was* intrigued.

In October 2021, I rode the train to Philadelphia and met Kim for lunch. Kim (who was 33) said she had never heard of the word ectrodactyly until she was in her twenties.

Ectrodactyly is also known as split-hand/split-foot malformation, or lobster claw hand, according to the National Institutes of Health. The NIH describes it as a hereditary limb malformation involving median clefts of the hands and feet, "which gives the appearance of a lobster." It occurs in about one in 90,000 births.

Kim considers her disability to be relatively mild, in the grand scheme. Her right hand is normal, but her left hand has three fingers. Her left hand has a thumb, and two other fingers, but the middle one is not usable. She said this has not hampered her career as a journalist and an author, because she can type with eight fingers. She can also disguise her disability, if she wants to. "At the end of the day, I have a visible deformity that's practically invisible if I stuck my hands in my pockets," she said. But she admitted that opening jars with a disabled hand is "fucking annoying." She gets her boyfriend to do it.

Back in 2019, she wrote an eye-catching story for *Vox* about her experience training at the Coney Island Circus Sideshow's Sideshows by the Seashore. She learned how to breathe fire and also how to eat fire, which is more dangerous. "As every cell in my body screamed, I stuck out my tongue, drew the fire into my mouth, and closed my lips around the torch in one measured motion," she wrote.

Kim used to live in New York, and she discovered the sideshow while visiting Coney Island with her boyfriend. She attended a four-day training session for $1,500, with seven other students, to learn the secrets of the sideshow. Her trainer was Adam Realman, as he calls himself, a sword swallower and diehard Coney Island fanatic who led the class. (His real name is Adam Rinn, and he has since been promoted to artistic director of Coney Island USA, following the tenure of Dick Zigun.) She learned a variety of tricks, like walking on broken glass and reclining on a bed of nails.

The experience was a turning point for her. At the start of the Coney Island class, standing in a small crowd, Adam called out if anyone was "natural born." She was the only person who raised her hand. When that happened, she felt an epiphany rush through her. "This is an asset, this aspect of me that I always downplayed," she said. "This gives me an edge. That was such a good thing to feel after a lifetime of hiding my hands in my pockets."

She'd always known her condition was rare. "You don't see people with lobster claws walking around," she said. She'd only met a couple of people with ectrodactyly, including a guy she encountered at a metal show. She said he was "kind of cute" and she figured they would make "a cute kind of handy couple." But he "turned out to be a Nazi," she said, so she moved on.

But the sideshow had enlightened her with a new perspective. At Coney Island, her disability was spotlighted as something rare *and* special, which elevated her from everyone else in the room. "They actually valued this weird thing about me, which has always been a complicated part of my life," she said. "Being part of the sideshow world, there is something different about me that is cool, and I don't have to hide it." The sideshow people were the first to treat her like she was lucky to be born that way.

Kim said that she didn't feel unlucky, necessarily, and she tended to downplay her disability. "It hasn't affected my love life," she said, by way of example. "I dodged a bullet. Having eight fingers is not that big a deal. You don't need ten fingers, that's excessive." She said it's no impediment to her writing, either. "Honestly, I type really fucking fast," she said.

We were eating lunch at an Asian restaurant as she said this, and I was typing down her words on my oversized laptop, stumbling over misspellings and jumbles of letters, hyper-conscious of my ten fumbling fingers. She once wrote a critique of *American Horror*

Story: Freak Show, a TV show featuring a fictional institution in Philadelphia called the American Morbidity Museum that collects wet specimens of sideshow naturals. Sound familiar? It's a creepy shout-out to Mütter. She was offended by the show's over-the-top portrayal of a man with ectrodactyly, with outsized prosthetics for his hands. Evan Peters - an actor who appeared in 100 episodes of *American Horror Story* - played Peter Darling, the sideshow performer with ectrodactyly. Peters was fitted with costume claw hands with the fingers fused to form V-shapes, like the Vulcan greeting on *Star Trek*. "The prosthetics were exaggerated to the point where it was a little offensive," Kim told me. "We look interesting enough where you don't have to make a buffoonish cartoon character." I asked her about a scene where the character with ectrodactyly gets his hands amputated and put on display at the Morbidity Museum. "That was kind of visceral," said Kim. It reminded her of when she visited the Museum Vrolik at the University of Amsterdam, which has a vast collection of human remains, including wet specimens with birth defects. "There was a huge collection of oddities and there were a couple of hands in a jar that looked a lot like mine, and that was the strangest feeling," she said. "My hands, that someone would display in a jar as a monstrous curiosity."

I wanted to see what she thought of the real Mütter Museum, which had similar displays. As it turned out, Kim had been to the Mütter Museum many times while growing up. It had been years since her last visit. When she lived in New York, she worked at the Morbid Anatomy Museum in Brooklyn, which was like a miniature version of the Mütter. It had human skulls and a fetal skeleton, specimens of experimental taxidermy including a skeletal jackalope, and realistic medical sculptures including an unforgettable recreation of a newborn baby being extracted from a vagina with a pair of forceps.

After lunch, we walked the short distance to the Mütter. The weather was crisp and sunny. We walked through Rittenhouse Square, a botanical park crowded with people and flowers, and made our way to the Mütter Museum, an imposing Victorian mansion that's like a mausoleum with its collection of skeletons, death masks, tumors and growths. We donned our COVID masks and went in, and entered a room lined with rows and rows of old skulls. I hadn't seen so many skulls since I'd been to the catacombs beneath Paris. Each skull bore a label stating where and when the person died and how. The skull of a 19-year-old man had a label saying that he killed himself a century ago when he caught his girlfriend cheating on him. "Oh honey," said Kim, sympathetically.

A glass case contains part of Einstein's brain. Another display case contains a post-autopsy cast of Chang and Eng Bunker, the conjoined twins who were circus celebrities in the 19th century. The case contained a cast of their heads and torsos, exhibiting the taut rope of flesh that bound them for life. Beneath the cast, a wet specimen displayed their connective tissue, floating in a dish of fluid at the bottom of the case.

The nearest wall had a larger case with shelves of jars containing mutated fetuses floating in fluid from the Victorian era.

"Oh, this is my section, the congenital defects," said Kim, approaching the fetuses with missing limbs. "It's really something, seeing yourself in a jar." One of the jarred fetuses had its legs fused, like a mermaid. There was also a plaster cast of conjoined twin babies that were joined at the pelvis, with one head facing one direction and the other head facing the opposite. The child had four arms and three legs. Born in 1870, the baby lived for an astonishing 13 months. Kim approached the plaster cast of the long-dead child. "Things could have gone way different," she said, contrasting her deformity to the children in the jars and on the wall. I asked her how it made her feel, looking at the jars of human specimens lined up on the shelf of this esteemed medical museum. "It makes me feel that I don't matter," she said.

Kim is a self-described "labor nerd," with an obsessive interest in workers' rights stemming from her roots in the New Jersey Pine Barrens. Her dad was a construction worker and her mom was an X-ray lab technician. She has spent much of her career covering the modern labor movement. She also covered the deadly clash in Charlottesville, Virginia, between white supremacists and anti-fascists in 2017.

In her *Vox* story about sideshow training at Coney Island, Kim wrote an illuminating explanation of the hierarchy of sideshow performers. "At the top of the ladder are the 'natural borns,'" she wrote. She explained how her trainer, Realman, referred to the natural borns as "the crème de la crème of the sideshow."

I contacted Realman shortly after his promotion as artistic director of Coney Island USA and asked him to explain the hierarchy. "Traditionally, the sideshow had three tiers of performers, the Natural Born, the Self Inflicted and the Working Act," he wrote in an email. "The Natural Born performers were considered the royalty of the sideshow and were often the highest paid performers in the show, the reason being that they were truly rare. The self-inflicted performers were the ones who chose to alter their bodies. Heavily tattooed and pierced performers would fall into this category, ranked just beneath the natural borns in the hierarchy of sideshow performers. Finally, the working acts, the sword swallowers, fire performers and other variety acts were beneath the other two. These are skills that anyone can learn with enough determination."

Sideshow naturals are rare. "I've trained a few little people, but Kim was the only one with ectrodactyly," said Realman.

The self-inflicted performers who manufacture their differences often go to extreme lengths to transform themselves through tattoos and surgical modifications. For example, Erik Sprague, AKA the Lizardman, split his tongue with a laser, filed his teeth into fangs, implanted demonic ridges into his brow, and tattooed his body green with the word FREAK across his chest.

The working acts breathe fire, eat razor blades and walk on broken glass. But in the world of sideshows, that's nothing special. Even the fire eaters get scant respect. Realman is a sword swallower and human blockhead with no disabilities. According to his description of the hierarchy, Realman inhabits the lowest rung. That doesn't mean that working acts are easy. Realman said that teaching anyone to eat and manipulate fire is "extremely nerve-wracking." He begins the training with an unlit torch. "If I feel that the posture, breathing or grip aren't perfect, the torch will not be lit," he said. "With Kim, it took a little more time until both of us were comfortable with lighting the torch, but the extra time paid off. Once Kim felt comfortable gripping and manipulating the torch, she handled it beautifully and progressed nicely."

Kim went from covering the sideshow to joining it. "I went in initially as a reporter or whatever, but I totally got sucked into the process of it," she said. She performed at Coney Island once during the winter of 2019, as a test run for the 2020 summer season. "I was planning to be part of the show," said Kim, who specialized in fire eating, hammering nails into her head and walking on broken glass. She also did an act called "mousetrap tongue," but she balked at sword swallowing, which "looks fucking hard." She was gearing up for a quasi-career as a sideshow performer to "add to the unorthodox collection of how I make money and spend my time. There aren't that many lobster girls in the world, so I have that going for me."

But then the COVID pandemic hit, killing tens of thousands of New Yorkers and canceling live performances while flattening her dreams of being a Coney Island sideshow performer.

"The pandemic year, that was supposed to be my first season," she said. "I'm devastated I couldn't do it. I was really psyched to do it."

Instead, she continued with her writing. In 2020, she wrote a unique story for *Allure* about visiting nail salons and empathizing with the workers who manicured her three-fingered hand.

In Coney Island and in nail salons, her hand stands out. But when mingling with coal miners, she wasn't the only one with missing fingers. As a reporter covering labor rights, she interviewed striking miners in West Virginia, and none of them gave her the side eye for having fewer body parts.

Sometimes she's sought by people for her disability. She said that an artist once approached her with a deal to make castings of her hands and sell them and split the profit. She turned him down, telling him, "You sound like one of those 19th-century hustlers trying to get somebody to sell their freak baby to the sideshow."

The naturals interviewed for this book sometimes have a hero, a predecessor with the same sort of disability who managed to succeed against all odds as a popular entertainer with a positive legacy. For Aaron "Short E. Dangerously" Wollin, his muse is Johnny "Eck" Eckhardt Jr., who was born in 1911 and became a famous and successful entertainer, starring in *Freaks* in 1932. For Mat Fraser, an actor on *American Horror Story: Freak Show* who was born with shortened arms and missing thumbs from thalidomide-induced phocomelia, his inspiration is Stanislaus Berent, a Coney Island regular who performed for 50 years as Sealo, the Seal Boy. Sealo and the late Ward Hall, the former owner of the sideshow World of Wonders, brought a court case against their home state of Florida because of a law prohibiting the exhibition of "crippled or physically distorted, malformed or disfigured" people in circuses or sideshows (according to Hall's 2018 obituary in the *New York Times*.) Ward and Sealo won the case in 1972.

But for Kim, she's stuck with Grady Stiles, Jr., an infamous sideshow natural with ectrodactyly, a convicted killer who was murdered in 1992 by a hit man hired by his abused spouse. While not exactly a role model, Stiles led an interesting life. Kim sent me photos of her visit to the Graveface Museum in Savannah, Georgia, comparing her three-fingered left hand to a plaster cast of Stiles' splayed hand.

Kim also has a more permanent tribute: a lobster tattoo. When I asked about it, she lifted her shirt there in the Mütter Museum to show me. She has a beautifully-inked blood-red lobster piece a foot high, tattooed into her side, as if it were crawling up her torso.

This happened in a room next to the gift shop with a modern-day exhibit on the surgery of female anatomy, complete with life-like models and videos of post-birth vaginas being sewn up with needle and thread. As we chatted and strolled amid the display cases of bones and preserved flesh, our conversation wandered onto the subject of hook suspension. She told me that she pays people to put hooks through her knees and then suspend her upside down in a room that looks like a gym, and she languidly spins around that way. She showed me a video on her phone. Her muscular boyfriend was helping her do it. I asked her if it hurts. Yes, it hurts, she said. She has scars on her knees from it. But it gives her a sort of thrill that is hard to explain.

She was not the only sideshow natural to experiment with suspension. I later met another natural, Nati Amos, who practiced hook suspension as well. I was told that it was becoming popular in the sideshow scene.

Kim had told me over lunch that there were twenty students in her high school class, and two of them were disabled – her, and a wheelchair-bound boy with osteogenesis imperfecta, a condition known as brittle bones. His name was Erik Paluszak, and he eventually became a sideshow performer too, under the moniker Velvet Crayon, with the Philadelphia-based Squidling Brothers Circus Sideshow and the Coney Island Circus Sideshow.

Growing up in the wilds of New Jersey, Kim said that kids in the tiny town where she was raised "got tired of calling me 'E.T.' somewhere around the middle of first grade." Later, when she was 14, a friend knitted her a customized pink fuzzy glove. She said the locals got used to her left hand and eventually stopped noticing it altogether.

The Pine Barrens of South Jersey are considered backwoods and remote even though New Jersey is the most densely populated state in America. She's from Chatsworth, an unincorporated community in Woodland Township, tucked into a stretch of forest located inexplicably between Philadelphia and Atlantic City, like an oasis of Appalachia on the teeming Eastern Seaboard. She described the area as "very rural and very isolated" and said that her family has "lots of guns."

"It's beautiful and barren," she said of the Pine Barrens, a sandy stretch where farmers figured out how to grow blueberries and cranberries. "They call them the barrens for a reason. I grew up half an hour from the nearest grocery store. There are still dirt roads in my town. It's kind of the land that time forgot. It's where the Jersey Devil lives."

The sideshow experience was a transformation for Kim because her three-fingered hand became like a rare jewel. She could flaunt it like a peacock's tail while becoming part of sideshow history.

"I think it's been a really powerful reclamation," she said. "You're part of this whole legacy, and it feels really good, because the rest of the world doesn't even know you exist. Freak, that's been a loaded word for a long time, but some people have decided to take it back, like the word queer."

Kim said that it's unfortunate that the exploitative history of the sideshow looms so large in its history. "That's what most people think of, the horrible things that were done to our people back in the day," she said. But she sees the sideshow as an endangered art form, like vaudeville. "It's not something people think about in a modern context, and it's unfortunate, because I think it's pretty cool," she said. Are sideshows exploitative? Ultimately, she said, it boils down to personal freedom and choice. "I'm controlling my image; I'm controlling myself," she said. "Whether you want to pay to see it, is up to you."

At this point in her life, her three-fingered left hand has become an important part of her natural born identity. I asked her: if she was given the chance to have two normal hands, would she do it? "If I got three wishes and I could change anything about me, I wouldn't change my hands," she said.

Chapter 3

The Seal Boy

"As a disabled actor, will I ever be seen as just an actor, or will I only ever be seen as a freak who acts?"
- Mat Fraser, from his 2001 documentary *Born Freak*

The day before I got married, in July 2010, I took our small crowd of wedding guests to see a real live freak show. And at Sideshows by the Seashore was an honest-to-God freak show on a Möbius loop that continued all day, a series of never-ending performances by tattooed tarts and pierced punks, prancing their way through burlesque acts, breathing fire, walking on broken glass, hammering nails up their noses, lying on beds of nails and cramming themselves inside boxes of blades. We paid admission and entered a room with bleachers and a stage, and that's where I first saw Mat Fraser, an Englishman who has since become the number one natural in the modern American freak show scene.

Mat looked dapper when he strode on the stage, a good-looking chap with a classically sculpted face, made for cinema. He was wearing a blazer and shorts, smiling and dancing to a jaunty pop song, when halfway through the ditty, his arms unexpectedly fell from his sleeves, clattering on the stage. His arms weren't real! They were prosthetic! Then he threw off his blazer, revealing his naked upper torso. He actually did have arms, but they were short, with no thumbs.

Now that he had our attention, Mat began to play the snare drums, hunching towards them with a pair of stick brushes so that his shortened arms could reach the skins and make that *whisk, whisk* sound. Mat then stopped playing and introduced himself to the audience, in a crisp English accent, as Seal Boy. In observance of sideshow tradition, he explained his condition in a classic narrative style. He has phocomelia, a birth defect based on the Greek word for seal, a reference to his flipper-like limbs. In his case, the deformity was caused by thalidomide, a painkiller that was used by pregnant women in the 1950s and early 1960s to fight morning sickness but with nightmarish results. The drug wasn't properly vetted before it was unleashed on the European population, and they didn't know its evil secret until the damage was done. Thousands of children were born with thalidomide-induced phocomelia and other defects before people realized that the drug was causing the deformities, and it was taken off the market.

Mat radiated with confidence as he explained his condition with the articulation and self-awareness of a trained theater actor who has appeared on stage a thousand times and the salacious, punk rock pizzazz of a burlesque dancer who has gone carnie. Despite his obvious physical deformity, he looked like a TV star. We didn't know it at the time, but that's what he would eventually become, playing a sideshow natural on a show viewed by millions.

But not at first. Earlier in his career, Mat had attempted a more traditional route as a television actor. "I wanted to launch myself on the world because I wanted to do a TV show," Mat told me over lunch one day in Manhattan in 2021, more than 10 years after I'd seen his performance at Coney Island.

But that's where he hit a wall. Mat auditioned for numerous television gigs but was constantly turned down, and while he was never told that he was rejected because of his disability, it was hard not to see it any other way. "I saw what that meant: they don't want me on TV," he said. "Let's go to where I'm really welcome, the freak show." He likes to say that his "flippers" brought him to the freak show. He discovered its untapped potential as an edgy art form that walks a provocative line between exploitation and self-empowerment.

Mat was born in England in 1962 to professional actors who divorced when he was young after his dad came out as gay. His mother took him to live in bucolic New Zealand for a brief time during the 1970s. This was an idyllic phase in his childhood and Mat said the New Zealanders insisted on including him in everything, including sports like softball. But after just a year and a half, he and his mother returned to England.

Mat spent much of his time living in London, and he still has a flat there, though he also lives in New York, somewhere in the Lower East Side, an energetic tangle of people and buildings with a well-earned reputation for dark bars, gritty music and experimental art. Mat lives with his wife, Julie Atlas Muz, a performer; she is the theater director at the Abrons Art Center dubbed by the *New York Times* as the "the royalty of burlesque." They have performed together, doing simulated sex scenes on stage while wearing *Meet the Feebles*-style costumes. They were also married on stage at the Abrons Art Center, in 2012.

Years later, in December 2021, I watched a Panto musical performed on that very stage called *Dick Rivington & The Cat*. It was written by Mat and directed by his wife, and he also performed as a drummer in the three-piece band in the orchestra pit. Unfortunately, the COVID pandemic would bring the curtains down on *Dick* before the season was through.

Before he became an actor, Mat started as a disability rights activist, writing angry poetry and turning it into rap. "I wore really long dreadlocks; I probably stank. I was in a reggae band. We toured Holland and got paid in food and weed."

We had just met for the first time, at his predetermined rendezvous spot. Mat Fraser made his grand entrance, riding through the park on a vintage single-speed bike with high handlebars, known among bikers as suicide bars. Mat rested his hands, with his short arms, upon these elevated handles. He managed to look completely distinctive even in a place like Alphabet City.

As Mat rode up to the corner, he was immediately approached by three people who had seen him on TV but they couldn't remember where. "*American Horror Story: Freak Show*," said Mat, and he obliged their requests for selfies with a smile and a short chat.

By the 1990s, Mat had embraced acting, his parents' profession, as his true calling. But nobody ever said that being a professional actor was easy. Nobody ever said that being disabled was easy, either. What do you get when you meld the two? Mat tackled this question in 2001 with a one-hour documentary called *Born Freak*, directed and produced for British television by Paul Sapin.

"As a disabled actor, will I ever be seen as just an actor, or will I only ever be seen as a freak who acts?" he mused in the documentary. Then he imagined himself as an action movie star, using his martial arts skills to rescue a damsel in distress from a couple of thugs. But they – the thugs *and* the damsel- just laughed at him.

In this film, Mat explained how he became fascinated by freak shows and eventually joined Coney Island's Sideshows by the Seashore, in a way that almost seemed inevitable. It started when Mat, as the narrator, explained how he started to research freak shows and he came across an old photograph that really "grabbed me," as he put it.

It was a picture of Stanislaus Berent, a 20th-century freakshow performer with phocomelia who went by the stage name of Sealo the Seal Boy. He had hands without arms sprouting from his shoulders. He was born in Pittsburgh in 1901, long before thalidomide came into existence, so his phocomelia was not induced by a chemical during pregnancy but was a naturally occurring birth defect. Sealo had a lengthy freak show career, performing at Coney Island and other venues for most of his adult life. He eventually retired to Gibsonton, Florida, a magnet for retired sideshow performers. As Mat points out in *Born Freak*, several states had outlawed freak shows including Florida. In 1973, Sealo challenged the ban in his home state and won in Florida Supreme Court. He died a few years later, in 1980, in a hospital in Pennsylvania.

In Sealo, Mat had found an inspiration and a muse, a like-minded disabled activist who embraced the sideshow as a way to make a living. He had hands without arms but still managed to saw lumber and shave himself as part of his performance. "My whole life is because of him, my whole voice life, my writing life," Mat told me, as he used his teeth to rip open sugar packets for his coffee. "Sealo gave me my voice as a disabled actor." He wrote a play about him in 2001 called *Sealboy: Freak*.

In *Born Freak*, Mat explained how he stumbled upon the idea of playing Sealo, in a real live freak show at Coney Island, where he decided to resurrect Berent's show as a tribute.

In the documentary, Mat meets the legendary Ward Hall, who once employed Sealo at his sideshow, the World of Wonders, and who allied with him in the court battle to legalize freak shows in Florida. Hall, who died in 2018, offered Mat $1,000 a week to work his sideshow, but Mat held out for his meeting with Dick Zigun, co-founder of Coney Island USA, a non-profit that runs the Coney Island Circus Sideshow and Sideshows by the Seashore in the same building where Sealo once performed. "If you're going to be Sealo, this is the place to be Sealo, right here," said Zigun in the documentary. "You got the job."

Mat gave it some thought, noting that "Everyone wanted me as their freak." He talked to an old friend of Sealo's who insisted that Sealo "got laid a lot" in the sideshow business. Mat found himself back at Coney Island to accept Zigun's offer to do the Sealo act, 14 times a day during the summer season. He wore suspenders, chomped on cigars, shaved his face and sawed wood, on the very stage where Sealo had done the same. But he did not enjoy being outside on the bally platform and barking like a seal to attract paying customers, calling the experience "exhilarating and distressing." But they sold so many tickets.

He couldn't get away from it. He returned to Coney Island for years afterwards, continuing to perform. He also did a cameo appearance at The Happy Sideshow in Edinburgh, Scotland, as the Thalidomide Ninja, breaking a brick with his head while clad in nothing but black briefs.

Mat, who is unafraid of getting naked on stage, compared sideshow work to being a stripper, as a theatrical experience for developing one's acting skills, because it's all about using your body to maximum effect with the audience. Like other naturals who have done sideshow work, Mat told me that it was easy for a "born freak" to take center stage and get top billing, compared to firebreathers and glass walkers who aren't disabled. "Some poor guy who's got half his face burned off, and his lungs burned up, and he's been fire breathing for 20 years, he's got to take second place to me," Mat said.

Mat's film caught the attention of David Mitchell and Sharon Snyder of the University of Illinois at Chicago. In 2005, they published an academic critique of *Born Freak* in the *Disability Studies Quarterly*.

The authors buried their distaste for freak shows under a pile of heavy-duty academic language. They credited the film with making three research findings: (1) "the distinct possibility that no viable place in the professional world for a disabled actor exists outside of some freak show context" (2) "even a systemic critique of the freak show offers little salvage from its dehumanizing effects" and (3) "the economic motives of the freak show mire participants in a base, pornographic activity that significantly compromise arguments about professional agency within modes of capitalist spectacle."

Mat told me that he has defended the artistic integrity of freak shows to Paul Longmore, a well-known disability rights advocate, history professor and director of the Institute of Disability at San Francisco State University. Prof. Longmore, who had lost the use of his arms from polio, died in 2010 at age 64. "He considered freak shows to be a denigration of the civil rights movement," said Mat. "I was trying to get him to recognize that not everything is black and white."

As Mat finished lunch, the waitress brought a to-go container for my Moroccan eggs. Seeing that I was busy with my laptop, Mat packed up the meal for me, bending towards the food to accommodate his short arms, pinching the edges of the crinkly aluminum container.

Chapter 4

The Poison Pill

"The indelible buds,
Knuckles at shoulder-blades, the
Faces that
Shove into being, dragging
The lopped
Blood-caul of absences."
- "Thalidomide," from the *Collected Poems* of Sylvia Plath

Mat views the sideshow as a legitimate artistic expression with a rich history and tradition. There's something appealing about the bohemian lifestyle, something edgy and sexual. He told me that it's like going to a fetish show, where "a girl wants to fuck you because you have flippers." As a punk performer with a penchant for burlesque, Mat likes to get naked on stage. When Mat does wear clothes on stage, it's often something skimpy, like black briefs. He's inviting the audience to check out his body. He's rattling expectations of what's considered normal or abnormal. "To me, the two things that people think you can't do when you're disabled is fight and have sex," he once said in a documentary. "So I've got a black belt, and I'm really good at shagging."

He loses no opportunity to sexualize himself through art. As he explained in that interview, the physical pleasures of life are important and we should indulge in them, consensually. "And we should all have as much of a party as we can, because we might get knocked over by a bus tomorrow and I want to live life, to live it to the fullest."

While building his career, he realized it was difficult to avoid being cast as a disabled character, so he took ownership of the situation. In 2005, he wrote *Thalidomide, A Musical!!* He said it started as a joke but then it became a real production in London. He starred in his own show, quite naturally, and his co-star was Anna Winslet, "sister of you-know-who" as the *Guardian* put it. The newspaper called it an "exuberantly bad taste comedy" and a "manically physical show." For Mat, it was a new way to sound his rage against the pharmaceutical manufacturers that had dumped their dangerous product onto the expectant but unsuspecting mothers of the world.

"Yeah, I am angry about the way those corporate bastards got away with it," Fraser told the *Guardian*. "And finally, I'm getting to stick the knife in."

One would think that thalidomide was conjured up from Hell. And maybe it was. The drug was developed in Germany by a company called Chemie Grünenthal, which was founded in 1946, literally in the ruins of World War II.

Thalidomide, patented in 1954, was a nausea treatment prescribed to pregnant mothers, primarily in Europe in the 1950s and early 1960s, that caused nightmarish deformities in their babies, including missing or stunted limbs, blindness and brain damage. *The Thalidomide Catastrophe* by Martin Johnson, Raymond Stokes and Tobias Arndt estimates that 25,000 thalidomiders were born alive, though many of them died before their first year. The toll on families was brutal. Some mothers suicided and it has long been suspected that some thalidomiders were allowed to die, shortly after birth.

The FDA eventually approved thalidomide years later for patients with multiple myeloma and leprosy. It is also used to treat leprosy in Brazil. At least 600 surviving thalidomiders were born in Brazil in the 1970s when the drug's dangers were well known. According to *The Thalidomide Catastrophe*, a thalidomide baby was born in Brazil as recently as 2010.

The book contains black and white photos of thalidomiders as smiling children, with brief captions describing their accomplishments later in life. There's a photo of a boy with a sharp, inquisitive look, who appears healthy in almost every way, except that he's holding a tennis racket with diminutive arms. The caption reads: "Mat Fraser, aged 6. Mat went on to become a professional actor and musician."

Mat told me that he had visited Brazil back in 2004 to make a British documentary called *Happy Birthday Thalidomide* and he met some of the thalidomide children. He also met lepers who took thalidomide. At one point, he encountered the drug itself. "I held the drug that caused my deformity in my hand," he told me.

The documentary *Happy Birthday Thalidomide* aired on British television in 2004. "The drug that shrunk my arms will be 50 this year," narrated Mat in the film. He explained how Britain is synonymous with thalidomide. (One tally counted 524 surviving thalidomiders in the United Kingdom in 2003, which is exceeded only by Brazil, with more than 600, and Germany, with 2,901.) "We're as British as boiled beef and carrots," he said.

The documentary includes footage of an infanticide trial in Belgium in 1962, where Suzanne van der Put was found not guilty of killing her thalidomide baby. Her supporters packed the courtroom and cheered the verdict. That was the year that Mat was born, in January 1962, three months after thalidomide was taken off the market. His mother said that when Mat was born there was a "heavy silence" in the delivery room and she feared he was dead. She was relieved when a doctor told her that her son was alive but with short arms.

In the movie, Mat mused about the standard of living for British thalidomiders who have received compensation for the drug, noting that "The worst of us still have a small flat." When I interviewed a German spokeswoman for Grünenthal, the company that manufactured the drug, she said that compensation for thalidomiders can range up to €8,400 a month, depending on the severity of the deformity. Grünenthal spokeswoman Fabia Kehren said the compensation for British thalidomiders is not handled by Grünenthal but is paid by the liquor distributor that sold thalidomide in the United Kingdom. That distributor was eventually acquired by Diageo, which took over the trust.

"We have always taken this legacy extremely seriously and we have a long track record of providing financial support for thalidomide-injured people in the U.K.," said Diageo spokeswoman Rebecca Perry via email.

She said the company has increased contributions to the trust over the years "to reflect the changing needs of its members" and has set aside funding until 2037 "to ensure that long-term financial support is available." The 2022 annual report of the Thalidomide Trust said they paid £19,244,000 to 450 beneficiaries, for an average of £42,764.

This sort of money would go farther in Brazil than it would in England. The purpose of Mat's doc was to go to Brazil to find the new thalidomiders. The drug is used as a treatment for the open ulcerating sores of lepers, and there are thousands of lepers in Brazil. The Brazilian government allows thalidomide for lepers but it's under strict control. Birth control is mandated for women taking thalidomide. But so long as women are still taking it, there is always a risk.

Mat flew to Rio de Janeiro and found some thalidomiders born during the second wave in the 1970s. Their mothers were prescribed it for leprosy. He went to a nightclub with two of them, including a man in a wheelchair with no legs, and was impressed by how well-adjusted they seemed in the party atmosphere.

Mat explained to me that thalidomide is an amazing drug for certain things, and he said this without irony. He seemed amazed by the twisted reality of a drug that could do so much harm, and so much good. In the film, he visited a leper and he asked to look at her thalidomide pills, and then he was holding the drug in his hands: Talidomida, 100 mg. The warning on the box said it can cause children to be born without arms or legs. After watching pain-wracked lepers take thalidomide and then slip into chemical contentment, he said that he couldn't begrudge them for taking it. "But it is pretty fucking weird."

Mat's quest to find Brazilian thalidomiders led him to Claudia Maximino, president of the Brazilian Thalidomide Society. He met her for lunch at a classy restaurant, and she was carried to the table, crutches in tow, by a porter. She is supposedly one of the first thalidomiders born in Brazil and her limbs are not fully formed. The two of them had natural chemistry and easy familiarity.

Claudia fought for the compensation rights of thalidomide victims in Brazil. Mat traveled with her in a van across the pampas to visit a little girl in a rural shack with shortened arms. Claudia wanted to find out if her mother, a sugar cane farmer, took thalidomide when she was pregnant. If so, she could try to get her compensation. But sadly, Brenda's mother couldn't unearth a prescription or any other proof. "It's the worst part of Claudia's job, having to tell desperately poor people that they're not going to be able to get compensation," said Mat in the movie. "You see, it's ironic. If you're proven thalidomide, you're likely to be well off, certainly compared to the millions who struggle against poverty."

Mat ended the film by meeting cancer patients in England who were taking thalidomide to relieve their symptoms. But Mat, whose father died of cancer, was still worried that people weren't taking the side effects seriously enough. "I worry even more about the rush for profit," he said. "That was the problem the first time round."

Chapter 5

American Horror Story

"Sex and drugs and rock n' roll looks like a pretty good lifestyle to me, if your alternative is to be kept in the back room in Alabama."
– Mat Fraser

Mat eventually hit the big time, but his career took a circuitous route to get there.

It seems like there are two types of actors: movie stars, and everybody else. There are also two kinds of musicians: rock stars, and everybody else. The career of an artist can be fun, but it can also seem like an endless slog to nowhere. Mat told me about his exploits in the 1990s as a foul-smelling dreadlocked drummer touring Holland and getting paid in weed. He said it was weird being a stoner in England "because you were the only one." As a part-time New Yorker, he was still getting used to legalization. "Now, there's a dispensary near the Slipper Room," he said, referring to a Manhattan club that's a magnet for sideshow people.

He once told the *Guardian* that during a typical Monday night in front of the TV he would get blasted on "half a crown of Charlie, an eighth of black and one of those little quarter bottles of blue-labelled 50% Smirnoff." He later explained to me that "black" was a reference to black hashish, which was the premiere way to consume cannabis in Europe. He explained that "Charlie" was cocaine. "I was hell-bent on getting wasted all the time, and happy people don't do that, do they?" he said.

He eventually toned down the narcotics for the sake of his health and shifted his physical prowess towards martial arts, becoming a black belt in taekwondo. "I love a good tear-up," Mat said. "I'm angry. I'm a furious person. I like to hit things. So martial arts and drumming are perfect for me." He defied the stereotype that disabled people can't fight. "I don't want to get my nose broken, but other than that I'm good for it," he said. As a professional actor, he needed to preserve his face.

In 2009, Mat starred in an indie film called *Kung Fu Flid: Unarmed But Dangerous*, playing a vengeful family man who fights gangsters in a brothel. The movie is hard to find, but YouTube clips reveal lots of blood and screaming. Mat's "cripsploitation" flick is a feature-length realization of his self-parody from eight years before in *Born Freak*, where the villains and the damsel-in-distress laughed at his high-kicking attempt to save her. *Bizarre* magazine, a now-defunct British glossy that was dedicated to tattoos, breasts, extreme body modification and other fetishes, dubbed him "Bruce Willis with flippers."

Mat radiates an intense, edgy vibe. He told me about a recent incident in a city park, where a muscle-bound man mocked his disability and Mat yelled at him to "SUCK MY DICK!" He narrated this anecdote so emphatically that he practically rattled the dishes on our café table. Mat said he was relieved, though, when the bully backed off.

I asked him about his fighting style. How did he compensate for his short arms? "I try to keep things at legs' length," he said. Mat has studied kick boxing and krav maga.

Mat trained at Tiger Schulman's Martial Arts school to prepare for a fight in Japan, where he watched bloody matches between disabled fighters. "They all had profound cerebral palsy," he said. "They all want to fight. It's part of their culture. Blood was spilled." There was a one-armed fighter who only had one move: choking out his opponent with that one arm. Mat is aware of his own limits on the mat. "I don't have thumbs, so I don't have locks," he said. "You learn the physicality of the body and what's possible." His short arms make it difficult to defend himself when his opponent closes the gap and gets too close. What does he do then? "I bite," he said.

In 2014, just three years after we saw him perform at Coney Island, Mat Fraser scored the gig of a lifetime with the popular TV series *American Horror Story: Freak Show*. He played a sideshow natural with phocomelia named Paul the Seal Boy. Paul was a character that Mat was quite literally born to play. Having performed in a real sideshow as a seal boy, he fit the role like a four-fingered glove.

This was a breakthrough for Mat. By moving his sideshow act from stage to television, he increased his audience from about 30 spectators to 3 million, as he put it. At the Coney Island Circus Sideshow, he performed for years in a small theater before dozens of audience members seated in bleachers. He did the live act many times, but it was fleeting and ephemeral. When he appeared on television, he only had to perform once for the camera, and his act was recorded and perpetually replayed.

More importantly, on TV he was performing for the masses and not simply sideshow fans. *AHS* debuted in 2011 as an anthology series, where each season depicts a different set of characters in a different location: a haunted house, a haunted hotel, an insane asylum, a coven of witches, a slasher summer camp, or a sideshow. The show's star-studded marquee includes Lady Gaga, Dylan McDermott, Angela Bassett, Neil Patrick Harris, Evan Peters, Kim Kardashian and other celebrities. *AHS* is on Netflix. An actor will sell his soul for a break like that.

"Best job of my life," said Mat, who appeared in the fourth season, titled *Freak Show*, about a murderous traveling sideshow in 1950s Florida. When Mat mentioned an audience of 3 million, he was being conservative by half. More than 6 million viewers reportedly watched the debut episode in October 2014, starring Kathy Bates as the bearded lady and Jessica Lange as an aging Marlene Dietrich-type who runs a carnival with a ridiculously high body count.

As a seasoned pro with decades of experience, Mat was able to own his role and capitalize on his success. He worked alongside prominent actors as an accomplished peer. He brought an invaluable status to the show as a natural born who cut his teeth at the Coney Island Circus Sideshow. He was also a well-read researcher on sideshow history and culture.

This was the culmination of what he had strived for: mainstream success as a disabled actor through the sideshow forum. "That was the best job I ever had, I'm not going to knock it," he reiterated about *AHS*. "It got me a foothold, it got me my next job, it got me my agent."

I realized that Mat had become a star when I was reporting for CNN in 2014. A large screen dominated the atrium-style newsroom of CNN's Columbus Circle office and showed a teaser of *AHS: Freak Show* with a troupe of sideshow naturals eating and carousing in a mess tent. It was much like the bustling mess tent that we had at the Big Apple Circus in the 1980s, where the troupers gathered at folding tables to eat meat and potatoes sizzled by a frizzled old trapeze artist. The *Freak Show* camera panned over the cast of naturals and lingered on Mat Fraser, front and center, their bona fide seal boy.

AHS: Freak Show was set in Jupiter, Florida, in a time when sideshows were still common in America, but their heyday was peaking. Television was taking center stage as the primary source of entertainment. The *Freak Show* season featured a serial killer clown, a psychotic prep boy, sadistic cops, and a wandering troupe of naturals who can't get through an episode without murdering somebody or getting murdered. The body count in *Freak Show* is so high that it's amazing the characters can find enough dirt in the woods behind the carnival to bury all the bodies.

The show is not intended to be an accurate depiction of the 1950s, and it's riddled with deliberate anachronisms. For example, Lange's character sings a David Bowie song as part of her act, and Peters sings a song by Nirvana. These anachronisms emphasize the surrealness of an itinerant sideshow, which doesn't fit into a particular time or place but exists as a separate world of its own, wherever it pitches a tent.

While *Freak Show* was set in Florida, Mat told me it was filmed at an old cotton plantation in Louisiana. The film set looked rural and authentic. The sprawling tents of the carnival were assembled on the banks of a creek. In true Southern style, the tents, trucks and ropes were overgrown with weeds, vines and bushes.

Mat said the Louisiana film location had sat idle for several weeks before filming, allowing the jungle to creep in and take over. "It was a genius move on the part of the art department, whether they intended it or not I don't know, because all the vines had wound their way around the posts," said Mat. "The cars were overgrown." I told him that in real life the circus rarely sat in one place long enough to get rooted, quite literally, in the bayou like the set on *Freak Show*. But it was a cool effect for a horror show.

Mat viewed the set as an opportunity to indulge in sideshow research. "When I had an hour off, I'd lean on the tent pole, take a vape hit, talk to the real carnies," he said. He said that when Jessica Lange arrived, she exclaimed, "Oh my God, I think this is the best set I've ever been on." He became friends with Lange, who played a dangerous matron named Elsa Mars. On the show, Lange's character Elsa was hooking up with Mat's character Paul.

Paul was a nattily dressed Englishman with a fedora hat and vest. Mat credited this hat as helping to expand Paul's role on the show. Mat told me that Paul was originally meant as a minor character, but his presence gradually increased throughout the season until Paul became one of the most significant characters.

He said that Paul was originally cast with just one line, "You're on in five, love," which he said to the sideshow matron, played by Lange, right before her act. For the scene, the director told him to say the line and place his fedora on his head. But Mat's arms were too short to follow the instructions. "I can't literally do anything with my hat, because my hands can't reach my head," he said. So, he ducked his head and tossed the hat onto it with a theatrical flourish. "I flipped up my hat and it looked like a thing. Jessica said, 'That guy can act, you should give him more work.'"

He said they ramped up his presence on the show as a more developed character. In fact, they made Paul the Seal Boy into a romantic lead. He was the lover of the character played by Jessica Lange, and also the lover of a character played by Meryl Streep's daughter, Grace Gummer. "Suddenly I was two-timing Jessica Lange with Meryl Streep's daughter," he explained. This led to considerable drama, as the shotgun-toting father of Gummer's character didn't appreciate his daughter necking with the Seal Boy.

On the show, Paul delivers a monologue where he laments his conundrum as a pleasant-looking man whose potential is marred by disability. "I have the face of a pretty lad; I have a handsome face," said Paul on *Freak Show*. "Can you imagine this mug on a normal body? I could have ruled the world."

I took this monologue to be a metaphor for Mat's life. But when I mentioned it, he dismissed the scene, as if embarrassed by it. He said the show's creators wanted to fake-tattoo him, which he thought was a bit overdone for a character who was already a natural born, but he went along with it. He balked, however, when they wanted to fake-tattoo his face, which he felt was potentially damaging to his looks and career. "I wouldn't get tattooed on my face," he told me. "That was the deal breaker."

He said that's why they made him do a monologue about how he's got a beautiful face and his short arms are the only obstacles between him and world conquest. "I know that's them punishing me for not wanting to get my face tattooed," he said. He complained that the monologue makes him "sound like some cocky fucker." Mat said, "I don't really think that and now everybody's going to think that I think like that."

They ended up fake-tattooing Gummer's face instead, in a scene where her father punishes her for cavorting with a sideshow natural. Mat said that removing her tatts after the shoot was a miserable process for her. "They're pulling this shit off this lovely young lady's face," he said.

AHS allowed Mat to showcase his talent to millions of mainstream TV viewers. It changed his life. "I'm very grateful to *American Horror Story*," he said. "But it wasn't perfect."

Some of the natural born characters on *Freak Show* were played by non-disabled actors who relied on special effects and makeup. For example, the show slapped a fake beard on Kathy Bates and she became a bearded lady. The beard looked authentic enough, and Bates was convincing in the role, but she was not a natural born.

The show relied on special effects for conjoined twins Bette and Dot Tattler to be played by just one actress, Sarah Paulson.

The Tattlers are introduced as characters hidden in a backroom at their mother's house in the Deep South. A freak finder, who recruits naturals for sideshows, rescued the Tattlers from the back room, and they went on the road.

The Tattlers discovered that sideshows are places where naturals can fit in and have a good time. One of the girls is horny and the other's a prude, resulting in amusing banter. But the prude eventually comes around, and the Tattlers awaken to the provocative power they have over men. Once they set their sights on a lover, the double-headed seductress uses an unforgettable pickup line: "Two souls, two mouths, devoted to you, to pleasing you, it could be that way always." These characters began as innocents, but they were sexualized in their unique way, like the conjoined twins Electra and Iphigenia in Katherine Dunn's *Geek Love*.

Life gets complicated for naturals who join sideshows, and their world expands, for better or for worse.

"Sex and drugs and rock n' roll looks like a pretty good lifestyle to me, if your alternative is to be kept in the back room in Alabama," Mat explained. "It's a great fucking life, and it's equality. But like all circus life, it fucks you up."

Mat wasn't the only natural on the *Freak Show* cast. The show was like a 21st-century version of the 1932 movie *Freaks*, which showcased some of the leading sideshow naturals of the day. The *AHS* show featured several little people including Jyoti Amge from India, who wore baby-sized clothes and spoke with the high-pitched voice of a doll, and Ben Woolf, a natural with pituitary dwarfism who was cast as a chicken-biting geek. Unfortunately, Ben didn't enjoy his newfound success for long. In 2015, the year after *Freak Show* debuted, he was hit by a car and killed while crossing the street in Los Angeles.

The show also featured a character named Legless Suzi, played by an actress named Rose Siggins, who was born with sacral agenesis, the same condition as Aaron "Shorty" Wollin. Her legs were amputated when she was two years old. She eventually married and had two children. But like Ben, she didn't enjoy her *AHS* success for long as she died in 2015, the year after the season aired. Her friend Bryce Graves, the owner of Hellzapoppin Circus SideShow Revue, said that she went to the doctor for a routine checkup but died after surgery from complications to her kidneys. "Ben's death was really tragic, and Rose's was contentious," Mat said, referring to her fatal complications at the hospital. I asked him if the cast believed in a *Freak Show* curse. "The rest of us stayed alive, so the curse was only a fleeting thought, which passed," he said.

Chapter 6

Black Scorpion

"I have been exploited, but not in sideshows or freak shows. I've been exploited by United States of America capitalism, in the workforce, and insurance, medical, anything but sideshow. Yes, I've been exploited."
- Black Scorpion

When I met Kim Kelly in Philadelphia, she mentioned another sideshow natural born with her so-called "lobster" condition. "Have you talked to Jason Black?" she asked, as we walked through Rittenhouse Square to the Mütter Museum.

It was a natural question for her to ask. Jason Black, AKA Black Scorpion, is a member of the 999 Eyes Freakshow in Austin, Texas. He wears a big, black bushy beard, a tutu and angel wings in his act. He was born with ectrodactyly, the same condition as Kim, though his condition is more pronounced, with three fingers on each hand and three toes on each foot. Kim and Jason both performed at the Coney Island Circus Sideshow, but not at the same time, and they had not crossed paths. Kim said that people with ectrodactyly rarely encounter other people with the same condition. I asked Black Scorpion if he knew Kim. "I have not had the pleasure of meeting Kim Kelly," he said, "but she seems like an amazing writer, a great student of sideshow, and someone I would like to meet someday if given the opportunity."

Black Scorpion isn't just his stage name; it's his alter ego as an artist, an existential eccentric, an irreverent clown, a sideshow philosopher, a put upon survivor, and an unrepentant nonconformist. He is one of the best-known sideshow naturals in America. *Sideshow and Other Carnival Curiosities*, a book by Ripley's Believe It or Not!, depicts

Jason in a candy-stripe pink outfit and a pink bandit mask, walking on broken glass with his bare feet. In addition to Coney and 999 Eyes, he's performed at Museum of the Weird in Austin. His acts include swallowing balloons, escaping from handcuffs and "hammer hands."

I reached out to Jason Black in March 2022, initially through his friend Erik Sprague, AKA the Lizardman, who also lives in Austin. "He can be a little reclusive at times (like all of us really)," texted Lizardman. I had better luck when I contacted Mat Fraser in London, who had helped Jason land an audition on *American Horror Story: Freak Show* in 2014. Jason was hired, not as an actor with ectrodactyly but as a consultant to an actor without ectrodactyly, who played a character with ectrodactyly. The actor, Evan Peters, wore prosthetic ectrodactyly hands.

When I spoke to Jason Black, he was beset by medical and financial burdens. Live performances ground to a halt during the pandemic and 999 Eyes was hibernating. He had retreated from the stage – or rather, the stage retreated from him. He temporarily lost his means of making a living and existed in limbo. At the outset of our conversation, Jason had one condition: that I address him only as Black Scorpion.

Black Scorpion sent me a video on April Fool's Day, 2022. It opened with Black Scorpion rifling through a Dumpster like a bear. He was looking for food, he explained. In the next scene, he stood in his tutu under an expansive oak on a green lawn with a nondescript building in the background, presumably in Texas. The weather was bright and sunny there.

Black Scorpion was wearing big sunglasses, mismatched socks, a blue-and-yellow tutu and a pair of angel wings. He explained, in a raspy voice, that the founders of 999 Eyes (which he pronounced as nine hundred ninety-nine eyes) had conjured the idea at Burning Man, and he had helped them build and expand it.

"Why am I in a freak show?" he said while waving his hands. "I don't know if you noticed, but I was born with ectrodactyly. Now, just because you're born with ectrodactyly doesn't mean you're going to join a freak show." But he explained how the bad reputation of sideshows is an undeserved holdover from the past. He said that naturals had recently transformed sideshows from "pre-conceived negatives into a beautiful giant positive."

He sent me a video of his hammer hands act. He held a hammer in his right hand, and he pounded his left hand as a live audience screamed. He looked like he was smashing his fingers, but he wasn't, really. He was wearing a glove on his left hand, and he yanked it off to reveal that his hand was split, forming an empty space in the middle. His ectrodactyly "claws," as he calls them, fill only three of the fingers in a glove, leaving two of them slack, which he stuffs with "severed Halloween fingers" to make them look real. He hammered the fake fingers on his left hand three times before the big reveal. He said that he does everything in his act three times.

I asked him about his getup. He emailed a photo in which he was wearing his trademark angel wings, bandit mask and tutu, with circus banners in the background for PegLeg the Clown and the Leopardman. He wore a green glove on his right hand, an orange glove on his left, and a Dunder Mifflin T-shirt. He explained in an audio recording that he wore the tutu for practical reasons. "It's the way I feel comfortable dressing," he said. "I have overactive sweat glands and pants kill me."

But he wore angel wings for a loftier purpose, as a tribute to his Renaissance hero, who was reputedly natural born. "Leonardo Da Vinci had syndactyly on his drawing hand," he said, referring to a theory that da Vinci was born with two fingers fused and that he had represented Jesus Christ that way in his most famous painting. "He even depicted Christ as having syndactyly in 'The Last Supper.' But his friends warned him that the folks who paid for the painting wouldn't be happy about that. So, he drew a line to separate the fingers."

He added, "I always loved the way he painted angels."

About one in 90,000 babies are born with ectrodactyly, according to a 2009 paper by the National Library of Medicine, which refers to it as split-hand/split-foot malformation, or SHFM, or "lobster claw hand." The word ectrodactyly is based on the Greek words ektroma, which means untimely birth, and daktylos, which means finger. The severity ranges from one person to the next. Kim's left hand has three fingers. She can put her hand in her pocket and walk undercover through crowds with no one noticing that she's a natural. She calls this "passing."

Black Scorpion explained how ectrodactyly affects not only his hands and feet, but also his teeth, fingernails and hair follicles. "It is a twist in the DNA. It's the same thing that causes cleft palates," he said. "It affects your hair. It affects your ears, nose and throat, all that."

He said that ectrodactyly affects the keratin in his body, which makes fingernails, hair follicles and tooth enamel. He said the enamel on his teeth is thin which makes them wear away quickly to get eaten by stomach acids. He said that he has three implants because his teeth have been destroyed by the effects of ectrodactyly. He sent me a dental photo of his remaining teeth, displaying how the dentine was wearing away. He also emailed an X-ray of his skull, a silvery blue image of his cranium with the jaw yawning open, showing missing teeth and what appeared to be a cleft palate. In all my interviews as a journalist, this was the first time someone sent me a photo of their skull.

He also explained how walking on triple-toed feet is bad for his posture and damages his spine. "I have to go to a chiropractor every other day, and that is *expensive*," he said. "Insurance doesn't cover a lot of these issues. So, if you're born different, a lot of times you are born in the hole. You are in debt, and you are not getting out of it. That's why I Dumpster-dived today. Sometimes you eat a little cardboard pizza. It might not taste great, but it really fills the belly."

Black Scorpion said that his job on the set of *American Horror Story: Freak Show* was to help the actor Evan Peters research his role as a sideshow natural with ectrodactyly. The character's name was Jimmy Darling, and his stage name was Lobster Boy, an unsubtle reference to the real-life Lobster Boy, Grady Stiles Jr. Black Scorpion sent me an image of Evan Peters wearing his ectrodactyly gloves. And then he showed me a juxtaposition image of Black Scorpion's hands, in the same pose. "You'll notice that they basically copied my claws and merged them into his," he said. "They might have had a little Grady Stiles Jr. claws in there, as well. But I believe that as a mold maker, as an artist, as a writer, as a graphic designer, that they basically took a picture of my hand and merged them with his and came out with the creation that way and built a mold from a graphic rendering."

But the fake hands looked larger, for sure. Kim Kelly wrote a story for the feminist website *Jezebel* criticizing *AHS* for making the Peters' fake claws look "monstrous." She later told me that people with ectrodactyly look "different enough" without such garish exaggerations.

I asked Black Scorpion if they overdid it with Peters' claws. He shrugged it off: "It's basically '80s Saturday morning cartoons fantasy. It's cute. When I finally watched that season of *American Horror Story*, I just thought it was precious." He was being sarcastic. He was acknowledging that TV is fundamentally unreal. The cruel irony is that the nondisabled actor, not the sideshow natural, got the job playing the sideshow natural.

"I didn't get the role," he said. "They had a tight budget and sometimes I just ask for too much money. I want to be able to eat the next day, I want to be able to get dental care, things like that. It's too much money to ask from Hollywood."

I asked Black Scorpion about his audition, and he sent a video clip that looked like a grindhouse flick with Black Scorpion in face paint shouting, "I SHOULD BITE THEM OFF. I SHOULD BITE THEM OFF. I SHOULD BITE THEM OFF." The brief clip ended abruptly but it was fascinating, and I wanted to see more. But I suppose *AHS* would have desired something less sensational and more conventional.

"There's a lot of pain behind that *American Horror Story* audition, a lot of pain," said Black Scorpion. He was experiencing the angst of a man who had flown close to the sun, but success had slipped away, rattling his confidence. He didn't get to play a sideshow natural on TV. He didn't get to be a star. A real star, wearing large fakes of his hands, played him instead. "It's really hard when your dream is to be an actor, artist, musician, Chef Boyardee impersonator, and every turn you're shot down like Dick Cheney's hunting partner," he said. I asked why he was rejected. He theorized that either he's "not as talented as I think I am" or that "America and the corporate machine does not reward talent. It's one or the other, or maybe it's both, I don't know."

Perhaps the audition was too weird for a mainstream TV show. But there's nothing normal or appropriate about *AHS*, which depicted a man with ectrodactyly getting his hands amputated (while he's still alive) and displayed in a museum. Kim Kelly found the scene visceral and offensive. Having this happen to a character with ectrodactyly seemed worse than having it happen to a character without. Perhaps because they're so rare. I asked Black Scorpion about the amputation of Jimmy Darling's hands and their exhibition in a glass display case at the fictional Morbidity Museum. "I didn't finish the season because they got to the part where they cut off the Lobster Boy's hands, and I was like, I'm out," said Black Scorpion. "I don't even know if I got to that part; I just found out that's what happens." But again, he shrugged it off. "You know, it's fantasy, it's horror," he said. "I don't think they overdid it."

Even if Black Scorpion missed his chance for mainstream success, he remains one of the most well-known performers in the 21st-century sideshow scene. But in the years following *AHS*, ectrodactyly took a toll on his health. His medical and dental bills were piling up, and Black Scorpion was making and selling castings of his hands to pay them off.

Natural casting is a sub-niche. Kim Kelly told me about a run-in with a guy who offered to make casts of her hand to sell them and split the cost. She got creeped out and rejected him. But later, she had a different sort of encounter. She visited the Graveface Museum in Savannah, Georgia, which had an exhibit on Grady Stiles Jr. featuring a claw cast of his ectrodactyly hands. She photographed her three-fingered ectrodactyly hand juxtaposed against the four-fingered plaster cast of the Lobster Boy. The resulting photo is a sideshow treasure.

Black Scorpion told me that he hadn't sold casts of his hands to this niche market in a while, but he would have to resume the practice out of necessity. "I have not been able to as of late, and I do still need medical funds," he said. "It is something that will never end for me." Making and selling claw casts is part of his hustle, and the money goes to pay medical bills, as doctors try to keep his body from falling apart. "Here's a little advice I have to all the listeners out there: If you are born different, be born to rich parents, OK?" he said. "It's a lot easier to keep your teeth when you've got money."

Black Scorpion made casts out of Hydro-Stone gypsum cement or silicone. He painted the Hydro-Stone casts to look bronze or silver, but the silicone casts look like they're sheathed in soft pink skin. "I made some claws that are made of silicone, and those are more lifelike," he said. "More wobbly and tobbly and bobbly." He referred to them as "siliconey," like Coney Island.

I asked him to elaborate on his claim, which he had made in an earlier message, that the casts could be used as marital aids. "I made a joke about those silicones being marital aids, as in getting your wife off in the middle of the night," he confirmed. "I've never done that, but I hear a lot of people are interested in doing that with silicone hands, but they just don't want me [to be] part of a picture. They just want my hands."

For Black Scorpion, the specter of exploitation looms large ... but it has nothing to do with claw casts. "I have been exploited, but not in sideshows or freak shows," he said. "I've been exploited by United States of America capitalism, in the workforce, and insurance, medical, anything but sideshow. Yes, I've been exploited."

Performing allows him to become the artist he wants to be, to become independent and autonomous, his own director, his own manager. "Freak show is where I'd say I commanded, more than I was put upon," he said.

He said sideshows weren't all bad, despite their historical reputation. There were examples of evil sideshow slavery, like with Joice Heth and the conjoined twins Millie and Christine McCoy, who were treated as property, not people. But there were also sideshow naturals who thrived, like Tom Thumb and Prince Randian. "A lot of people just think freaks were exploited, but that's really not the case," he said. "In a lot of history, freaks actually ran the show."

It's important to remember that naturals had slim prospects in the working world and turned to sideshow as a means of making a living. This was the case with Joseph Merrick, the Elephant Man, who became an itinerant showman to escape the oppressive misery of the workhouse.

"I don't think I've been exploited in freak show, but yes, I have been exploited in the American work force," Black Scorpion reiterated. "Working in the real world is where I, and almost everybody else I know, has been exploited."

The natural born performers are an elite troupe in America, a handful of individuals warding off sideshow extinction. 999 Eyes hibernated through the pandemic and Black Scorpion didn't perform for two years. While unemployment was widespread, he suspected prejudice against performers who were born different. "In America we act like we're progressing, but in reality, we're falling backwards," he said.

Glass walking, one of his stage specialties, is a metaphor for trying to make it. "Basically, you have to crawl across broken glass just to get a chance in Hollywood," he said. "I mean Mat Fraser would know more about that. He's the only one of us who made it that far, personally, that I know."

Black Scorpion longed to perform again. It's an opportunity for him to educate people on the experience of being born different in America. He tells them how "tortuous it can be" dealing with the medical system and trying to climb out of the hole from the financial fallout of ectrodactyly health problems.

He eventually got his wish. When COVID restrictions finally lifted, 999 Eyes restarted its live shows and Black Scorpion was performing again. By December 2023, Black Scorpion said they were planning to expand: "Exciting events are upon us for the 999 indeed," he said by email. "The plan is to open our own building, the Freakhouse, on the east side of Austin."

As a disabled performer, Black Scorpion considers sideshow to be more important than light-hearted "ha-ha gigga google" entertainment. He explained that his act is humorous, but it also has meaning: "It is very important to me that I leave a path of positivity for those that are treading the same trail that I ride upon."

Chapter 7

The Bendable Girl

"We give people who live normal lives a sense of wonder."
- Camille Zamboni, foot archer-contortionist with Ehlers-Danlos syndrome

It was a dark and stormy Friday night in Atlantic City, New Jersey, in May of 2022. A pixie, with a long black ponytail and pointy elf ears, appeared on stage with the Hellzapoppin Circus Sideshow Revue. She wore a little black outfit with fishnet stockings and she carried a black bow and arrow. She stood on her hands and raised her legs in the air, balancing upside down while holding the bow and arrow in her bare feet, her toes curled around the shafts and the string. She aimed her archer feet at a target onstage behind her. Still standing on her hands, she pulled back the string with her toes and let fly the arrow, striking the target dead center. It didn't seem possible, shooting a bull's eye with her feet backwards and upside down. But then again, the Bendable Girl has a superpower.

I was in Atlantic City because Short E. Dangerously was there with Hellzapoppin, playing a small venue called Bourre, which doubled as a Thai restaurant. The streets of Atlantic City were deserted, not just on the side road past Bourre to the boardwalk but on Pacific Avenue past the looming monoliths of Bally's and Borgata, which glowed in the fog. It was a dreadful night to wander outside, and most people stayed home. Bryce "The Govna" Graves said he sold 73 tickets that night and only about half of the customers showed up. They were rewarded with a spectacle: Lucian Fuller, the unicyclist who juggles knives while blindfolded; Willow Lauren, a sword swallower who also eats razor blades; Shorty, who jumps on broken glass and does one-armed handstands; and Camille Zamboni, the contortionist who shoots a bow and arrow with her feet.

Normally, Shorty jumps on flaming glass. He was disappointed because he couldn't ignite the glass this time, thanks to the venue's safety-conscious but restrictive fire code; Bourre wouldn't allow it. "I feel like, without fire, it cheapens it," he told me after the show. It had been nearly a year since I saw him and he looked older, by more than a year. It was another year of COVID with sky-high inflation, gun violence and international volatility. Hellzapoppin continued to book shows, but it wasn't easy. The Govna, founder, ringmaster and human blockhead, ended that night's show by asking for donations to help get down the road. "This is a dying art form, and we are doing our best to keep it alive during the pandemic," he said on stage, wearing his top hat, long braids and Alice Cooper-style mascara. As the show was winding down, The Govna danced a little jig with Shorty, holding the half-man to his chest.

After the show ended, I approached Shorty, who was still on stage, signing a fan's copy of a Ripley's Believe or Not! book, *Sideshow and Other Carnival Curiosities*, which contained a two-page photo spread of Shorty doing a handstand on bowling balls. In the book, Shorty explained how his hero, Johnny Eck, the half-man who starred in *Freaks*, "paved the way for guys like me." Shorty, who plans to surpass Eck's legacy, propped himself on his elbows onstage as he jotted his name and a quick note for his young fan while her dad looked on. He wore his trademark cowboy hat and black leather biker vest with a big patch that read: Texas Hippie Coalition: Family Member.

Shorty finished signing and stood on his hands. Since he was onstage and I was standing next to the stage, we were at the same height, more or less. He introduced me to their new performer, the contortionist foot archer. "She's a natural," he said, meaning that she is natural born, like him.

Her name was Camille Zamboni. "My parents gave me a circus name," she said. "This is my first tour." Back in her hometown of Pittsburgh, she billed herself as the Bendable Girl.

Camille is slim, pale and tattooed. Her archery burlesque act was beyond the scope of what most people can do: standing on her hands and balancing on her arms while shooting a bow and arrow with her feet, gripping the bow and arrow and the string with her prehensile toes with enough strength in her feet to pull back the string with the arrow and release with force and control. After shooting the arrow and hitting the target, she did a split, still standing on her hands, and still holding her bow aloft with her foot. She then placed her free foot, the one that had pulled the bowstring, near her mouth and kissed it.

"I wanted to take contortion and hand balancing and make it very playful," she explained later. This is how she came up with her unforgettable grape-eating act. "I eat grapes from my toes," she said. She stands on her hands while holding a bunch of grapes between her toes and bends her back and legs to a pretzel and feeds herself with her feet. "I go into different contortions and positions and make it as complicated as I can. The grapes, they go everywhere, because the ones I don't eat, they fall off the vine."

Her feet take center stage. "Some people don't like feet," she explained after the show, while the crew was decompressing in the tour bus. "Some people like feet a lot." She looked at her friend Shorty. "He doesn't like feet; go figure," she said.

Her flexibility and balance are impressive. To the observer, her contortions appear impossible, but they are explained by her superpower. Camille was born with a condition that makes her stretchy and extra-flexible, for amazing potential as a contortionist. She has Ehlers-Danlos syndrome, which causes joint and skin elasticity. She demonstrated this for me by pinching the skin of her neck and stretching it like bubble gum. Her skin is also translucent, with blue veins visible beneath. "Under the lights, you can see all my veins," she said.

She said that Ehlers-Danlos syndrome loosens the ligaments in her body, which allows her to twist and bend herself into a human pretzel. This was her natural born superpower which allows her to do things that most of us can't. But nothing lasts forever and, over time, she said, her ligaments will deteriorate with age.

She wasn't the first natural with Ehlers-Danlos to appear in sideshows. James Morris, born in Copenhagen, New York, in 1859, was able to stretch out his skin by 18 inches, and his specialty was to pull the skin of his neck up over his nose like a turtleneck. He joined Barnum & Bailey in 1880 and was paid $150 a week (which is what I made working for Ringling as a vendor 109 years later, in 1989.) They called him the Rubber Man, or the Elastic Man. He was sometimes confused with another natural performer, a contemporary named Felix Wehrle, AKA the Elastic-Skin Man.

Camille was new to the sideshow scene. She said she used to be a nurse, and then she was a gymnastics coach and she also worked on the *American Ninja Warrior* TV show, helping to design the obstacle courses and the curriculum. She was a Hellzapoppin fan, seeing a dozen shows before Graves signed her on for the tour. She was 29 years old and had two kids, ages 10 and 6. Her parents took care of them back in Pittsburgh while she toured with Hellzapoppin. "I have parents who live very close to me and they help me out a lot," she said. "My parents are a blessing in my life."

I met with Hellzapoppin after the show in their tour bus, in a parking lot across the street from the restaurant. They needed time to tear down and unwind before the interview, so I waited in my car parked near the Excursion RV that served as home to Hellzapoppin while on tour. This is the same vehicle they were touring in last year, when I first met them in Clifton, N.J. I imagined The Govna parking this beast at his tree farm in north Florida during the off-season. But for now, the Excursion sat alone in the parking lot, with the glowing smear of casinos in the foggy distance. Coming from New York, I was struck by the wide-open spaces of Atlantic City, the dearth of cars, and the freedom to park just about anywhere.

It was still raining. I figured that Shorty would have to walk on his hands through this nasty weather. I had noticed that he had his rugged black gloves with him. He wore those when he walked on the sidewalk, to save his precious hands for the glass.

As I sat waiting in my car, I saw Camille jog lithely through the rain towards the RV, the lights of Bally's looming in the distance. She had her bow in one hand and a quiver of arrows in the other, looking like a ninja. She climbed into the RV.

Twenty minutes later, Shorty texted me to join them in the Excursion. I didn't see him go in the RV but he was already there. He must have slipped in right after the show, before I staked the place out. The Excursion was a sanctuary from the rain and quite spacious inside, like a trailer, but it filled up quickly. It was designed to house the crew, with bunks along the walls and a bathroom in the back. Rain was drumming hard on the metal roof and they were scarfing down road food. Shorty was on the carpeted floor of the RV, perched on his elbows and eating mac n' cheese with chopped hot dogs. Willow, the sword swallower, was eating microwaved food out of a Tupperware container.

Shorty had shed his hat and vest and was smoking weed from the same green bong that appeared in my *High Times* profile about him. Camille had changed into a silvery pullover and puffed on a vape pen. I noticed that she had elf ears. This was from body modification, not Ehlers-Danlos.

According to the Mayo Clinic, symptoms of Ehlers-Danlos syndrome include overly flexible joints and stretchy, fragile skin. "This can be a problem if you have a wound that requires stitches, because the skin often isn't strong enough to hold them," said the Mayo Clinic on its website.

The Mayo Clinic described the syndrome as a group of inherited disorders affecting connecting tissues, primarily skin, joints and blood vessel walls. A more severe version of the disorder, called vascular Ehlers-Danlos syndrome, can cause the walls of blood vessels, intestines, or uterus to rupture. "Before vascular Ehlers-Danlos syndrome can have serious potential complications in pregnancy, you may want to talk to a genetic counselor before starting a family," said the Mayo Clinic, noting that the vascular form of the disorder is relatively rare, compared to the common version known as "hypermobile."

"It had always been an issue with my joints," said Camille, who had once accidentally dislocated her hips, but then discovered that her joint flexibility allowed her to "push it with yoga," which prompted her to experiment with contortionism. Six years ago, she became obsessed with handstands and then started balancing on hand placement poles and posting videos on YouTube.

"I started doing contortion and hand balancing for a local show in Pittsburgh and I noticed that I made people cringe, and I liked that," she said. "Anytime I made people cringe, I would take that shape and push it as far as I can." She said that one of the cringe-worthy acts was taking her foot and jamming it up into her rib cage.

Now, she can dislocate her joints on a whim, and pop them back in again, without visible pain. She demonstrated this skill during the interview when she popped out the joint of her shoulder, and it almost seemed to float under her tattooed skin, and she popped it back in again, like a Lego brick. She was smiling at her backstage parlor trick. She said that some people get freaked out by her casual dislocations, but sideshow performers take it in stride. They've already seen it all. "That doesn't bother me, your shoulder popping," Shorty told her.

Camille had decided, while still in her early 20s, to "make use of" her condition by learning the various skills and talents that she puts to work on stage. "Otherwise, I would not have even known that I could do these things," she said.

Camille said that archery is her newest act. It's something that she "played around with" over the last several years, much to the consternation of other city folk. "The neighbors don't like that I do archery in my backyard, but it's my yard," she said.

While it was easy to shrug off her neighbors, she found the physical pain hard to deal with. "Every time I did archery, it hurt, with handstand foot archery, and my back would be so sore afterwards, and I would talk myself out of doing it," she said. She got sidelined by two spinal fractures in 2019 which she blamed on "overuse from contortion." But she finally had surgery, and after that the pain stopped.

Camille had joined the Pittsburgh Circus Arts Collaborative, a local collective of performers. She became infatuated with sideshows in general, and with Hellzapoppin in particular, after she discovered them in 2018 at Riot Fest in Chicago. "I saw this circus tent with this big devil head and I went in and the show blew my mind," she said, referring to the demonic façade with a fanged mouth that Hellzapoppin uses as its gateway to shows when touring with metal bands and festivals.

Shorty and Bryce noticed that Camille wasn't just a casual observer. She was studying them because she wanted to join them. "I had done contortion," she said. "I thought, I'm going to be there with them. I want to be in this show in particular." Graves recognized her talent and hired her for the spring tour of 2022. She put her skin in the game.

The experience taught her there are two kinds of audience members: the ones who watch sideshows, and the ones who *are* sideshow. "We give people who live normal lives a sense of wonder," she said. "And then there are people who see our show who say, 'That's me!'"

But the downside of touring is that she missed her kids. She said her daughter had attended one of her shows the other night. Her kids had grown used to her practicing foot archery in the backyard, but that was the first time her daughter saw her do it onstage. She was expecting to see both her kids the following night - which was the night before

Mother's Day - at their upcoming show in Stroudsburg, Pennsylvania. "I will probably cry a little bit, but you can't shoot bow with tears in your eyes," she said.

Hellzapoppin also featured non-natural working acts like Lucian Fuller, who can juggle three knives while blindfolded on a 10-foot unicycle. Without the blindfold, he can juggle five knives or five torches or a chainsaw with two balls. "The chain is spinning when I juggle," said Lucian. "It's live, it's real, it's super dangerous." At the A.C. show, he cranked Rammstein while juggling on a unicycle and ripped off his shirt to reveal nipples crossed with black Xs of electrical tape. He described the stunt as punk comedy. "The great thing about sideshow is that it feels like the street," he said.

I asked Graves what it was like touring a sideshow with two naturals during a quasi-apocalyptic pandemic that had killed nearly a million people at that point. He was blunt.

"Touring in a pandemic is extremely difficult," he said, sitting on a bunk in the RV. "It's terrible. We are surviving. If I wanted to make money, I wouldn't have gotten into this business. We do it because we love it. But there is no money to be made right now."

His friends chimed in. "I do it for the glory," said Shorty. "I used to do it for the chicks. Now not so much."

"I do it for the screams," said Camille.

But even as Graves complained about the difficulties of touring during sky-high gas prices and booking venues during an infectious pandemic, he also had a sense of badass pride at emerging from quarantine in early 2021, to venture into the frontier. "We were the very first national touring act in America after COVID," he said. "We were the only touring act in America for the first few weeks."

He said that other acts were afraid to tour, and Graves was afraid that Americans would be too afraid to attend his show. "Everybody is living in fear right now," he said, so he called his tour "Face Your Fears." He said that others in the entertainment industry were watching them, like canaries in a coal mine, to see what would happen, and then follow their lead. Are they going to make it through a tour without getting sick? Are people going to show up?

He said that Americans did, in fact, face their fears, and they sold out every show back-to-back from February to August 2021. "It was insane," he said. COVID restrictions and requirements for masks and vaccinations varied from state to state. They started touring in Florida and they headed north towards New York. The city was ravaged in the early days of COVID, with tens of thousands of New Yorkers dying in March and

April 2020. "When we came to New York, people looked like they had been through a war," he said. "They had the look of fear." New York was one of the more restrictive states, corralling vaccinated versus unvaccinated groups of fans into separate sections of the venues. But California was even more restrictive. "California was fucking awful," he said. "Only the vaccinated came to our show."

And then, late in the summer of 2021, a new wave of infections from the Delta variant swept across America. The entire cast got sick on the second-to-last day of the tour. They went back to Florida, where Hellzapoppin is headquartered at Graves' tree farm near Gainesville. They tested positive and went into quarantine. Shorty returned to his home in Daytona. (A self-described metalhead jock skater punk, Shorty used to drive modified race cars in Daytona, which is how he ended up there.) They theorized that they caught COVID at some of the last shows they played in Iowa and Colorado, which didn't mandate masks. "Five hundred people in this theater and it was sold out," said Graves, referring to a venue in Grand Junction, Colorado. "They were screaming and yelling and there were plumes of spit coming at you."

After a hiatus, they returned to touring in 2022. Venues reopened as the death rate for COVID eventually dropped, but so did attendance. He said that venues where they used to bring in 350 to 900 audience members were now down to 100 to 300 attendees. "Seventy-three people paid to see our show," he said, referring to the night's show in Atlantic City. "I can't even break even at 73."

This drop in attendance accompanied the worst inflation since the 1970s. Gas prices were rising like never before, a problem when driving an RV cross-country. He said it cost $420 to fill up the tank and go 550 miles. "If we break even at the end of the tour, I will be ecstatic," he said.

Graves also told me that he was about to turn 50, and his daughter was pregnant. He was about to become a grandpa.

It was past midnight. Shorty pulled out his phone and showed me a video from Sturgis, South Dakota, where he was shooting an FN assault rifle at an outdoor range on a grassy field with rolling hills. He was lying down in the grass to shoot the gun, propped up on his elbows, just as he had been lying on the stage to sign the Ripley's book. He pumped rounds from the semiautomatic, hitting metal targets in the distance.

I asked him what it was like, being on tour during a pandemic. "Everybody has lost their goddamn minds," he answered. He said that phones had made it so convenient for people to post their opposing opinions on social media that it'd transformed Facebook into a fight club. "It's turned into, you either agree with me, or you hate me," he said. "There is no middle ground anymore where people can come together. You either agree with me or you're wrong."

Willow said the ongoing point of contention on social media for Hellzapoppin was that the sideshow tours with naturals. "We still get Facebook messages all the time: "Shame on them for dragging Shorty around and parading him," said Willow. She said that some people took offense to a video, posted on the Hellzapoppin website, of Riot Fest in Chicago in 2018, where Shorty was stage diving and crowd surfing while wearing a helmet. "They think that I'm being forced," said Shorty, who insisted that he is not being exploited. He said that he approached Graves for the sideshow job, and that he is doing exactly what he wants to do.

He said that in sideshow history, the natural born performers were at the top of the circus hierarchy. In the "legitimate shows," they were the ones who made the most money. But aside from the sideshow, job options could be slim for naturals. "What people don't understand is that, for a lot of natural performers, they can't just go into a McDonald's and get a job," said Shorty.

The sideshow, he said, was a better alternative to sitting at home. "This provides them a way to go out and earn a living and have a life that they would not normally have," said Shorty, who lives partly on disability income. "If anybody is exploiting anybody, I'm exploiting myself."

Graves leaned from his bunk to chime in, his long braids hanging forward. "You're not exploiting yourself," he said. "Just because you don't have legs, that's not why you're on this show." Then, his walkie-talkie crackled. It was 2 a.m. I bid farewell, stepped down from the RV and into the rain. I got into my car and drove north into the howling night.

Chapter 8

Life After Freak Show

"But I, that am not shaped for sportive tricks, nor made to court an amorous looking glass, I that am rudely stamped, and want love's majesty, to strut before a wanton ambling nymph..."
- Shakespeare, *Richard III*

On July 25, 2015, the year following his breakthrough gig on *AHS: Freak Show*, Mat Fraser recruited an eclectic troupe of natural born performers and brought them together for an edgy arts festival that served as the culminating achievement of his theatrical sideshow career. He called it Cripfest.

At first glance, it looked like Mat had created his own sideshow, by bringing together far-flung naturals to appear in artistic performances. But the event also featured conference-style discussion panels. And he gave the event a proper sense of gravity by holding it on the 25th anniversary of the passing of the Americans with Disabilities Act, the anti-discrimination law requiring government buildings that receive federal funding, like schools and courthouses, to install handicapped accessible accommodations, like wheelchair ramps.

Mat, the curator, had the high-minded sensibility to hold the event at the prestigious Brooklyn Academy of Music, better known as BAM. By holding it in such a venue, he commanded respect. Furthermore, Cripfest was sponsored by the British Council, an organization that promotes British culture abroad, which gave it the royal stamp of approval.

Cripfest was an all-day arts festival, according to the website description: "Professional disabled artists present performance, visual art and video works with celebration, agitation and Cripsploitation – while reclaiming their identities as part of a larger movement of creative artists who are reshaping the notion of disability in our world, away from the inaccurate performances of disability on Broadway."

The marketing poster for Cripfest was like a punk rock flyer, depicting the American flag and a Union Jack with Mat dominating the foreground, shirtless and grimacing, brandishing his arms. In the ad, he promised "more deformity than in Bradley Cooper's worst nightmares." Cooper had recently starred in a Broadway performance of *The Elephant Man*. He didn't use makeup or prosthetics, so he didn't have the huge swollen head of John Hurt in the David Lynch movie. Instead, it was just Cooper, wearing nothing but a loin cloth, acting like Joseph Merrick. A partially naked heartthrob playing the Elephant Man.

Mat, in his promotion of Cripfest, had called it "dangerous, transgressive, and amazing." He sounded like he was on the bally platform once again, only this time, it was his show, held in an elegant, venerable opera house in downtown Brooklyn. The event began with a panel discussion, "Getting Disabled Performers Cast in Popular Media." The panelists included Mat, who was qualified to discuss this topic, having recently starred in *AHS: Freak Show*.

The performers included Bill "Crutchmaster" Shannon, who break-danced on crutches; Nati Amos, a Coney Island sideshow veteran with amniotic band syndrome who called herself the Patchwork Girl; and Jessy Yates, a burlesque stripper with cerebral palsy who billed herself as "Cerebral Pussy." (Her mentor was Mat's wife, burlesque queen Julie Atlas Muz.) Cripfest also featured a punk band called The Spazms, starring Mat as drummer and Kim Kelly's old high school classmate Eric Paluszak, also known as Velvet Crayon, who plays an arsenal of instruments including guitar. (Kim covered the event for *Jezebel*.)

Having made his mark and established himself in the disabled artist community, Mat was ready to move on to something new.

Mat returned to the stage with a mission. He cast himself as a traditional character in a traditional role, but with his unique twist that gave it a new life and made it unforgettable, even if some critics didn't know quite what to make of it.

He returned to an act he had done before, *Beauty and the Beast*, the 18th-century French fairytale adapted into 19th-century opera and a 20th-century Disney movie, followed by another Disney movie. Mat created a 21st-century theatrical version with his wife, whom he met backstage at the Coney Island sideshow in 2006. In *Beauty and the Beast*, they were often naked and either shagging or simulating. They did explicit runs of this production in 2010, 2014 and again in 2016 in various places, including London, Chicago and New York. They performed at the Abron Arts Center in the Lower East Side, where they were married on stage in 2012 by Dick Zigun.

This was no Disney movie. Mat was dressed in an outlandish costume, with curved ram horns, hairy satyr legs for pants, and prosthetic steampunk arms, but little else. Mat and Julie romped about the stage either partially or fully nude. A *New York Times* review of the 2014 performance said that Mat and Julie worked their way through "an impressive variety of sexual positions," making it sound like an Amsterdam sex show. It was edgy stuff, not so much because it had sex in it but because it featured a disabled actor in a show with sex in it.

A cautious but clearly excited *New York Times* description from 2010 makes it sound like phantasmagoric porn: "The show's outrageous elements all derive from sexual explicitness: a film of a talking clitoris (you read that correctly), the onstage nudity, a very funny scene in which each actor simulates oral sex with fruit of increasing sizes, and an equally over-the-top scene that provides the, er, climax." Mat told me that the production was inspired by *Meet the Feebles*, a demented but brilliant puppet film directed by Peter Jackson early in his career when he was still directing horror movies in New Zealand.

From there, Mat moved on to Shakespeare.

In 2017, Mat was cast in the titular role of *Richard III* for a live theater production in England. This was a brilliant casting choice. Shakespeare depicted Richard III as a disabled character, a hunchback with a "withered" arm. Shakespeare used his disabilities as props for his villainy, to show us how nasty and wicked he was, which complicates the moral ambiguity of playing this character and of Mat's choice in taking on the challenge.

Shakespeare's famous play begins with a monologue from Richard III. Mat delivered the lines like he'd been waiting his whole life to speak the words of the Bard:

"But I, that am not shaped for sportive tricks, nor made to court an amorous looking glass, I that am rudely stamped, and want love's majesty, to strut before a wanton ambling nymph, I, that am curtailed of this fair proportion, cheated of feature by dissembling nature, deformed, unfinished, sent before my time, into this breathing world, scarce half made up, and that so lamely and unfashionable, that dogs bark at me as I halt by them."

Over the centuries, actors have depicted Richard III in various ways. In the 1980s, he was portrayed by Sir Antony Sher, who used crutches and a fake hunchback as props. Sher used the crutches as weapons, implements of intimidation, and phallic tools for referencing sexual innuendo (as explained in *The Oxford Shakespeare* introduction for *Richard III*.)

Casting a disabled actor as Richard III is rare. Mat didn't need crutches, and he didn't need a fake hump. "I don't have to start performing my own impairments," Fraser told the BBC in 2017. "I can just be, in my body. I don't have to make any flourishy hand movements to show my wonderfully crippled hand, or prance about on a stick or anything to illustrate the point." Mat seized the performance with both arms and wallowed in monstrous villainy. "It's very freeing, precisely because I don't have to worry about any political correctness," he told the BBC, allowing him to be "as horrible as possible."

The *Guardian* rated the performance four stars out of five with a review that a true Englishman would understand: "Casting Mat Fraser in the title role was a striking choice, not so much because the actor was born with phocomelia (underdeveloped arms caused by the drug thalidomide) but because he was born in the south of England. Yet Fraser plays on his outsider status brilliantly, creating a sense of a man bitterly aware that he will never fit in."

The critic was taking a contrarian tone, by choosing to emphasize Mat's southern pedigree, rather than his disability, which was clearly the centerpiece of the show. But in fact, the performance took place at the Hull Truck Theatre in Hull, in the North of England, where Mat's Essex accent would mark him as an outlander. The provincial nuances of England are rooted in ancient times and taken extremely seriously. (If you think otherwise, think of modern football fans.) The critic took this opportunity to make a joke, to distract us from the unpleasantness of writing about people's disabilities.

Richard III was the last English king to die in battle, killed by the forces of Henry VII. Some historians have argued that Richard III was actually not that disabled and wasn't deformed as Shakespeare depicted him. Revisionists had long favored the view that Shakespeare's *Richard III* was a pro-Tudor PR hit piece depicting him as an evil, child-killing scoundrel who usurped the throne from its rightful heirs and, therefore, deserved to die. While Richard III probably murdered his young relatives, the crimes remain unsolved, and not everyone agrees with this unflattering depiction. Richard III has fans in England and elsewhere, including the Richard III Society, formed in 1924 to provide a more "balanced assessment" of the reviled king, based on the belief that further research into Richard III "would reveal a very different character from the evil caricature of Tudor propaganda," according to its web site.

Scholars are trying to untangle the lasting misrepresentation created by Shakespeare centuries ago. They believe that Shakespeare's depictions of his disabilities were exaggerated to make them seem grotesque. For example, Richard III in Act 3 says, "Then be your eye the witness of this ill. See how I am bewitched. Behold, mine arm is like a blasted sapling withered up."

Historian Annette Carson, who participated in the exhuming of Richard III's remains, believes the scene in Act 3 where he thrusts out his withered arm "has no factual basis," as she put it in her book, *Richard III: The Maligned King*. She blames the Tudors for his lasting notoriety, and for "believing that an ill-formed body was the outward manifestation of an evil mind," as she wrote in her book. She downplayed his disfigurement as scoliosis placing his right shoulder higher than his left. She described Richard III as having "sound and straight" limbs.

"Stories of Richard as a deformed one-armed hunchback are disproved by his well-attested prowess in battle, and no one who is known to have seen him even mentioned deformity or disability," she wrote, noting that in Richard III's last mounted charge he "single-handedly" killed Henry Tudor's standard bearer and unhorsed his bodyguard, Sir John Cheyney, a "man of outstanding strength and fortitude."

It was easy to dismiss this theory until 2012, when historians including Carson exhumed his skeleton from beneath a monastery parking lot at the site of a Medieval battlefield and discovered that he wasn't as disabled as often depicted. She wrote that Shakespeare's play was finally exposed as propaganda "with the myth of the withered arm and hunchbacked body now dispelled by Richard's own mortal remains."

Richard III's supporters in England consider him their rightful king, whose throne was usurped violently from him by the Tudors. His fans still refer to him, affectionately, as King Dick.

Mat and I met for lunch again in December 2021 at the Essex Market in the Lower East Side. Mat picked the place: a comfortable, open restaurant with roomy booths and good food. He had lived in New York since 2009 and his home was close by, near the theater where he was about to stage a musical production.

I asked Mat about his life after *AHS: Freak Show*, including *Beauty and the Beast*. It reminded me, vaguely, of a French erotic horror comedy from 1975, *La Bête*, where an actress in a Marie Antoinette wig performed a baroque strip tease to harpsichord music while fleeing an aroused beast in the woods, ripping off her clothes piecemeal to slow down the creature.

"I'm saluting her vagina while we're naked," said Mat, describing the explicitness of his onstage performance with his wife in *Beauty and the Beast*. For Mat, it seemed like the climax of his artistic career, like he had crossed a line. Which isn't to say the line was good or bad. But it was a line, which left him wondering what to do next. "Where do we go from here?" he said. "We did the most explicit thing. Let's go the other way and do a show for the whole family that has no tits and cock in it. For the Trump era." He and his wife had decided to do a kid-friendly show. "I don't have kids, don't want kids, but wanted to have contact with kids," he explained.

So he wrote a ribald dance musical based on the old English style of panto, short for pantomime. He explained that panto comedies are family shows but also kind of trashy, with lewd references disguised by puns, gags and double entendres so that only the adults will get it. They used to be popular in Britain as live theater, but they were largely phased out by television, particularly shows like *Benny Hill*, which appeal to the same tastes and desires. But panto shows still appear in places like England and Ireland during the Christmas season. In fact, a panto show was performing in New York that afternoon, just a few blocks away.

Mat wrote the show and called it *Dick Rivington & the Cat*, inspired by an English folk tale of a similar name. Mat was seated in front of the stage, on a stool in the band pit, which consisted of a three-piece band with Mat as drummer. The show starred a natural born performer with dwarfism named Tyler West, who played a cat named Tommy and was dressed in a black-and-white cat costume. "I also need regular stroking," purred Tommy, lifting his arms and grinning lasciviously as an attractive actress scratched his furry stomach. West's face was painted black and white, and he had pointed ears and a tail. West was a clown from the Bindlestiff Family Cirkus.

The party came to an abrupt end later that month, just before the holidays. COVID was resurging with Omicron, a less lethal but more contagious variant. The thirty cast members were being routinely tested, and Mat was bracing for the inevitable. And then, one day, someone got a positive test result and they had to close the show.

It was disappointing to see such a fine performance shut down for events beyond their control. But Mat's versatility demonstrated his long and storied career. Sideshows had played a central part, but he also played drums in bands, acted in live theater, acted on television, created documentaries, wrote musicals and performed naked in a raunchy show with his wife. What would he do next?

After the untimely end of *Dick Rivington & the Cat*, Mat was returning to his flat in London, for his long-scheduled surgery. He was getting his left hip replaced. He was approaching 60, and the hips typically burn out prematurely for thalidomiders who rely heavily on their legs and feet to overcompensate for underdeveloped arms. "Listen, if there's a piece of shit on the countertop, I'll pick it up with my toes and drop in the bin, where you just pick it up with your hands," he explained. "It's just quick and easier with my toes."

He was getting his left hip replaced in January 2022. A spokeswoman for Grünenthal told me that they assisted thalidomiders in the United Kingdom by providing them with funds for hip replacements. She said that thalidomiders "used up" their joints because some of them use their feet to eat, to write or to paint. She said that in some cases their joints are "completely deformed" as they approach 60, like Mat, who was born during the height of the thalidomide epidemic in 1962.

After a few weeks of convalescence, Mat was back at work. We had meant to reconnect in New York, but he was busy in London, getting back-to-back acting gigs for the BBC. This was after years of hustling as a disabled actor who couldn't get roles on TV.

"Hi mate, I got super busy in the last month, fielding 5 different TV jobs," he emailed me in May 2022. "Things have really changed for disabled actors in the UK."

A few months later, *Dick Rivington & the Cat* returned to the stage for the holiday season.

Chapter 9

Tyler West

"I try to be a funny guy who happens to be short, [rather] than a short guy who happens to be funny."
- Tyler West

Tyler West performed as Tommy, a feline clown, in *Dick Rivington & the Cat* during its run in New York in December 2021. Tyler, a natural born little person, was cast as the titular tuxedo cat. He wore a shaggy suit of black and white, with a tail and a furry hood with cat ears. He wore black and white face paint. He was hilarious, energetic and fun. He blended comedy with acrobatics. The cute cat also shared a private connection with the audience. Tommy seemed a bit sharper than the other characters onstage and he shot the audience knowing glances. They were in on his jokes, including raunchy quips that went over the kids' heads.

I finally interviewed Tyler West nearly three years later, in November 2024. I asked him about his role onstage as a natural who has performed in circuses. "I identify as a clown, that's what I feel I am," said Tyler over Zoom. "As a clown you have to have some comfortability with the audience laughing at you."

Tyler was 29 years old at the time of this interview. He was born with dwarfism and stands four feet, three inches tall. He had just moved to Las Vegas from New York. The background setting on his Zoom call showed a clean but featureless room in a residential unit. He said it was temporary housing, as part of his new job with Spiegelworld, an entertainment company with multiple locations. He was located at the Atomic Saloon

Show, a Western-style act featuring sultry actors in skimpy outfits at the Venetian Resort on the Strip.

He had kicked off his career in New York as an actor, comedian and clown. His slick website depicts him in a suit and bow tie with his mouth open, holding what appears to be a cocktail shaker. "Half the Size but Double the Fun," said the website, which includes a plug from the *New York Times* as "The most exhilarating show I have seen all year."

He said that being on stage is an opportunity to be the most powerful person in the room. He decides how people perceive him. Self-perception and the attention of strangers are two different things. "It's something that we forget about until the mirror is brought up to us," he said. As a little person, he gets pissed off when he's riding the subway and strangers take pictures of him. In public, he does not give them voyeuristic permission. But as a clown, he is inviting their attention, and he controls the comic narrative. "I'm letting you laugh at me," he explained.

He said it's a "weird dichotomy" because he gets frustrated with how naturals are represented, but at the same time he performs as a clown, where he invites people to laugh at him. But he tries to guide their perceptions of him and to influence their preconceived notions of little people in general.

"I think dwarves and little people have it the hardest because in pop culture we're represented as mythical creatures and beings," said Tyler, who cultivates a mainstream appearance offstage. He cited Peter Dinklage as an example of a successful artist with a diverse and complex acting career who has transcended stereotypes about little people.

Tyler is no stranger to the dry desert cities of the West. He is originally from Tucson, Arizona. His father was a dentist and his mother was a receptionist. He grew up thinking he would be a Muppeteer, but his arms were too short. He became an actor instead. He graduated with a B.F.A. in acting from the University of Arizona and then moved to New York to kick off his career.

He said that being a little person helped him stand out amid the scrum of actors in New York. "It was the thing that got my foot in the door at first, just because it brought attention to me, and it does make me memorable, so I don't mind it," he said. "I don't mind using my disability placard because, you know, it does set you apart from the rest."

But being a natural born isn't enough. One must have skills. He can juggle, roller skate and stage fight. He has acrobatic talents, including cartwheels and the worm, which he performed as Tommy the Cat, balancing on his furry stomach yoga-style while bending the rest of his body into an arched plank, hands and feet pointing to the ceiling of the theater, rocking like a curved seesaw on his furry stomach. He was in four circuses: Circus Flic Flac, Giffords Circus, Circus Flora and the Bindlestiff Family Circus. He also performed at the House of Yes and the Slipper Room, avant-garde nightclubs in New York that are frequented by sideshow performers.

That's what brought him to *Dick Rivington*. "Mat Fraser's disability is much different from mine," said Tyler. "He surrounds himself with disabled people, who he learns from constantly," said Tyler. He said that when Mat speaks, he listens, because it comes from actual experience. "He's just much more aware, and much more on the zeitgeist of all that."

Mat and his wife recruited Tyler in 2021 and cast him as Tommy, with specific designs as to how to portray a natural born on the stage.

Mat was a drummer with the band offstage. Tyler was the sole natural on stage, and the only little person. "I was the only dwarf that was represented as the cat," he said, "but there were average-height people represented as rats." He was referring to the tall actors in their full body rat suits who towered over Tommy. Still, as a cat, he occupied a higher tier in the hierarchy than the lowly rats. This was no accident. Tyler noted that Mat and Julie's casting selections were purposeful.

Tyler said Mat can pick up on perceptions from the audience, and how people might see an actor presented on stage in a certain way. Tyler said that Mat was able to put him into "the most powerful presentation" on stage.

"Every choice on that show was made with a lot of thought, and so Tommy the Cat was the most powerful person on stage," said Tyler. He explained that Tommy occupies a unique role because he's the only character who can communicate directly with the audience and empathize with them, while also interacting with the other characters on stage. "I think the character was like a genie figure from *Aladdin*. He's the character between the two worlds. No one in the play can understand him but the audience can."

Tyler has not been in a sideshow, though he's performed in circuses, and the circus has a long history of exhibiting naturals. "When I work in circuses, I try really hard not to be the butt of the joke," said Tyler.

He has seen other little people cross a line that he will not cross and do things that he will not do. "I haven't dressed up as an elf or leprechaun or whatever and I try not to," he said. "There are some people who are like nihilistic capitalists, a gig is a fucking gig, if it pays it pays." But he will not debase himself. "There is a really clear path that I could go down but choose not to go down," he said. For example, he does not like the "mini" trope of little people performing miniature versions of rock bands or celebrities because he said they lower the standard for little people, just as minstrel shows diminish the standard for people of color. He once worked with a troupe of little people in Germany who performed as miniature tributes to a famous German band. He liked them personally, but he didn't like what they were doing. "If they're happy with it, then they're happy with it," he said. But Tyler believed that they had reduced themselves to a height joke. "There are better ways to get out in front of an audience than this," said Tyler. He spoke carefully, not wishing to personally criticize other naturals. I told him that I interviewed a little person who toured with Mini Kiss. "They're really wonderful people but they're caught in those traps of being the mini version of another," he said.

Disabled people are often at odds with the built world. He related an anecdote from when he visited the Museum of the City of New York and used the bathroom, where sinks were lowered for kids. Tyler experienced a rare moment where he was able to wash his hands in a public bathroom without having to stretch up to reach the faucets and the sink.

Some little people do not consider themselves disabled. But Tyler, inspired by Mat, acknowledged himself as disabled, as part of a greater effort to make the world more equal.

"I consider myself a disabled artist because there are parts of the world that are inaccessible to me," he said.

I met Tyler a few months later in Las Vegas. I was staying at Circus Circus, where sideshow performers Jackie Molen, Crystal Lockhart and Erik Sprague once worked at the Fright Dome. Tyler was seeing a show with a friend who used to work at the Big Apple Circus. We met downtown in front of the Plaza at the end of Fremont Street, which was illuminated by digital skyroofs the length of city blocks. Sexy strumpets in skimpy outfits cracked whips and jiggled to pounding music. Musclebound shirtless men in tight jeans hoisted tourists to pose for photos while holding the American flag. A massive humanoid in a gorilla suit danced in the street with tourists and posed for selfies. The street was lined with neon T-shirt shops, restaurants and bars.

Tyler had the night off from Spiegelworld to see a drag king's performance. I asked him to compare Las Vegas to New York. He said he lives a 9-to-5 life in Vegas, and everybody drives. "I miss New York," he said. "I miss the people. I miss the walking. I miss walking out just to get a coffee."

But in Vegas, he was living the life of a professional performer because he cut his teeth back in New York, where Mat Fraser mentored him on the methodologies and philosophies of disabled actors. "He's bringing down the elevator for all of us," said Tyler.

Chapter 10

Coney Island

"The Homicides felt that the movie *The Warriors* was based on them, and when it opened at the Ocean Theater in Brighton Beach, the gang packed the theater and went wild, breaking down all barriers between art and reality. The male gang members were known for their black hats, which were stolen from Hasidic Jews, crushed, and wrapped with bandannas signifying the gang's colors."
- *Coney Island Lost and Found*, by Charles Denson

As any film fan will tell you, the Warriors were a fictional Coney Island gang that traveled up to the Bronx for a citywide multi-gang meeting, only to get framed for the assassination of the top leader. They spend the rest of the night jumping turnstiles and riding graffiti-covered trains, pursued by skinheads, Baseball Furies and seductive pistol-packing Lizzies. When the survivors finally make it to Coney, the leader, Swan, takes one look at the depressing graffiti-covered ruins and says, "This is what we fought all night to get back to?" The answer is yes.

Coney Island, the honky-tonk beach at the city's edge, its sands strewn with trash and its boardwalk packed with the unwashed masses, is home to the Coney Island Circus Sideshow, one of the few sideshows left in America that inhabits a permanent location. It's a bona fide freak show, meaning that naturals do perform there. But not always. Sideshow naturals are hard to find.

The bally is where Mat Fraser used to bark like a seal, drawing record numbers of ticket-buyers in the early 2000s. But there were no naturals at the Coney Island Circus

Sideshow in the spring of 2022. There was an eclectic troupe of performers nonetheless. They beckoned to curious tourists from their bally platform on the sidewalk outside the sideshow, next to its main entrance. Niki B. the Talking Doll, a tattooed Goth with long black hair also known as Pink Velvet Witch, serenaded passersby with promises of bizarre acts and entertainment. The Velvet Witch invited an onlooker in a Goosebumps T-shirt to come up to the bally platform and fasten another performer, Cyclone Jack Sullivan, into a straitjacket, from which he deftly escaped, Houdini-style. "Thank you, Goosebumps," cooed the Velvet Witch.

Other cast members shared the bally with them: LaReine the Thrill, the raven-haired priestess of pain, a sword swallower restrained in a buxom corset and fishnet stockings; Obsidian Absurd, a mermaid with long red hair and shiny green sequins and a jaunty little costumed tail; and Alaska the Lost Boy, an aerialist with striking blue hair, a matching blue tiger tattoo, and a scarlet felt cape that clashed with, but also complemented, the color ensemble.

The spectators filed into a dark theater with several rows of bleachers that could seat nearly a hundred. The audience started small, with ten people or so, including two children, but gradually grew during the show, as more ticker holders wandered in during the breaks and occupied the bleachers. Cyclone Jack, with his beard, frizzy blonde hair, cowboy outfit and straitjacket, warmed up the crowd with toilet jokes for the kids. Then he used a grinder and a machete to spray sparks into his bearded face and open mouth.

La Reine the Thrill, the self-described "pain-proof goddess," took the stage and announced, in traditional sideshow style, that she'd undergone a series of facial reconstruction surgeries, starting when she was a little girl. "I have a very special relationship with metal," she said. "I'm going to have to acquaint you with the metal in my skull." She invited a lady up from the audience to feel the screws in her bones, beneath her skin. "That's all I need you for, to verify that I have screws in my face," she said. The lady confirmed that, yes, she could feel them. The goddess sent the lady back into the audience and then stuck a pair of scissors up her nose. Then she swallowed a sword, bending forward as she consumed the blade.

The next act was Obsidian Absurd, who glittered with blue and green sequins. She leaned forward, her red hair tumbling down, and poured shards of glass, blue and green, onto the stage like water. She walked on broken glass, and she walked on the sharp edges of scimitars while balancing swords on her hips and her head, all while jiggling her mermaid tale. Then, Obsidian Absurd climbed into Twisto, a coffin-sized box known in the business as a "blade box." Alaska slid broad blades into the slots of the box, one after another, like a giant knife block, while Obsidian Absurd hid inside, unseen by the audience. Alaska invited spectators to pay a dollar and come onstage to get a close look at Obsidian, her body twisted between the blades. Obsidian stuck her hand out through an opening in the top and waved. "Hi Mermaid," I said to her, "That looks uncomfortable." She replied, "It's like a New York apartment."

The audience continued to add spectators between acts. The bleachers filled up as the show went on. Blue-haired Alaska came onstage in a red velvet cape and stripped it off, revealing a striking blue tiger tattoo on a muscled thigh. Alaska wore a leotard, the sort of outfit worn by a dancer, or an athlete, or an aerialist. Alaska blew up a blue balloon and popped it on the nails to show their sharpness, then pranced provocatively on the bed of nails, bare feet standing on the spikes.

The bed of nails is a common stunt in sideshows and other institutions, including my kung fu school. It is often dismissed, by people who haven't done it, as a trick of displacement, where the many tiny points are displaced across the body to minimize pain and damage. But this is easier said than done. Performers who survived the bed of nails say there's pain involved, and you must power through it. Mat Fraser told me that getting on and off the nails is the hardest part, because at some point you have to put a lot of weight on just one small area, like your butt, and then it feels like you're getting impaled. Mat said getting on and off the bed of nails was particularly challenging for him because he has short arms. After the show, Alaska told me how to withstand the nails: "Meditation."

Alaska brought the sideshow to a climax with an aerial act, climbing and descending from ropes and ribbons and chains, spinning on a suspended ring, and dancing with the practiced forms of an artist-acrobat. Alaska was the star of the no-natural show.

Adam Rinn, artistic director of Coney Island USA, said that he made a conscious decision to include an aerialist in the show, even though it's not a classic sideshow act. He had taken this decision seriously. He knew that Coney Island is the epicenter of American sideshows. "Who defines what a sideshow is?" he asked. "Who's making the rules for what sideshow is? I'm making the rule for what sideshow is. We can do whatever we want." He had a point. Sideshow is an evolving art form.

The show ended after Alaska's act, and customers began leaving through an exit that took them past the gift shop, which sold a selection of carnie-related merch. A man and a woman asked the security guard if the show was over because they had only joined halfway through, and he told them that after an intermission, the show would re-start and they could watch the whole thing again. Theoretically, with the price of admission, ticket holders could watch the show ten times if they started early enough in the day. It's quite a grind for the performers, who must do the same act many times, day after day. But landing a job as a paid staff performer with the Coney Island Circus Sideshow was a cool gig for off-Broadway. Some performers would return year after year.

The show ended with a "What is it?" gimmick, in the spirit of P.T. Barnum's notorious Feejee Mermaid, a jackalope-style humbug of creative taxidermy which he marketed in New York City in the 1840s as a gigantic sexy mermaid, though it was actually a shriveled Frankenstein creation, the torso of a monkey carcass sewed to a fishtail. Coney Island USA didn't employ the same sort of deceptive marketing for its end-of-show exhibit, but it didn't need to. The customer reaction was good enough, and the $1 price was too cheap to argue.

The "What is it?" sign was beside a dark closet that guests could enter after paying a dollar. "It's gross," whined a bearded hipster, as he exited the closet where they hid the mysterious exhibit. Naturally, I was intrigued. It was a wet specimen, a slab of flesh in a jar of fluid, like at the Mütter Museum. It was a piece of meat with teeth, a marine mutant in a greenlit jar with a backdrop of an old newspaper clipping about an unidentified horror found on the beach.

Coney Island's sideshow history goes back to the 19th century when it was a decadent playground known as Sodom by the Sea with an elephant-shaped hotel that eventually burned down. In the early 20th century, Coney was the Disney World of its day, with a boom-and-bust succession of amusement parks and hotels. But by the 1970s, its violent crime, arson and toxic waste made it a waystation to nowhere, a ruined beach at the end of the world.

This was the context in which *The Warriors* was made. The movie provides a 1979 time capsule of New York crumbling into ruin, like the fall of Rome. Crime was only going to get worse, peaking at 2,244 homicides in 1990.

But one of the upsides to urban decline is that apartment rents also decline, so artists and musicians can afford to live there, and the city becomes way cooler. Coney was irresistible to a cadre of artists who couldn't afford Manhattan. One of them, a Yale graduate named Dick Zigun, co-founded a sideshow in Coney Island in the 1980s. And it's still there.

Coney Island (which is not really an island, but used to be) is at the bottom of Brooklyn, where the beach melts into the Atlantic, and where massive freighters and cruise ships pass by, going to and from New York Harbor. Native Americans were the first to inhabit the neighborhood 12,000 years ago. In 1643, English pioneers began settling the area they called Coney Island, named for the wild rabbits that lived there. (The rabbits are still there. They live under the boardwalk.)

Its boardwalk is world-famous, and its skyline is dominated by the towering Parachute Jump, a retired ride where the structure is still maintained for posterity as a gigantic museum piece. The amusement parks, Steeplechase, Dreamland and Luna Park, are iconic (even the ones that burned down a long time ago.) There used to be an attraction called Shoot the Freak, where tourists shot paintball guns at dodging teenagers in *Mad Max*-style battle armor in a trash-strewn alley, but that's gone too. But the Wonder Wheel, built in 1920, is still there and still turning. The Cyclone, which opened in 1927, is the oldest still-functioning roller coaster in the world, built partly out of wood, which gives it that clickety-clack sound. Nathan's Famous Hot Dogs, which has been selling franks since they cost 5 cents back in 1916, is famous for its annual hot dog eating contest on the Fourth of July. The Polar Bear Club's annual New Year's Day Plunge has been going since 1903. Ruby's, a famous dive bar on the boardwalk, has been open, more or less, since the fall of prohibition in 1933. The annual Mermaid Parade is a burlesque art extravaganza that has become the neighborhood's biggest event since Zigun co-founded the nonprofit

Coney Island USA in 1980. He would march in the parade wearing a bowler hat and an old-timey bathing suit while beating a drum. His baby, the Coney Island Circus Sideshow, is one of the few places in America where you can see a genuine freak show.

Zigun's sideshow was originally located on the boardwalk, a prime spot for a bally. But it was moved in 1995 to its current location, one block inland at 1208 Surf Avenue in the Childs building, with a stage for a sideshow, a green room, bathrooms, a gift shop and the Freak Bar, and with a museum upstairs. Zigun was replaced by Rinn as artistic director in 2021.

The Italian Renaissance-style Childs building was built in 1917 but didn't stay there. According to Charles Denson in his book *Coney Island Lost and Found*, the building was jacked up in 1921 and moved 30 feet to make way for W. 12th St. when it was "carved through to the beach." The building still has its barrel-tile roof and corbel brackets. The outside walls have always boasted banners advertising things like "snakeology" and "Electra" and "strange men" inside. They've been updated over the years with pictures of cast members including Mat Fraser, Jackie the Human Tripod and the Lizardman. The entertainers come and go, but Sideshows by the Seashore (as it is also called) is the only fully operating sideshow in America to be rooted in one place year after year, with paid staff and a rotation of performers.

"We are the only permanent ten-and-one circus sideshow in the country," said Rinn, in an interview in April 2022 at the Freak Bar, a funky watering hole that adjoins the sideshow, decorated with 1950s-retro furniture and bric-a-brac. He explained that 10-in-1 means 10 shows for one price. The customer pays a set price and gains admission to an endless series of repeating acts, like a Möbius strip.

"There are other traveling shows and there are nightclub acts and there are other performances, but this is the only permanent housed sideshow in the country," he said. He described World of Wonders as the last traveling tented sideshow, and he described Hellzapoppin as a nightclub act (though they also perform rock concerts, festivals and other outdoor venues.)

Rinn is a teacher who moonlights as a sword swallower and human blockhead whose stage name is Adam Realman. Rinn had a gray beard that made him look like a cross between a pirate, a wizard and a bear. He wore tinted glasses, a black T-shirt that said Coney Island Laser Show, and a pair of clunky silver rings. One of the rings had a demon face. The other was shaped like a hand.

The Freak Bar was bustling. "It's like a cacophony in here," he said, in his native New York accent. He said that his day job, as a teacher of kindergarten and first-grade health and physical education at a New York school, and his second job at Coney Island USA, keeps him "working around the clock."

"These worlds do not meet," he said, referring to his jobs as a sideshow director and a teacher for little kids. "There is no intersection between the two worlds."

But there is some crossover, actually. The Coney Island sideshow is family-friendly, and kids are welcome to attend the show with their parents. He said the shows include gross-out acts with a comedic twist. Sword swallowing is one of the scariest and most dangerous acts.

"There's a certain level of discomfort, certainly, for the audience to watch," he said. "When they're watching these things, they're squirming in their seats." He said the goal is to have the kids walk away from the sword-swallowing act saying, "Wow, that was cool!" instead of hysterically crying with an enraged parent shaking his fist and going, "What the hell did you show my kids?"

He said that some sword swallowers, especially the ones you see on TV, take it to the extreme, swallowing curved swords and doing backflips. Rinn shakes his head at stunts like that. "Swallowing a sword is dangerous enough," he said. "If you can't marvel at the fact that I'm putting 27 inches of steel down my throat without doing a backflip, then sorry, there's nothing I can do that's going to impress you."

He teaches these carnie skills at Coney Island USA's Sideshow School. That's where he trained Kim Kelly to eat fire in 2019.

"Sideshows still are sort of a fringe art," he said. "They're still not as mainstream as magic, as circus. They're called sideshow for a reason, I think. Part of it is to bring sideshow to a new generation of people."

He sat at a Formica booth in the Freak Bar with a commanding view, through plate glass windows, of the street scene on Surf Avenue and the side street (West 12th St.) leading to the boardwalk, where performers on the bally stage performed stunts for tourists, beckoning them inside with their banter, their charm, their weird hair, their costumes and other eccentricities.

"I want to get asses in seats," said Rinn, watching the bally and thinking about the sideshow's recently-ended pandemic hibernation. "It's been two years."

The sideshow had been in operation for nearly 40 years when COVID arrived. "I was appointed associate artistic director just pre-pandemic," said Rinn. "Then we hit March [2020] and the world shut down. And then *we* were shut down. And then it was basically: What the hell are we going to do?"

In the summertime, Coney Island is a funky, tattooed, sunburned party of skin, sweat, music and beer. But in the winter, it can seem like desolation, with only the Polar Bear Club and the Russians from Brighton Beach willing to swim its frigid waters. With COVID-19, an extra-long *Game of Thrones* winter came to Coney. When Kim Kelly did her fire-eating performance in December 2019, that was the last live show at Sideshows by the Seashore until the spring of 2022. COVID caused the venerable establishment to close its doors for more than two years.

"The first year, there was nothing to do," said Rinn, explaining how the sideshow attempted several re-openings but had to shut their doors every time a new variant appeared, causing a spike in infections and mortality to roll through New York. "In 2021, we opened, then closed, and we opened, and we closed, and at a certain point we said the risk isn't worth the reward, and we shut it and were done."

At the dawn of the pandemic, Zigun was still running the organization as artistic director. He had lived in the Surf Avenue building upstairs from the sideshow. He had planned to retire there, but at the end of 2021 he was terminated from the organization.

He was replaced by Rinn, who was promoted to artistic director at the start of 2022 to oversee the grand reopening.

Rinn credits Jim Rose with mainstreaming the modern sideshow. Rose led a Seattle troupe of tattooed, pierced-up performers who committed acts of self-torture, including the Amazing Mister Lifto, who hung cinder blocks and beer kegs from piercings in his nipples and penis, Tim Cridland The Torture King, a bed of nails badass who impaled himself with skewers, Bebe the Circus Queen who tempted suffocation in her Plastic Bag of Death, and Matt "The Tube" Crowley, an ex-pharmacist who used a stomach pump to feed himself beer, chocolate and ketchup through a seven-foot nasal tube and then extract his "bile beer" for an audience member to drink. Rinn said that when the Jim Rose Circus Sideshow appeared with Lollapalooza in 1992, it returned sideshow culture to the mass American consciousness. But this time, it was different. Rose had inspired a new image for sideshows, with fewer naturals but more self-modified performers, with emphasis on punk-style gross-out stunts of self-punishment. "Playing with pain," as Mat Fraser put it, in his documentary where he performed with a group of non-natural Australians who called themselves the Happy Sideshow.

Sideshows without naturals feel *unnatural*. There were no natural borns at the Coney Island Circus Sideshow in the spring of 2022. Rinn said that Xander Lovecraft, a little person, was planning to join the show that season, but he had developed medical problems back in St. Louis.

The seasonal lack of naturals was just a temporary vacuum for Coney Island. Its history is synonymous with sideshows and there's a long list of naturals who performed at Coney in the 19th, 20th and 21st centuries: Stanislaus Berent, who performed as Sealo the Seal Boy; Mat Fraser, who also performed as Sealo in a series of tribute shows; Jason Black as Black Scorpion; Kim Kelly as Greta the Lobster Girl; Erik Paluszak as Velvet Crayon; Jackie Molen as the Human Tripod; Jesus "Chuy" Aceves as the Wolf Boy, from a Mexican family where dozens of members have a hairy condition called hypertrichosis; Crystal Lockhart as Lil Miss Firefly; Erik Sprague as the (self-made) Lizardman; Eli Bowen as the Legless Acrobat; Xander Lovecraft as Xander Lovecraft; William Henry Johnson as Zip the What Is It? (a famous microcephalic "pinhead" who rescued a drowning girl at Coney in 1925); Minnie Woolsey (who appeared in the movie *Freaks*) as Koo Koo the Bird Girl; Sarah Houbolt of Australia, also as Koo Koo the Bird Girl (she performed as a tribute to Minnie); Otis Jordan (who changed his persona from Frog Boy to the Human Cigarette Factory); Prince Randian as The Living Torso (and also the Snake Man, the

Human Worm, the Sausage Man, the Pillow Man, the Human Torso, the Caterpillar Man); Serpentina, a woman who was boneless except for her head and arms and went by Nature's Strangest Living Enigma; Jennifer Miller as Zenobia the bearded lady; Antonio J. Torres Jr. as Koko the Killer Klown; and the little person Nik Sin.

Lionel the Lion-Faced Boy was one of the most famous Coney Island naturals. Hair, eight inches long, covered his body like a lion's mane. He was born in Poland in 1890 as Stephan Bibrowsky with a condition called hypertrichosis, or "werewolf syndrome," abnormal hair growth all over the body except for his palms and soles. Lionel started exhibiting in Europe when he was four years old and came to America in 1901, where he toured with Barnum and Bailey for five years. He went back to Europe to continue exhibiting until he returned to America in 1913. All roads lead to Coney Island, where he spent 15 years performing his gymnastic skills for millions of spectators at the Dreamland Circus sideshow. Lionel's extensive tented exhibit boasted three separate banners showing pictures of the hirsute natural. Members of the audience asked him why he didn't shave, and he replied that he was paid $500 a week.

There were three major amusement parks in the history of Coney: Steeplechase I, from 1897 to 1907, Luna Park, from 1903 to 1946, and Dreamland, from 1904 to 1911. Some parks burned and were rebuilt.

Many of these performers were based at Dreamland, including Eli Bowen, a father of four who died in his Dreamland living quarters in 1924, at age 79. He was a legless performer who rode a bike tandem-style with his natural born friend Charles Tripp, who had no arms. Bowen would grip the handlebars and steer while Tripp would pedal the bike with his legs.

Dreamland loomed large in the history of sideshow, particularly for little people. The amusement park featured Lilliputian Village, a showcase community of 300 little people, including the most famous one of all, Charles Stratton, better known as Tom Thumb, the prodigy of Phineas Taylor Barnum, the impresario of natural borns. They also called it "Midget City," though the m-word has since been condemned as an offensive slur. Old photos show groups of little people posing as couples, the men in suits and the women in long flowing Victorian dresses with frilly bonnets. The city had its own police and fire department but was eventually overshadowed by a groundbreaking but bizarrely situated scientific exhibit of incubators, where tourists gawked at premature babies being kept alive in the new contraptions.

Sideshows, on a smaller scale than Dreamland, continued to be a regular feature at Coney up until the 1950s when they were banned by reformers who believed that the naturals were being exploited. Also, the urban planner Robert Moses hated sideshows and loudspeaker bally marketing which he considered too trashy for Coney. Moses was one of the most powerful public figures in New York history and usually got what he wanted.

I asked Rinn if he thinks sideshows are exploiting the natural born. He said that nobody at Coney is being forced to do anything. "We all make choices; your choice is to work here or not to work here," he said. "Your choice to work within the field of sideshow is your choice."

He said that throughout history, sideshows provided opportunities to people with disabilities that they wouldn't otherwise have. "If you were born different 100 years ago, there were laws in some places that said you could not leave the house, you could not go out in public," he said. "The sideshows were the only places where people like this could get work. Were some of them exploited? Sure. But in many places, the sideshow performers were paid more than anyone."

He explained his philosophy on recruiting naturals for the show, which was similar to what Bryce Graves said about Hellzapoppin. Being natural born, by itself, just wasn't good enough. They need to have talent. They need to have skills.

"If you're good on stage, we'll give you a job," he said. "You need to have a quality act, whether you are born different or not. Impress me. We're not in the business of putting people on stage just to exploit. They're not meant to be gawked at. They also have accomplished talents."

Chapter 11

Freak Finder

"Everyone's happy when the wizard walks by."
- Black Sabbath

Jellyboy the Clown slid a sword down his throat, commanding the attention of a packed audience at a saucy Brooklyn nightclub known as the House of Yes. He stood on stage in front of a live Tesla coil, crackling with a halo of raw electricity, with a sword handle projecting from his mouth, the blade buried inside him. The clown bent towards the oscillating current, coaxing the volts towards him. A hot jolt of electricity arched from the Tesla coil to the sword hilt jutting from his mouth, forming an electric bridge between machine and man. He had turned himself into a human lightning rod, from the inside out.

I shadowed Jellyboy one night in the summer of 2022, during his whirlwind tour of New York and Philadelphia while visiting from Iceland. He had been in the sideshow business for about 20 years and had traveled the world. He co-founded the Squidling Brothers Circus Sideshow with his brother, Matterz Squidling. He and his brother once had a house in Philadelphia for sideshow naturals to live in. He had served as a modern-day "freak finder," a sideshow recruiter for naturals. He used to be a recruiter for the Coney Island Circus Sideshow.

Jellyboy wore white face paint with jagged black stripes that matched his partially shaved beard. He wore a baggy black suit with a flat crowned fedora. He had a shuffling walk and a dusty demeanor, like the road clowns from the Great Depression who wore a shade of black that was darker than dirt. He had decorated his suit with pictures mimicking the banners and placards of the Coney Island Circus Sideshow.

Jellyboy swallows swords, a gun, a flamethrower and even a sword attached to a strange furry puppet. The clown was driving around New York in a beat-up van full of carnival props that could have doubled as weapons in a zombie apocalypse.

He invited me to have tacos with him after the show, and then he drove me in his van over to his next show in Manhattan, at the Slipper Room, the burlesque haunt of Mat Fraser, Velvet Crayon and Illustrated Penguin. He fired up the van and drove through the crowded streets of Williamsburg, working his way around drunken revelers, leaving the bars and lights behind as he rolled along the dark streets at the edge of the neighborhood, making his way towards the bridge to Manhattan. Jellyboy explained that in his days at Squidling, he became friends with Crayon and Penguin. Dick Zigun eventually recruited him to run the casting for Coney Island. He worked there from 2017 to 2021 and was adept at recruiting naturals.

"I was a talent scout," he said. "I found all these freaks, and all these freaks would find me."

It struck me as something Ward Hall would say: the late, legendary freak finder from the World of Wonders. I asked Jellyboy how he became an impresario for the natural born.

"When I got the job at Coney Island, I reached out to everyone I know," said Jellyboy. And then he pulled off a remarkable stunt for a 21st-century sideshow. He recruited a natural born lineup of five performers at Coney, his so-called Dream Team: Nati Amos, the Illustrated Penguin, Xander Lovecraft, Velvet Crayon and Sara Houbolt, AKA Koo-Koo the Bird Girl from Australia. She had fashioned her act in tribute to the original Koo Koo the Bird Girl, AKA Minnie Woolsey, who appeared in the 1932 movie *Freaks*. He said they got her a work visa and flew her to New York. He said that she did an aerial act over a bed of nails, blindfolded, to prove that she was legally blind, because otherwise the spectators wouldn't believe her.

He told me about other naturals he'd met: Chuy the Mexican Wolf Boy, Jane Hash, Samantha X, Lil Miss Firefly and Jackie the Human Tripod.

And then, in 2019, he recruited Kim Kelly, who had just learned how to breathe fire at the Coney Island sideshow school. She was signing on for the summer as Greta the Lobster Girl. "We were going to give her a shot," he said. "Grind shows are not for everybody." He was referring to the all-day Möbius strip of shows, one after the other, 10-in-1.

In the winter of 2019, they were excited about the upcoming 2020 season. And then COVID happened, and the world shut down. But not forever.

Three years later, Jellyboy parked his van in the Lower East Side and we walked along the sidewalk rolling his beat-up suitcase containing his swords and flamethrower through the thriving crowds of Saturday night. It's hard to stand out in New York, but Jellyboy manages. Strangers on the street smile when they see the shuffling clown. During his act at the Slipper Room he played *The Wizard* by Black Sabbath, with its famous lyric: "Everyone's happy when the wizard walks by."

Jellyboy returned to Philly that night, rolling into the city as the sun was rising. Two weeks later, he was back in Iceland.

Chapter 12

The Patchwork Girl

"You can think that my life is poor and sad because I'm in the circus, but it's not; I have a cool life and I'm OK. People have a hard time with me being a happy person."
- Nati Amos, the Patchwork Girl

"One undergraduate professor told me that because of my disability, no college would ever hire me as a teacher. I guess he thought he was helping me face the hard facts."
-*Why I Burned My Book*, by Prof. Paul Longmore, San Francisco State University

It was a cool, cloudy Sunday afternoon in September 2022. We sat outside at a little round table at a café in the Upper East Side, across Fifth Avenue from Central Park, and just a few feet from the Guggenheim Museum. The café was in an old stone church with buttressed columns like a Medieval castle.

I asked Nati Amos how many fingers she had. She laughed. It was an awkward question, but I honestly couldn't tell. She explained that this was a conundrum for some people, trying to guess. She had turned it into a sideshow act.

"Quick, figure out how many fingers I'm holding up!" she said, amused at the chance to do a sideshow trick. She held up her hands and spread them out, pink and stubby, like latex mittens.

"The answer," she said, "is all of them." She laughed. The joke is that she actually has ten fingers, more or less. Mostly less. Eight of them are tiny digits ending at the first knuckle. She has two full fingers, the index finger and thumb of her right hand, so she can form the OK sign. But while her hands look different, they're unexpectedly dexterous, as if full-developed fingers move beneath the skin. She picked up a coffee cup in each hand, lifting it up and down. "This is a five-dollar act," she said.

We each had our own pot of coffee resting on the table in front of us. The pots were made of thick clear glass and shaped like fishbowls, with circular bodies and short fat openings at the top. They were like smaller versions of the glass carboys I used to brew beer in college. They were filled with steaming black coffee. She lifted one pot by the neck, her hand wrapping around it like a sock. She lifted it easily, even though she only has one full finger and one full thumb. "People would pay five dollars to watch me lift shit," she said. "So, you're getting a free show."

Just prior to our lunch date, I had seen her approach from a distance, unmistakable in her white and black striped shirt and matching winter cap. She was walking with a cane along Fifth Avenue, the white edifice of the Guggenheim looming behind her like a gigantic layer cake. She came all the way from the Bronx on the subway to meet with me, at my request. She had chosen this café as an approximate halfway point between where we each live. I figured the least I could do was buy her lunch.

Nati is a scientist and a lab technician with a bachelor's degree in biochemistry from Roosevelt University in Chicago. She is also a natural born sideshow performer who specializes in fire. She was born with amniotic band syndrome. "That's an archaic term," she said when I brought it up. It is a rare and complex condition, difficult to label.

I asked her to describe her act. Like other sideshow performers, she had experimented with different ways of shocking and delighting. The bed of nails. The straight-jacket escape. The flaming, twirling rod dance. The fire staff. And mind-blowing mundane stuff like lifting a coffee pot.

Mundanity has a place in sideshow tradition. She told me that in Coney Island in the 1800s tourists would visit Lilliputia, the Dreamland amusement park staffed by hundreds of little people living in a model community, going about their routines as cops, firefighters, railroad conductors, lifeguards and laundry washers. They rode on ponies and a little train. "People would go to Lilliputia and they would watch the little people do mundane things," said Nati.

She explained how some sideshow naturals do simple tasks for the amazement of the audience. For example, she said that Mat Fraser would sometimes shave as part of his show, which is no mean feat for a man with short arms and no thumbs. Jason Brott, AKA the Illustrated Penguin, would get dressed for an office job as part of his act, which he managed without the benefit of arms, just a pair of hands sprouting from his shoulders. Of course, the mundane acts are part of a broader repertoire of talents. Mat is a trained theater actor and a drummer, while Jason is a drummer and a human blockhead. Short E. Dangerously jumps on flaming broken glass. Black Scorpion hammers his hands. Xander swallows a balloon. The Bendable Girl shoots a bow and arrow with her feet while standing on her hands. The Lobster Girl eats fire.

"The longevity of a natural born is to have an act," said Nati. "Something to accentuate their oddity." Mundanity is not Nati's style. Her style is much hotter than that. "In my case, that happened to be fire," she said. "I like fire. Who doesn't like to blow shit up?" There are many ways for a pyromaniac to play with flames. Nati chose the fire-twirling rod. "It is challenging and dangerous," she said. "Especially when you don't have fingers."

A *Vice* profile in 2016 described her sideshow acts as laying on a bed of nails, escaping from a straitjacket while reciting *The Glass Menagerie*, and dancing to a PJ Harvey song while twirling a metal flaming staff with two fingers. *Vice* described her performance as "flirty, mischievous."

Years later, Nati still performs in sideshows occasionally. The fundamental question is: Why? "Needing to make money and not being able to find a job," she said. (At that particular time, she was between jobs, though she soon returned to her profession as a lab technician.) She said that if she's going to get gawked at by strangers, she might as well monetize it. "I look weird anyway, and if people are going to stare at me for free, they should pay," she said. Some sideshow naturals aren't shy about trying to monetize their disability, though in her case it's more of a side hustle than a full-time job. Either way, it did not seem like a path to riches.

She said that it wasn't easy, scraping together a living as a sideshow performer. "It's a grind," she said. "They don't call it a grind show for nothing." Nati referred to the classic 10-in-1 show, where a customer buys ten acts for one ticket. The shows go on all day, and customers can wander in and out, so it's ideal for meandering tourists at Coney Island.

She said that a good strategy is to get a couple of good paydays and live on that for a while. But you're going to have to work for it. "You can get lucky and get a corporate act, and corporations will sometimes want an extreme act," she said. As with most things, she's said it's all about networking. "Even now I get calls for gigs," said Nati, who did a fire act that summer. "If I have the time, I'll do them."

In the traditional sideshow style, the naturals explain their condition to the audience. Nati said that amniotic band syndrome is actually a multi-faceted condition that has no "special linkage," as she put it.

"The idea is that the very small spindles that are used to create the developing fetus in the amniotic sack usually disappear, but mine didn't, and they wrapped around the facial feature," she said.

She said the spindles cut through the developing tissue of the fetus like a string on a needle threading through warm butter. Amniotic band syndrome is a rare birth defect that can happen when the amnion, or the inner layer of the placenta, is damaged during pregnancy, according to an online description from Johns Hopkins Medicine. Sometimes this creates fiber-like bands of tissue that tangle around the fetus, restricting blood flow, and causing deformities. "In some cases, strands can tangle so tightly around the limbs of a fetus they can amputate them," according to Johns Hopkins. "For example, a band that passes over the face has been associated with cleft lip and even cleft palate." It can also kill the fetus.

Nati said she was also born with a club foot, and one of her early surgeries was to try to repair this foot, by breaking and resetting it. "My foot is essentially a broken foot," she said. "The foot was already broken; they just broke it more." When I asked her how many surgeries she's had, she laughed, as if I'd asked her to count the hairs on her head. Then she calculated an average of six to eight surgeries per year, since her birth in 1986. "With all the surgeries I've had," she said, "pieces of my hips have been used to paste together parts of my nose, and parts from everywhere. I'm a patchwork of tissue. Nati made from Nati."

She was born in Mexico City, though her parents had planned to birth her north of the border. "I was born premature," she said. "For all intents and purposes, I was going to be born here [in the U.S.]; it just didn't happen." Her parents moved her to the U.S. eventually, where she has lived most of her life. They moved when she was practically a newborn because the life-saving medical care she needed was unavailable in Mexico. Nati paraphrased her Mexican doctors: "They said, 'You should go to the U.S.; we don't have anything for her here. She will die here.'"

Mexico City in the 1980s, with its cartels and poverty, wasn't hard to leave behind. She grew up in New York and San Diego. She started undergoing surgeries when she was two months old, and the doctors had grim prospects for her living much longer than that. "They were not optimistic," she said. "They said we can try it, but we're probably not going to make it."

As she got older, the surgeries continued one after another. She got used to the pain. "You get desensitized to it to a certain extent, and that becomes a problem," she said. "I have a high tolerance to pain." She's endured dozens of surgeries and it seems to have affected her wiring. "Your body is constantly in a state of fight or flight," she said. She said her nerves moved slowly. "With pain, it took a long time for my body to tell me that something is wrong," she said.

While other patients rely on opioids, they were not an option for her. "I'm allergic to opiates; no heroin for me!" she said in mock glee while spreading out her arms theatrically, as if she were talking about ice cream.

One time, when she was in "immense pain," her brother gave her pot brownies, and the pain went away. But she usually copes by doing hook suspension. She met a friend at a party in the 2000s and he introduced her to it. He told her, "I think you would really enjoy it." She fell in love with hook suspension.

I told Nati that Kim Kelly also does suspension. She would literally pay someone to put hooks through her knees and hang her from the ceiling by cables. Kim would dangle from them upside down, twisting languidly over a hardwood floor. She made it look easy, but it reminded me of a Japanese movie, *Ichi the Killer*, where a yakuza tortured a rival by suspending him from hooks and pouring hot tempura oil on him. When I mentioned this movie to Nati, she nodded, smiling knowingly. "It's fun for me," she said. "It became a little bit like crack for me for a while."

She said that many of the surgeries throughout her life were to make her "somewhat tolerable to the human eye, as much as I can be." She considers the surgeries as an accommodation, something the doctors did for the non-disabled public. "All of these old guys would rip me up and put me back together as their Mona Lisa," she said. "So suspension was a way for me to take myself back. The suspension is something I was told is mine. It's just me and God. To me, it was just super-healing and helpful. It was cheaper than therapy."

Nati left home when she was 17 and joined the circus. She described herself as an "angry feminist punk" at that time. "I was very into constructive destruction," she said.

At first, she made her way to Seattle, got a job, and "did boring office shit." But she developed her skills as a performer and joined a small troupe called the Kings Cabaret, which she described as a smorgasbord of four or five people who would "do crazy shit." "That was my introduction to circus work and then it kind of escalated from there," she said.

When she was in her early 20s, she landed a gig with World of Wonders, a traveling tent show run by the now-deceased Ward Hall, a legend among sideshow hucksters who managed some of the most famous naturals of his time, and partner Chris Christ. (This was before current owner Tommy Breen took ownership of World of Wonders.) She lasted one season, shaking her head with amazement as she recalled the vagabond lifestyle of sideshow life.

Then she made her way to Coney Island to work for Dick Zigun. At that point, she had performed at the two most legendary sideshow venues with the two most legendary impresarios. She described Zigun as "like the grandpa that you love, but he's an asshole, but you love him anyway. If he believed in you, he would take you under his wing." She said this could lead to favoritism, one of the nuances of working in the microcosm of Coney Island USA.

Nati is also a gifted writer. She sent me the draft of a story in which she referred to herself in the third person, to temper the intensity of her memoir. She wrote vignettes about life as a natural born: "Her father would tell her that God had made her his living Dalí. It was the most exquisite compliment she could ever hope to get."

I asked her the question I ask all sideshow naturals: Do you think sideshows, less delicately known as freak shows, are exploiting or empowering disabled people? "It's a very fine line," she said. "The thing is, we're going to get exploited no matter what. We have no privacy. Exploitation? You walk out into the street, you're going to get exploited."

The decline of the sideshow, following the heyday of the mid-20th century, is blamed on multiple factors, including the ascent of television as entertainment, and the so-called do-gooders who wanted sideshows banned as an evolution in cultural tastes and civil reform. But Nati isn't buying it. "People who say sideshows are bad, these are the same people who would berate people for going on Social Security or welfare," she said. "What do you want? You can't have it both ways. Finding a niche for us to be self-sustaining, isn't that better than living as a dredge on the system?"

Capitalism is the driving force behind sideshows, carnivals and circuses. P.T. Barnum once wrote a book about it called *The Art of Money-Getting*. In truth, Tom Thumb became rich as a sideshow natural and even bailed out Barnum when he went bankrupt. He was the 19th-century equivalent of a movie star or a rock star. Generally speaking, I didn't get the impression from naturals that they were making a lot of money doing sideshow. Nati told me they try to live on a sprinkling of big paydays. But they were also doing sideshow for the rush, like Shorty, or the art, like Black Scorpion, or the tribute, like Mat Fraser. It's the same reason why authors write books, even if they don't make money.

"I think sideshow gave me a lot because it helped me come to terms with how people see me," she said. "The thing is, I'm never going to control how other people see me. The best thing you can do is do as much as you can with your narrative. And leave it there. Don't react, don't pick a fight, just do your art and leave it out there." She said her father once told her that people are going to see you, however they're going to see you, and you can't take it personally, because it's on them.

As she tries to read the minds of her audience, she figures some of them are thinking, "Thank God I'm not like her." If cynics are going to sideshows with the ableist attitude of pitying the naturals, she sees herself as doing them a service. "I gave them some appreciation for whatever shitty life they're going home to," she said. But that's not the way she sees herself.

"My life is fine," she said. "You can think that my life is poor and sad because I'm in the circus, but it's not; I have a cool life and I'm OK. People have a hard time with me being a happy person. I can't miss what I've never had. I don't know what it's like to have 10 fingers. I made a good life with what I have."

She mentioned an issue that is central to ableism, which is the superiority complex that non-disabled people feel over naturals. Ableism manifests itself as the creeping horror that non-disabled people feel when they see someone who is disabled, and sometimes they conclude that their lives aren't worth living. This is the philosophy of Peter Singer, an Australian academic who has advocated euthanasia for naturals. He's anathema to disabled academics like Alice Wong, an author with muscular dystrophy, and the late Prof. Paul Longmore, a historian who lost the use of his arms from polio at age 8. Disability activists argue that the bleeding hearts who want to do them a favor should improve the built world to be more accommodating, instead of killing them.

"If you're so concerned with my quality of life, then maybe make my quality of life better," said Nati. But instead, people tell her that naturals like her should be aborted. "People say I should die, or they say my mother should have killed me," said Nati. "They say, 'If my kid was like you, I would have killed her in the womb.'" She said that she has been accused, inaccurately, of being a crack baby, or to be more specific, "a poster child for crackheads." She said this hateful rhetoric has become emboldened in recent years.

She finds it bizarre that the majority are so resistant to helping disabled people, since many of them are destined to become disabled themselves. "Anybody could get disabled," she said. "You could get into a car accident. It's stupid to think that disability is only a problem for people who are disabled. You may get old and you may need a wheelchair. Us fighting for things like elevators and wheelchair ramps, you're going to benefit from this at some point in your life."

According to the Centers for Disease Control and Prevention, 26% of the U.S. population has some type of disability. That means that 87.3 million Americans are disabled, which is more than the population of Germany. The CDC says that 13.7% of the U.S. population has a functional disability to their mobility, meaning that 46 million Americans have "serious difficulty walking or climbing stairs." Yet people with disabilities are dismissed, ignored and overlooked, like an obscure tribe.

Public speaking might be her greatest talent. Nati's voice is soft and sometimes muffled, but she commands the stage with a smart delivery that challenges whatever preconceptions the audience might have of the four-foot-six Patchwork Girl. She was a speaker at TEDx, an independent offshoot of TED Talks, in Jersey City in 2014. She appeared on stage nattily dressed in a plaid tie and pocket hanky with a dapper vest, bowler hat and a deep purple shirt. She talked about her father. "He told me that no matter how smart, how intelligent, how clever I was, that might not be enough for some people to look past." Her father told her that she would have to work three times as hard as anyone else because she is a woman, she is Latina, and she is "seen as disabled."

Nati, with her bachelor's in biochemistry, works in wet labs with blood panels. Since she's a lab technician who conducts tests, the COVID-19 pandemic hit her like a tidal wave. She was in the city for the apocalypse, working at SUNY Downstate Medical Center and Kings County Hospital Center in Brooklyn as a research assistant, swabbing and doing intake for the hordes of sick patients.

"During COVID, we had to shut down, but we also had to do all hands-on deck," she said, while toiling at Downstate and Kings County hospitals. "We got hit hard. We had to use the cafeteria as a second waiting area. It was wild, wild. It was what I imagined war would be."

She was also starting a job as a lab tech at Mount Sinai Hospital in Manhattan, which got slammed as well. "A lot of people didn't want to come in, so I basically lived at the hospital for a couple months. I thought I was going to die. I thought, this is how it ends for me."

It was not an easy thing for Nati to enter the field of science. One might think that academia would be more accommodating to disabled people than hands-on jobs like construction, but that is not necessarily the case. Longmore wrote about his struggles to become a history professor for San Francisco State College. Every step of the way, he was told by academics that colleges would never hire him. He wrote a powerful essay, *Why I Burned My Book*, about how the earnings from his history book were threatening his access to disability benefits, so he torched it in a public display. He had written the book by pecking out the words with a pen clenched in his teeth.

"My story is not unique in terms of oppression," said Nati. "We're recognizing race and gender but not so much about disability. Disability is kind of a weird world to people because people don't know how to digest it."

Sometimes Nati herself has a hard time wrapping her brain around the word "disability," like when she's applying for a job. "Going into the job market now and clicking the disability box is really difficult for me because I don't know if that's going to help or hurt me," she said. "Disability is a code word for liability. But my disability does not prevent me from doing my job, so I always struggle with that."

Like Longmore, Nati embarked on her career with big plans to become a medical doctor, but she encountered hurdles. "When I wanted to go to medical school, I got laughed at. They said, 'You can't go to medical school; you can't be a doctor,'" she said.

"I'm really knowledgeable and I'm really smart and I'm really capable," she said. But she knows that some people have a hard time accepting her intellect at "face value," especially hospital patients who would encounter her as a bedside visitor during rotations.

"You have to examine patients, and I don't know about you, but there's not a lot of patients that would want me to touch them," she said, holding up her hands. She had accepted the fact that many patients don't want to be handled by a disabled medical practitioner.

"It's like that saying, when you make plans, God laughs," said Nati, who is Jewish. "And to be fair, I thought that with my intelligence, with all of the ingredients that would make me a good scientist, that I would prevail. Science, with its hardcore math and numbers and results and ideas, that's something I can do."

So she abandoned the idea of becoming a medical doctor. But she later regretted that decision when she learned of the DaVinci system of conducting surgery remotely, via robotic arms and video connections. "Had I stayed in medicine, I could have just used fucking robotics," she said. "But I let them talk me out of it, and that's what hurts more." She said that she wants to spend the rest of her life working in a lab and teaching. She also has big plans for higher education. "I want to get my Ph.D.," she said. "I could have three Ph.Ds. and it's not really going to matter. The reason why I'm getting a Ph.D. is because I want it, I want it, I want it."

Chapter 13

The Mayor of Coney Island

"Zigun and his drama degree from Yale University soon got the most ink. Reporters treated his sheepskin as an oddity, the same way they would a two-headed baby or an albino python. Zigun's academic credential usually appeared in the lead paragraph as if to reassure readers about the organization's freak show."
- *Coney Island: Lost and Found*, by Charles Denson

Dick Zigun, the unofficial mayor of Coney Island, co-founded Coney Island USA in 1980 and ran the place for about 40 years. He was a creative force behind Sideshows by the Seashore and the Mermaid Parade.

Back in 2002, author Charles Denson of *Coney Island: Lost and Found* asked Zigun what he planned to be doing when he was 70 years old. "I'll be semi-retired, a member of the board emeritus, and still have my home in the Childs building," said Zigun, when he was about to turn 50. "The young folks will be doing the balance of the work at the sideshow while I go back to being a playwright. I'll probably be doing exactly the same thing I'm doing now, chasing Koko the Klown down the street, cleaning the toilets, and doing the bookkeeping."

But when I met Zigun at the Coney Island Brewery 20 years later, just before he was to turn 70, he no longer worked at the Coney Island sideshow and neither did Koko. His tenure at Coney Island ended in 2021.

Koko was a diminutive, barrel-shaped clown, but according to Zigun he was actually a "very hardcore ghetto gangbanger" with a criminal record named Antonio Torrez Jr.

Zigun created his sideshow character the Killer Klown. A black and white photo in Denson's book shows Zigun on the bally wearing a bowler hat, a fat python wrapped around his shoulders, with Koko standing beside him, short and thick, his face painted white, wearing a prison uniform stenciled PROPERTY OF FLORIDA STATE PENITIARY. But that was a long time ago. Since then, Tony Torrez, his early sideshow star, had moved far away from the boardwalk. He lived in West Virginia and was "doing great," explained Zigun.

Zigun launched Sideshows on the Seashore in 1985, as a test to New York laws and public perception. "It wasn't even clear whether it was legal to open a sideshow," he said. He worked with John Bradshaw, a veteran performer who served as a one-man sideshow for Coney's first season. But Bradshaw wasn't natural born. They didn't feature a natural born performer in that first season, a decision that had more to do with availability than anything else. Sideshow naturals were rare, if they could be found at all.

And then they found one, down in Georgia. Bradshaw, with the help of colleague Dick Burnett, recruited a natural born performer named Otis Jordan, pulling him out of retirement from his hometown of Barnesville. He was born with arthrogryposis multiplex congenita, a rare defect causing permanent flexion of the joints, according to his profile on sideshowworld.com, which described him as "halfway between a human torso and an ossified man."

Jordan, born in 1926, was one of the very few sideshow naturals in America at that time, and he deserves credit for keeping sideshow alive during its near-extinction. Bradshaw once told the journal *Shocked and Amazed!* that sideshows relied on working acts "but what they really needed was a couple [of] good, strong features, nice looking freaks or human oddities, and feature that. I always had Otis and a bearded lady or a tattooed lady. Something different." He said that working acts, like fire eaters, support the main act, the natural born. "You have to be *born* a feature on a sideshow," said Bradshaw.

Historian Robert Bogdan interviewed Jordan for his history book *Freak Show*, which he published in 1988, when freak shows barely existed in America. "The framing device of that book begins and ends with Otis Jordan, the Frog Boy, who was forbidden to perform at the New York State Fair," said Zigun. "The accusation was that he was being exploited."

Freak Show explains that Otis was banned in 1984 from appearing in the Sutton Sideshow's Incredible Wonders of the World as part of the New York State Fair. Disability activists felt they were doing him a favor. The book cites Douglas Biklen, a disability studies professor from Syracuse University who referred to sideshows as the "pornography of disability."

Bogdan explained that Otis had been able to buy a small house in Georgia with his sideshow earnings, but now he was worried about having to go on welfare. Zigun said that Otis successfully sued the New York State Fair and he was allowed to make a living for a time, but it was a fleeting victory.

"By the early 1980s there were no sideshows anymore to employ Otis or anyone else," said Zigun. But that changed when Zigun and Bradshaw launched the non-profit circus sideshow in Coney Island. The first season, in 1985, had no naturals in the cast, but when Zigun and Bradshaw continued the sideshow for the second season, in 1987, they hired Otis the Frog Boy, thereby resurrecting the Coney tradition of sideshows with natural born performers.

Otis Jordan was, quite possibly, the last remaining sideshow natural performing at that time. The end of the line, languishing down in Georgia. When Zigun and Bradshaw offered him a job, Otis, who could not move his arms or legs, drove from Georgia to New York in his specially modified car. They decided that Otis needed an upgrade. A new image, that was more palatable to 20th century New York. "I worked with Bradshaw and

Otis to totally repackage him," said Zigun. "Given that he was a disabled Black man from the South, calling him a boy would be offensive. He didn't look like a frog."

This last comment might have seemed obvious, except that Otis' prior sideshow managers had marketed him as a cartoonish amphibian, for reasons that would only make sense within the warped perspective of carny hucksterism, a sort of perverted capitalism that does not operate within the boundaries of normal advertising. "There was a picture of him, green, sitting on a lily pad catching flies with a long tongue," Zigun explained. "We decided to do away with that. It was racist and disrespectful."

Zigun was inspired by Prince Randian, a sideshow natural with no arms and legs who appeared in the movie *Freaks*. Prince Randian could roll cigarettes and light them and smoke them using only his lips and tongue. His lack of limbs did not hold him back from getting married and having children.

Otis had arms and legs, but they were frozen in place. He could not move them, said Zigun, so it made sense for him to adopt Prince Randian's act. He was no longer the Frog Boy.

"We called him the human cigarette factory," said Zigun. "Unfortunately, cigarettes cause cancer, but he wasn't called a boy, and he wasn't hidden." He said that Otis could roll a cigarette and light it and smoke it with his lips and tongue. He could also make the cigarette disappear with his "sleight of tongue" magic tricks.

Zigun said that between shows, Otis would roll along the boardwalk in his motorized chair. This was new to him. His prior manager wouldn't let him go out in public, because he didn't want rubes gawking at him for free. Zigun insisted the public life was better for Otis.

He made it through a season without the city shutting down the show, and without significant conflict from the public. Then he realized it wasn't up to the cops, or up to him, or up to the government. "It was up to the press." He said that *Newsday* wrote the first print article about the sideshow, which Zigun described as positive. He described the press treatment as "a sideshow seen through rose-colored glasses," where they weren't exploiting anybody. "Nobody protested, and that broke the ice in Coney Island," he said.

The sideshow had finally been resurrected from his Coney Island hiatus, and long after its peak as a boardwalk attraction. This was 75 years after Dreamland burned to the ground just a few blocks away, incinerating Lilliputia, which Zigun referred to as "the mother of all sideshows."

Zigun said that when they started the non-profit "everything was on the books, everything was legit." This meant that employees, including sideshow performers, were eligible for unemployment insurance. He explained that unemployment insurance was key for seasonal workers.

I asked him: Are sideshows exploitative? Or are they empowering? "I never wanted to present anyone born different to come out on stage and get gawked at," he said. To empower them, you need to pay them, he explained, and you need to "treat them like rock stars." He mentioned how Gen. Tom Thumb became wealthy enough to bail out his bankrupt impresario, P.T. Barnum.

Sometime around 2000, Zigun was in the Childs building and he heard a knock on the door. He opened the door, and there was Mat Fraser. He had never met Mat and had never heard of him. But he noticed that he was natural born.

"My first words to Mat Fraser were, 'Welcome home,'" he said.

Zigun immediately decided to hire him. Ward Hall had the same reaction when he first saw Mat, a freak finder's dream, and offered him a job on the spot. But Mat hesitated at both these offers, as he explained in his documentary *Born Freak*. It isn't easy for a natural born disability rights activist to jump right into being a sideshow freak. It was crossing a line that was difficult to define.

At first, Mat stubbornly clung to the idea of the sideshow as an immersive theatrical experience. "He said that Coney Island was as real as it could possibly get," said Zigun. "He really wanted to explore that opportunity. I told him to shit or get off the pot."

So began a fruitful friendship. Mat worked there for a decade and discovered that Coney Island is a magnate for burlesque dancers, like Julie Atlas Muz, who he met backstage. "I introduced him to his wife Julie," said Zigun, "and as an officiate, I married them." The wedding took place onstage at the Abrons Art Center near Mat and Julie's home in the Lower East Side in 2012.

Zigun believes that 21st-century sideshows can serve as an opportunity for naturals, a style of live theater that gives them a taste of fame. "They have every right to have every opportunity to become a lawyer or an actor," he said. "Peter Dinklage has the right to become a world-famous actor. Within that same modern acceptance, they also have the right to go back and reinvent their role in circus sideshows and become rock stars."

Sideshow performers need strength and stamina to get through the ten-in-one schedule, day after day. Zigun said the workday ranges up to 12 hours, with a series of sixty-minute shows where customers can drift in and out. The mechanics of keeping the show going and keeping everybody in rotation without stopping can be complicated, because it's not just a game of numbers. It's a parade of personalities.

He said that performers during the sixty-minute cycle typically get 35 minutes where they're not onstage and they can take a break. But the juggling of so many moving parts can get thrown off balance "if any one act gets full of itself. If it gets on too long, that throws off the timing." This can happen with some of the more long-winded naturals, especially if they follow the traditional sideshow format of explaining their medical condition to the audience. "Feeling the need to talk and explain their personal history sometimes unbalances the show biz side," he said.

Zigun, like Jellyboy, acted as an impresario. He said the naturals came to him, more often than not. I told him that Xander Lovecraft had seriously considered working a shortened season at Coney that summer, even though he couldn't really afford the New York rent. Zigun cited this as evidence that naturals want to perform in sideshows, and it's not just about money.

I met with Nati Amos earlier that day and I asked Zigun what he thought of her fire twirling. She was inflammatory. "Nati came to me doing fire," he said. "But she not only set her costume on fire, but she also set the curtain on fire on a couple of occasions. So, it became important to work with Nati and position her definitively." He did this by outfitting her with a fireproof costume and hanging the stage with fireproof curtains.

He also worked with Jennifer Miller, who is not, he assured me, a bearded woman, but a "radical feminist" and a "woman with a beard." Like Mat, she did not enjoy exhibiting herself on the bally platform to lure gawking rubes into the freak show. "She found the most difficult part was to go out on the bally stage where you're playing with everyone walking by, trying to get them all to pay attention and potentially buy a ticket, and you're trying to include not only intellectual people who might have an enlightened attitude but also the most ignorant, and bring them all in at the same time," he said.

There's another problem with sideshows, that would no doubt constrain the ambitions of trained performers like Mat and Jennifer. "Nobody gets rich working in sideshows," he said. He said that a stilt walker could potentially make $600 for a two-hour act, but the most seasoned performer at Coney Island is going to make $200 a day or less.

The Woman with a Beard left Coney years ago. She still performs, but she has a serious day job in academia. Prof. Miller teaches in the humanities and media studies department at Pratt Institute in Brooklyn.

Zigun has worked with many naturals. He described Fraser as exceptional because of his stage presence. Zigun's successor Adam Rinn also gave Fraser high praises: "Everything he touches turns to gold."

Zigun also worked with Chuy the Wolf Faced Boy, a Mexican whose family carries a rare hereditary gene that causes hair to grow all over their faces and bodies. Chuy and some of his relatives work in circuses and sideshows. When Chuy worked at Coney, he couldn't speak English, but he demonstrated legitimate circus skills and walked on a high wire that they rigged above the stage.

Zigun used to book the Squidling Brothers for performances at Coney, and that's how he met Jellyboy and Jason Brott, the Illustrated Penguin. "The Squidling Brothers had brought him out with a little drum, with a little strap around his neck," said Zigun. He noticed that Jason didn't talk during his act. Jellyboy did all the talking for him. Only when Zigun met Jason backstage did he realize that he was articulate, with a cheeky sense of humor. But the audience had no way of knowing he was smart. "You've got to learn to talk for yourself," he told him.

But health problems got in the way of Jason's career at Coney. "He makes comeback after comeback," said Zigun. But he said that it's difficult to run a show and pay rent and try to make it through the summer when "your star attraction missed 40% of his acts because he has to do chemotherapy."

Zigun said the sideshow performers came from a range of artistic experience, training and education. Some needed more coaching than others. "I've had some very strong conversations with some born different about how to repackage their act," he said. For example, he didn't want Velvet Crayon wearing a panda mask. "How about a pair of sunglasses and a leather jacket?" he asked him. He described Black Scorpion as an amazing performer and he was impressed by his involvement in 999 Eyes, one of the few remaining sideshows. But he said that Black Scorpion would sometimes go on too long, and he would tell him, "I don't know why you're wearing the tutu."

He wanted his performers to think big, in terms of their image. "In the greater world of sideshow, there's no higher place than Coney Island to work," said Zigun. "It's a place where you can make a national statement."

With the help of Jellyboy, Zigun made a big statement in September 2019 when they assembled a cast of five naturals for a weekend stint at the 10-in-1. "We would do a weekend called Super Freak Weekend, which was nothing but naturals," he said. "Those were amazing shows the likes of which would have probably never happened anywhere."

Coney Island might be the only sideshow in the 21st century to have fielded five naturals at the same time.

Chapter 14

Woman With a Beard

"Step Right Up! See the Bearded Person!"
- *New York Times* headline from 1995

"Now, it's with a wink. It's part of a post-modern reconstruction deconstruction."
- Prof. Jennifer Miller, woman with a beard

Her apartment windows looked over the East River and the shimmering towers of Manhattan. It was the winter of 2022, and she'd been living in north Brooklyn for a long time. She remembers the old New York, before ex-Mayor Giuliani's crackdowns on crime that transformed the city, and before the terrorist attacks of September 11, 2001, that killed thousands and ruptured the skyline. She's nostalgic for the dirty, wild, artistic New York of the 1980s, when crime was bad but normal people could afford to live here.

Jennifer Miller and her partner have kept their apartment through perseverance, longevity and lawyers. That's how she survived the corporate era of ex-Mayor Bloomberg and the decades of stratospheric housing inflation that have turned New York into a city of the rich and the poor. This is how a knife juggler, who built her own circus from the ground up, can live in an airy, sun-drenched loft in a building inhabited by well-heeled hipsters in the cool but overpriced neighborhood of Williamsburg. The location is perfectly suitable for Professor Jennifer Miller of Pratt Institute, the esteemed art school in neighboring Fort Greene.

She refers to herself as a woman with a beard, eschewing the antiquated term "bearded lady." She greeted me at the door of her flat in the upper-floor hall, looking for all the world like Jesus Christ (even though she's Jewish) with a dash of Zappa. She had flowing brown hair with a full moustache and a rich, well-formed beard. But when she spoke, her feminine tone revealed her gender, crystal clear. She was, if there was ever any doubt, a woman. She was wearing baggy clothes, and her pants were clown-like, which reminded me that she was, in fact, a clown.

She invited me into her home, which was filled with plants and wooden furniture and throw rugs. The style of her flat was well-worn, uncluttered and unpretentious. I felt that I had been transported back in time to the simplicity and warmth of a 1970s hippy dwelling.

I reckoned she was about a decade older than me. The chin part of her beard was grey. But when I asked for her date of birth, a standard interview question, she turned me down gently. "A lady never tells," she said, smiling beneath her beard.

As an icebreaker, I explained that we had both been in the circus in New York City at the same time. Not too many people can make that claim, for whatever it's worth. I arrived in New York and joined the Big Apple Circus in 1989, the year that she formed Circus Amok, backed by grants and funding from the state. The *New York Times* covered her performance in Harlem in 1990. A grainy photo shows Jennifer holding a burning torch over her open mouth. "She confronts her audience head-on as a 'bearded lady,' in an amalgam of old-time vaudeville and feminist theater," described the *Times*. "'I am a woman with a beard!' she says, tugging as if to prove it is real. 'A woman with a beard, not 'the bearded lady!'" In the *Times* story, she dismissed the attempts of hirsute women to rein in their facial hair: "Pluck, pluck, pluck," she clucked, "as if these women were chickens!"

But that was a long time ago, and the times have changed. "My thing was a feminist rant," she told me. In recent years, she's backed off a bit. She explained that she no longer lectures women about shaving and plucking, if that's what they choose to do. But she wants to encourage hirsute ladies about their "potential to have a beard, if only they would pursue it."

In 2000, she appeared in *Born Freak*, a documentary starring Mat Fraser. I recognized her apartment from the video. The interview included an unforgettable shot from the lofty ceiling, looking down on Jennifer as she juggled knives that were curved like cutlasses. She threw the sabers with side-hacking motions to make it look like she was juggling sideways instead of up and down. Captured by the camera, the blades of the knives twirled back and forth in front of Mat's face. This style of juggling is called "chops," she told me. "It makes it look harder. I grab it at the knob and I spin it."

She left the room and disappeared into another section of the apartment and then reappeared with a trio of clubs that she started juggling for emphasis, adding the spin-throws that she referred to as chops.

I looked up at her ceiling and tried to imagine how they set up the video shoot, because the ceiling seemed shorter in real life, compared to the video. It was. A few years before, city codes had required her to "lower the ceiling," which explained why new ceiling panels covered up whatever was there before. The ceiling shot of Jennifer and her chops wouldn't be possible today.

When Mat met Jennifer, she had already performed at the Coney Island Circus Sideshow as a natural for a half dozen seasons and had established herself in this subgenre. Mat hadn't joined the sideshow yet. He was experimenting with the idea of joining and was seeking Jennifer's advice. She didn't sugarcoat it. She explained that it was a grind show with ten performances a day.

But for an actor who was born different, Coney Island also offered a unique experience. That is the insight that Mat was seeking from her, as one natural to another. He was asking for guidance about the sideshow experience, from the perspective of a natural who's been on the bally platform. There are few people in the world with that expertise. "It's deep work," she told him. "I think I was in your situation. I wanted to check it out."

I wonder if this drove Dick Zigun a little crazy, the fact that two of his star naturals, Mat and Jennifer, were performing in the freak show as an artistic experiment, rather than a way of life. But it's hard to find fault with their philosophy towards the freak show as a career building exercise, since Jennifer eventually landed a job as a professor at a respected university, and Mat became a TV star on *American Horror Story* and numerous BBC shows.

During her performances at Circus Amok and Coney Island, Jennifer would breathe fire and also eat fire. This struck me as particularly dangerous for someone with a beard, though I remembered that Jellyboy, with his experimental facial hair, is also a fire breather. Kim Kelly (who does not have a beard) considers eating fire to be scarier and more dangerous than breathing fire, because you must hold the fire in your mouth and let it burn there.

But there are different schools of thought on this pyrotechnic topic. Jennifer said that breathing fire, which she called "blasting," was more challenging. "I think blasting is hard on the body because some of the fluid will drip down," she said. "I was breathing fire, and I lit on fire a little bit."

Accidental self-immolation is a real risk with pyrotechnics. This is why Zigun made the Patchwork Girl wear a fireproof suit. She twirled fire at Coney and scorched the fire-resistant stage curtains. So why do sideshow naturals play with fire? Because the audience loves it, and the feeling is mutual. Incendiary acts thrill the artist. "It's great, to be around fire, and put it in your mouth and put it out," said Jennifer. "It feels very powerful."

But she wouldn't do the bed of nails. I was fascinated with this act because my kung fu school had a bed of nails. During an annual demonstration at the school, one of the kung fu instructors formed a human sandwich between two beds of nails. He was lying on one bed pointy-side-up, while the other bed was placed atop him with the pointy-side down. Another instructor stacked cinder blocks on the nail bed sandwich and smashed them with a sledgehammer, while the human in the middle barely flinched, and emerged from the ordeal unimpaled.

Jennifer said that the bed of nails can be a painful exercise, but that wasn't her main problem with it. "That's harder to do for a woman, because people want to see topless," she said. "The only way to do it is to take your shirt off. It's a sideshow aesthetic."

The bearded ladies, as they were called, were fixtures in the Old Timey sideshows, with facial hair, real or otherwise, that flowed to their ankles. They wore ankle-length dresses and gowns in those conservative times, to emphasize their femininity. Members of the audience sometimes demanded proof that they were women. They wanted to see what was underneath those Victorian dresses. The bearded ladies never had trouble attracting men. Quite the opposite. They often got married, sometimes to their managers.

Jennifer is proud of her queer identity and makes it the centerpiece of her show. I asked her to describe Circus Amok. It included not only "circus stuff," as she put it, but served as a suitable platform for political theater. "I was not trying to get anything across," she said, when I asked how she used the circus to express her queer identity. "I was just trying to make space for us to be ourselves. It's the same thing with the beard; it's not trying to hide where I am."

She said that Circus Amok is "giving space" to "liberationist ideologies" about gender, queerness, economic equality and race. When I asked her how she used the circus to express queer identity, she seemed to be talking her way towards an answer, and then she found it. "Queerness is this kind of cultural futuristic replacement of our world," she said. "There's always kind of a queer fantasia going on, a queer reality. Because we don't live in a queer culture and a queer world, we are having to fantasize about everything. It's kind of a utopia."

In her description, queer people were living in a world that is not set up for them, where they don't really fit in, and so they are creating their own world, an alternate reality within that real world, even though what they really want is to be considered an equal part of the real world.

Jennifer's beard can seem like a political statement, but the beard is all-natural: The politic statement is in the act of not shaving it. She started letting her beard grow when she was in her 20s as she was growing into her identity as a woman. She described the appearance of a woman with a beard as "almost a queer look at what being a woman is."

I referred to her beard as a disability, as I was testing the word to see how she would respond, but she shook her head, dismissing the label.

"Being a woman with a beard means nothing," she said, meaning that she didn't consider it much of an obstacle, relatively speaking, or maybe not an obstacle at all. Though she admitted that the beard can make her life tricky in public bathroom situations. "It means something in my trips to the bathroom when there's only a men's and women's," she said. "There aren't many women with beards."

The times have changed, but the rarity of bearded women remains the same. I asked her a question that didn't even exist back in the 20th century, when she launched her circus/sideshow career: What is your pronoun? "My pronoun is she," she said. "I'm sticking with the she because I've always felt very comfortable with the she. I also feel a real alliance with women and feminism." She also vacillates between pronouns. "But I can sometimes also embrace the they," she said. "There's a kind of liberation in the they sometimes."

Jennifer referred to such gender-neutral titles as "a utopian grab," meaning that it was an outstretched arm from the queer community towards the dream of a world where there was no pressure to assign any labels at all, to live completely free of any sort of sexual classification. Could this ever be achievable in a more enlightened futuristic society? "Maybe someday we will sometimes live in a nonbinary world," she said. "I would love to live in this gender mélange. It's a wide continuum of no one is really anything. People feel very committed to their feminism or masculineness, but I've always had a certain androgynism."

Bearded ladies, who often have a genetic condition called hypertrichosis, formed a popular subgenre of sideshow naturals in the 1800s and early 1900s. In those days, the concept and the reality of a woman with a beard were seen as a contradiction, and this is how the bearded ladies, as they were called, were exhibited, with long, flowing skirts that left everything to the imagination. Sometimes they even wore veils to conceal their beards. They were the very picture of Victorian modesty and domesticity.

"Except for the beards, these women represented the quintessence of refined respectable womanhood," said Robert Bogdan in his book *Freak Show*, noting that bearded ladies often took publicity photos posing next to their husbands. Some of the women would claim in their marketing that doctors had examined them to verify their female gender.

Some of the bearded ladies were quite famous, including Jane Barnell, who was born in North Carolina in 1871, exhibited in sideshows starting at age 12, and appeared in the film *Freaks*. She was married three times, went by the name Lady Olga and performed for more than 65 years, until her beard was long and gray.

Annie Jones was the queen celebrity of hirsute maidens. She would pose for publicity photos while admiring her long dark beard in a tall mirror. Annie was born in Virginia on July 14, 1865, just months after the end of the Civil War, and just one day after P.T. Barnum's American Museum burned down in Manhattan. She was first exhibited by Barnum when she was a baby. She earned $150 a week as "Esau," learned to play the mandolin and wore a veil in public. Her beard was valuable, and she didn't want to give away the show for free. Annie's life was intense and short. She was kidnapped by a phrenologist when she was a little girl but rescued by her parents six months later, married at age 16, divorced, remarried, invested in Brooklyn real estate, and died of tuberculosis at age 37. She was buried in Evergreen Cemetery, a sprawling graveyard in Brooklyn, to join the bones of dead luminaries like Jean-Michel Basquiat and Teddy Roosevelt's parents and first wife. She had spent the latter part of her life campaigning against the use of the word "freak." But cradle to grave, Annie lived in the shadow of the sideshow. "She had known no other life than that of a freak," wrote Bogdan.

I asked Jennifer the fundamental question I ask every natural: Are sideshows, less delicately known as freak shows, exploitative? Or are they empowering for disabled people? For her, the answer changes through the history of sideshows, which extends back to antebellum America, when circus showmen including P.T. Barnum exhibited slaves as freaks for the amusement and profit of free people. "The deeply racist history of sideshows is problematic without question," she said.

Slavery is the ultimate exploitation, and some of the most famous performers in freakshow history, including Julia Pastrana, Joice Heth and the conjoined "Carolina Twins" Millie and Christine McCoy, were slaves. Jennifer said that sideshows often stigmatized categories of non-white people, who were depicted as freaks or even aliens based on their race alone. For example, exhibitors depicted Pastrana as a "Semihuman" or "Ape Woman" (according to *Ripley's Believe It or Not! Presents Sideshow and Other Carnival Curiosities*.) In the early 20th century, Ringling Bros. and Barnum & Bailey Circus exhibited George and William Muse, Black American brothers with albinism, as "ambassadors from Mars." The John and Mable Ringling Museum of Art in Sarasota, Florida, displays a life-sized banner of the brothers, dressed in outlandish outfits and depicted in a Martian landscape.

Exhibitors portrayed women with facial hair, or disabled people, or overweight people, as freaks. Jennifer's fundamental issue with sideshows is this stigmatization. She doesn't consider herself to be a freak, even though she chose to perform in a sideshow.

"The idea that a woman with a beard was a freak is a problem," she said, referring not just to the old days, but her own experience at Coney Island. She described the bally as "good political theater." But it was hard to ignore the fact that she was in a freakshow, because there was a banner out front advertising: "Freak Show! Woman with a Beard!"

She laughed off her sideshow wages as "shit money," but she needed it anyway. And it's not just about the money. Whatever remains of the sideshow scene has turned itself completely on its head. Sideshows peaked in popularity in the early-to-mid 20th century, but then they nearly became extinct. State and local governments shut some of them down for offending people, and they were also competing with television. Sideshow naturals resurrected themselves in the 21st century as experimental artists, pushing the limits of sensibility and owning the stage. "Now, it's with a wink," said Jennifer. "It's part of a post-modern reconstruction deconstruction."

Of course, everyone has their own perspective on sideshow. To some performers, the sideshow might seem ironic, and they're letting you in on the joke. But to some naturals, sideshows are an abomination. "A short person who wants to be working in a bank would feel disgusted to see a short person advertised as a freak," she said. But Jennifer didn't want to work in a bank. She wanted to be in the circus, so she made one. For Jennifer, the art of self-exhibition, in a way that sensationalized her facial hair, was something new and exciting. "Bearded lady: so now it's out in the open," she said. "So, there was something empowering about that experience." It was a way of addressing her differences head-on, her way of telling the audience, "I know that you see that I have a beard."

But the sideshow no longer seemed like a proper venue for a woman with a beard. "It's hardly appropriate," she said. "Gender has changed, gender performance, gender presentation. It wouldn't even work anymore. Well hallelujah, a woman with a beard isn't even a freak category anymore! It's just another way of being."

The times are changing, and the sideshow, what's left of it, must change as well. The sideshow is not static. The acts evolve with the times. As an example, Jennifer said she used to perform with Mike Wilson, billed as the Illustrated Man, who would hammer a nail through his tongue before a live audience. The act was sensational, while it lasted. Audience members would gasp and faint, until one day someone yelled "It's pierced!" from the audience, and that sunbeam of reality ruined his show forever. Now everybody knew that he was simply sliding a nail through a tongue hole that already existed. "That was the beginning of the end of that particular act," she said. "That act doesn't exist anymore. Everyone is getting their tongue pierced."

She was using the parable of the tongue-hole as a metaphor for other acts that had gone the way of the dinosaurs. The so-called bearded lady doesn't seem like a big deal in an age where gender fluidity has become widespread. "I think there are so many people who are gender queer or nonbinary or gender transitioning," she said. "We're seeing a lot more of the in-betweens."

Professor Miller worked at Pratt Institute at the humanities department in the School of Liberal Arts and Sciences, teaching introduction to performance practices and improvisation dance. She had been full-time since 2012. She used her experience at Circus Amok to teach students how to make outdoor political spectacles. She has taught queer theater, disability studies and freak show studies. For the upcoming year, she was planning to teach a course on theater of the ridiculous.

Her experience at Coney has been invaluable for teaching at Pratt. How many people can claim to have the experience of wooing customers from a freak show bally platform? She said that she wore a veil during the first few years that she did bally in the 1990s. "The tradition was that you can't show them the product before you come in."

I told her what Zigun said, that she had a knack for appealing to a wide range of boardwalk crowds that might have included enlightened political activists and also sunburned drunks.

"[You] just got to see everybody as human beings, I mean that's the spiritual part of it and then you have to do a good bally," she said. "You've just got to be warm, you've got to be welcoming, you've got to tell them there's a good show inside. I think I learned a lot of good sleazy sales charm."

It takes courage for someone who is queer and different to put themselves out there, especially in these dangerous times. America has a mean streak, and queer people are often the targets of violence. The topic of hate crimes emerged at the end of my interview with Jennifer, as I was getting ready to leave, because New York had experienced a recent wave of anti-Semitic incidents. I packed up my computer and notebooks and put the empty teacup in the sink. As Jennifer escorted me to the door, she said that all the violence and threats versus queer people and Jews had made the world a scary place.

"I'm afraid to go out," she said.

But Jennifer was also getting ready to leave. She said it was time to walk her dog. A beautiful chocolate-brown greyhound named Pearl emerged from another room. I had been in the apartment for two hours and this was the first time I had seen Pearl. I didn't even know there was a greyhound in the next room. It was supple and sleek, a perfect biological machine of muscle and bone.

"I'm joking," Jennifer laughed. "I'm not afraid to go out."

No, she was not afraid to go out. I finally saw her perform in June 2024 at Coney Island.

If New York City is the center of the universe, then Coney Island is the edge of the world. I visited Coney many times in the summer of 2024. My daughter became obsessed with the Wonder Wheel and also the Sideshow Cat at the Freak Bar. One afternoon, after several hours on the beach, we walked onto the boardwalk and right into a live performance of Circus Amok. Prof. Miller was dressed in the purple uniform of a drum major with a tall hat and was juggling clubs with another purple juggler, and they were deftly passing the clubs back and forth before a crowd of spectators. Jennifer wore vibrant blue eye shadow, a brilliant dash of stage femineity. Her thick brown hair fell below her shoulders and her beard was thick and bushy.

They played a portable stage at the base of the Parachute Drop, a discontinued icon that was infamously scary and was known for making people scream and piss themselves with fear. It's a tall skeletal structure that can be seen from miles away. On summer nights, it lights up with shifting neon colors.

In the heat of the day, our attention was on Circus Amok, a kooky, queer-friendly troupe of experimental dancers who moved to a live band wearing makeshift metal hats with long curved, shiny streamers. A quartet of tall, thin men and women wore long dresses and moved amongst each other like dancing pillars. Miller shifted into multiple costume changes, from the purple drum major outfit to the robe of an old lady to a brilliant dress of shimmering gold. The show was there to celebrate differences, with a heavy LGBTQ-plus emphasis on pride. It was an outstanding show. Utterly real. I'm so glad my daughter got to see it.

Chapter 15

Illustrated Penguin

"It's not like someone's pointing a gun at a natural born's head and making them do this. We're all doing it so we don't go out of our minds, staring at four walls. It's not exploitative."
- Jason Brott

Jason Brott is a natural born from Baltimore. Like many performers, he is introverted and extroverted at the same time. He's a soft-spoken sideshow eccentric who is prone to flamboyant displays of body modification. He was born different, but being born different wasn't different enough for him. He is covered with tattoos, from head to foot, on his hands, neck and head. His face and other body parts are sprinkled with shiny steel piercings. He has stretched his ear lobes to accommodate fat O-shaped earrings. He has lifted weights with these earrings at sideshows. He sometimes wears his hair in a spiky mohawk nearly half as tall as himself. He sometimes sprouts a ponytail from the top of his head and shaves the rest of his skull so you can see the tattoos on his forehead. "I like to do skulls," he said, and he draws them all the time. He is a tattoo artist. He has the image of a marijuana leaf inked onto his stomach, the size of an outstretched hand. He has two big "rib pieces" of nurses, depicted as benevolent sexy angel-demons. He immortalizes these goddesses by inking their images into his living skin, putting his deep attachment on display.

Bryce "The Govna" Graves told me that Jason feels deeply for nurses because they have always cared for him. In a phone interview with Jason in the summer of 2022, he told me that yes, nurses have taken care of him his entire life, and he respects them for shouldering the most unpleasant burdens of their profession. Doctors make the nurses do their dirty work, he explained, like telling a patient that his pain meds have been cut off. "They put up with a lot of shit," he said, and since he was referring to those who deal with bed pans, it wasn't just a figure of speech.

When he first got into the sideshow business, Jason used to bill himself as the Penguin Boy. But then he got older and inked up, like *The Illustrated Man* from Ray Bradbury. "I am not a boy," Jason explained, so he changed his name to Illustrated Penguin. His friends call him Penguin.

Penguin's friends include Graves, Jellyboy and Velvet Crayon. Jason traveled widely with Hellzapoppin and performed with Squidling Brothers and the Coney Island Circus Sideshow. Lots of people know Penguin. He's a traveling crossroads of sideshow experience. He's a treasure trove of 21st century freak show lore who should be downloaded into a book before his knowledge is lost forever. He is aware of his impending mortality, which follows him like a shadow.

I asked Jason why he presents himself in such an outlandish fashion, meaning the tattoos, the piercings, the big earrings, a self-bifurcated tongue. He said that people are always staring at his hands, which sprout from his shoulders. Jason wants to give people a different reason to stare at him. "I thought if I got stuff that looked different, people wouldn't notice my hands," he said. "Also, it's a control thing. I can't control getting sick or having a kidney that won't work, so I get tattoos and piercings. I can control that." I remembered a story that Jellyboy told me, about the time that Jason sawed his tongue in half with a butter knife, while riding in a car on tour. Jason also has deliberate scarification on his wrists, in the form of raised, Frankenstein-style cicatrix, to make it look like his hands were cut off and sewn back on.

Jason was 36 years old at the time of our interview in 2022. Given his natural born condition, it's amazing that he had made it that far. To a large extent, medical technology was keeping him alive.

Jason was born with TAR syndrome, a rare condition that most people have never heard of. "TAR syndrome; Google it," said Jason. "It'll come up Thromboccytopenia-adsent radius syndrome. It's a long fancy word for shortened limbs and anemia."

TAR syndrome, according to the National Library of Medicine and the Children's Hospital of Philadelphia, is a congenital disorder marked by low platelet count and missing radial bones in the forearms. Of all the naturals interviewed for this book, Jason's disability is among the most severe. "I have hands that protrude out of my shoulders," he said. He doesn't seem to have any arms at all, though Jason insists that the arms are there, they are just very short and you can't see them. His arm bones are not straight. "All spiraled up like a little snake," he said. "The genetic code wasn't written up and it wouldn't form."

Jason is also short-statured, as a side effect of TAR. He said it is partly because of his "platelet issue" and partly because his legs were "crossed Indian-style" when he was born. He said the doctors broke his legs and reset them with pins to reform. To this day, Jason wears leg braces. "I am not a midget or a dwarf," he said. "I am just short because of the kidney problem, because of the legs."

Other naturals with TAR syndrome don't necessarily look like Jason nor are they affected in the same way. "There are many different versions of my condition," he said.

Jason said he started performing in sideshows in the early 2000s, when he was 20 years old. He toured with Hellzapoppin Circus Sideshow Revue in a Blue Bird school bus that Bryce had converted into a tour bus, like a freak show version of *The Electric Kool-Aid Acid Test*.

Hellzapoppin has performed thousands of shows over the years and Jason traveled far and wide in this troubadour lifestyle. "I've been all over the United States, I've been almost all over Europe, and I've been to Australia," he said.

He spent much of his time quietly observing the frenetic and social environment that was constantly shifting around him, as he moved from place to place, circus-style. "It was definitely a different life on the road," he said. "I was there, but mainly just watching, and smoking. It was a different town every night, a different crowd of people, parties. People thought we were cool. Some people invited us into their homes, let us crash at their place. I made friends that I still talk to. It was definitely a cool experience. But if you're a person who needs structure and routine, that's probably not the best environment." I asked Jason if he needs structure and routine. "As I've gotten older, and with my health issues, yes," he said.

Life on the road can exacerbate and complicate day-to-day hardships. And Jason has more than his fair share of those. Early in his career with Graves, they went to Los Angeles and stayed in a hotel room, where Jason had to administer a peritoneal dialysis. He said that Graves helped him input dialysis solution from a bag through a catheter into his belly.

"I used to be able to just pick up and go on the road, sometimes we were on the road six, nine months out of the year," he said. But now he has "kidney issues," as he puts it, and he's tethered to Maryland with its high-quality hospitals, where he's kept alive by dialysis three times a week. At that time, in 2022, he seldom traveled, and when he did, it usually wasn't far from home. The best he could manage for long-distance gigs was a quick roundtrip flight.

"I do shows every now and then," he said. "I'm not fully done [with sideshow,] but I won't go on long, extensive tours. If it's not a fly-me-in, fly-me-out kind of thing, or a weekend kind of thing, I won't perform. I haven't booked anything in a while. I don't actively look for gigs anymore."

He couldn't stray too far, or too long, outside a certain radius from Baltimore. He said he's dependent upon Medicare and Medicaid to cover medical costs. "A good portion of my stuff is covered, but some stuff is not," he said.

This is where Jason and other disabled people run into an administrative catch-22 that can stymie their careers and threaten their health at the same time. Gainful employment for disabled people threatens their eligibility for the medical benefits that keep them alive. "People say, 'Why don't you get a job?'" Jason told me. "If I get a job, I lose my benefits, and if I lose my benefits, I have no health insurance, and I'm screwed."

Sideshow performers tend to specialize in certain acts. Some breathe fire, some eat fire, some juggle knives, others walk on broken glass.

"I did human blockhead," said Jason, "and I also did an act called pierced weightlifting. I have ear lobes that are stretched and I would chain my ear lobes to a cinder block and pick it up and swing it around."

This reminded me of an act I saw at Coney Island, where a performer hooked his stretched earlobes to a carabiner that was hooked to a bowling ball and swung it around. I was afraid his lobes would rip and the ball would fly into the audience and smash a face. But the lobes held.

Graves told me that Jason was a drummer when he first met him, and he took Jason to Turkey to perform in a television show. But Bryce said it was only after they flew to Turkey, at the expense of the TV station, and had arrived at the station to perform, that he decided that Jason's drumming was underwhelming. There are some things that look good on TV, and some that do not. Graves came up with something else, immediately. In a private room at the station, he taught Jason how to shove foreign objects up his nose and how to use a screwdriver to thread a condom through his nasal passages, in one nostril and out the other. Jason performed it for the first time on Turkish TV, just minutes after he'd learned it.

Graves also described Penguin as the fastest texter alive. He won a speed-texting contest when he was in Turkey. He propped his phone between his hand and his shoulder and tapped away with his index finger.

In the years that followed, Jason became a seasoned sideshow performer with his own specialties. He would wear a black vest and pants with "weird writing," as he put it. "My main act, I lifted stuff with my ears," he said. "Cinder blocks, bowling balls, buckets and other objects that I thought were interesting."

He also picked up a bucket with his lip ring, and he ate fire and breathed fire. He was also training to be a sword swallower in Australia. A sideshow star from Down Under named Space Cowboy made a special sword for him with a two-point lever system, allowing him to bend the sword so he would be in position to swallow it, without the use of arms. But he never got beyond the practice stage, and he never swallowed a sword in a live act. There was an interruption in his sideshow career as he moved from Maryland to California and he lost some of his sideshow props and outfits. Sword swallowing is one of the toughest acts in sideshow, and he's wary about taking it up again. "Now that I'm older, I don't really do the shock stuff," he said.

Throughout sideshow history, some of the more disabled naturals would demonstrate, to the amazement of the audience, their ability to do mundane things. For example, limbless Prince Randian, who appeared in the legendary film *Freaks*, would roll cigarettes with his lips and tongue. This is no small feat, since many people are incapable of rolling a joint even with fingers and hands.

Jason had an act where he would dress himself for an office job. "I call it My Morning Routine," he said. It was an act where he merely put on clothes. It was his answer to all those people who asked if he could feed himself or wipe his butt. "People always ask me, 'Do I need help?' or 'Do I do things on my own?' I show people. I put on my shirt and tie, and I tell everybody, 'I'm ready for my job on Wall Street.'" (He said the tie was "pre-tied" so he could loop it over his head.)

I had been told that naturals have got to have an act, that you can't just go onstage and be a natural. But when I had lunch with the Patchwork Girl, she told me that naturals can perform mundane functions, without the use of arms, fingers, etc., to entertain and educate their non-disabled audience. I asked Jason what the audience thought of his Morning Routine. "They like it," he said.

Back in 2014, when he was 29, Jason made a sizzle reel that served as a show piece for his rapper persona, Lower Case J. In the video, he's wearing massive earrings, a big clunky piece of jewelry stuck in his body modified chin-hole, and tattoos on his face, hands and fingers. The video demonstrates his various skills: skateboarding in a sunblasted park; tattooing in a studio; performing on stage; hammering a screwdriver up his nose; inhaling a condom into his mouth and pulling it out of his nose. "I know I look a little weird and a little odd, but trust me ladies and gentlemen, I have had a very fulfilling life," he said in the video.

The video showcased how Jason accomplishes the more basic tasks of his day-to-day reality. He emerges from bed and steps into a pair of shoes without using his hands, then walks to the bathroom to brush his teeth, aided by the proximity of his hands to his face. The hard part is getting the toothpaste out of the tube. He rests the tube against the sink and presses his chin against it to squeeze the paste onto the brush, then taps the cap against his face. He can drink water from a bottle. He can feed himself, using a fork and knife to eat turkey with gravy and green beans. He explains how he wipes his butt, by folding the toilet paper against the edge of the seat.

Jason was born with dysplastic kidneys and had undergone two kidney transplants at the time, along with dialysis treatment three days a week. Supporters set up a GoFundMe page to raise money for surgeries. "Lowercase J is a ninja that I'm sure a lot you ninjas are familiar with from performing at the Gathering of the Juggalos and the Juggalo Psypher or performing on TV shows like Todd Ray's *Freakshow*,' said a website called faygolovers.net, referring to the Faygo-drinking fanatics of Insane Clown Posse and a reality TV series about a sideshow in Venice Beach, Los Angeles. "Now it looks like he's at the point where he needs a new kidney altogether, y'all."

Jason told me that he sometimes sings, and he also plays a custom guitar that is three-quarter scale, with three strings. He said that he also makes appearances as a motivational speaker. He speaks out against bullying, especially versus people who were born different. He tells his audience not to be mean. He urges people to be empathetic. He reminds non-disabled people that anyone could become disabled at any time. "If you ever see a kid getting picked on, stick up for 'em," said Jason. "You may wake up one day and you can't use your legs, or see, or be able to use your arms. You don't want people to treat you differently."

He tells young, disabled people to be strong, and to know that when they get older, their lives will get better, and it won't always be about people picking on them. He told me that natural borns have the same desires and interests as anyone else, ranging from playing video games to traveling, to having a girlfriend or a boyfriend, or even getting married and having a family. "Everybody wants the same thing," he said, "just to be felt like they're wanted, or to fit in or something, or to not be alone."

I noted that sideshow naturals sometimes score girlfriends by going on the road and performing. "I've been in relationships, absolutely," he said. "Ladies like me."

I asked Jason the fundamental question: Do you consider sideshows to be exploitative? "No more or no less than anybody who gets exploited at your regular job," he said. "It's not like someone's pointing a gun at a natural born's head and making them do this. We're all doing it so we don't go out of our minds, staring at four walls. It's not exploitative. People like to twist things, to make it exploitative. You make a living, party, meet women, meet people. If you didn't, you'd be stuck in a room watching cable or Netflix or playing video games."

When I first contacted Jason in 2022, he was living with his mother in Maryland after his stalled attempts to become a California cannabis farmer. This was after he put the brakes on sideshow life and moved from Maryland to California to be with his girlfriend. Jason had been training to be a sword swallower, and when he moved across the country, he lost props and outfits. He said he was ready for a career switch anyway. He had his eyes on a new undertaking as a cannabis farmer.

"I went to California and I was learning how to grow weed and I was in charge of 100 plants," he said. "I used advanced nutrients. It came out great, there was plenty of yield and stuff like that, so I was happy for going out there and doing that."

Jason said that his burgeoning cannabis career was going fine, but his romantic life was not, and one couldn't survive without the other if he was going to make it in California because of housing costs. "I had a girlfriend at the time and we broke up and I couldn't afford living there by myself, and I was staying on my friend's couch for a long time, and I came to the conclusion that I couldn't do that by myself," he said.

So he decided to move back East and live with his mother, in a suburb north of Baltimore. He took a quasi-hiatus from the sideshow scene. "I don't really talk to many natural borns, or very many people anymore," he said. "I'm kind of reclused, chilling it out. I live with my mom, and I get Social Security, not very much. I do shows every now and then."

Jason said that when he moved back to Maryland, he became a card-carrying member of the state's medical marijuana program. He enjoys dabbing, a super-potent way of inhaling concentrated cannabis, and has developed a high tolerance for his drug of choice. "I can smoke one of those king-sized cones to my face and still be up walking around," he said. He's gone to "weed flea markets" where people gave him dabs, and he astonished them by continuing to function. "People would be like, 'How are you still walking around?' I can consume quite a bit," he said.

He consumes cannabis for fun and medical purposes, and to relieve his anxiety. He would like to resume legal growing someday, if he gets his own place. "Weed is a touchy subject here," he said, referring to his mother. He said she does not like marijuana, and she makes this known as he regularly steps outside to smoke. "She was like: 'How many times a day do you smoke?'" he said. He answered, "As many times as I want."

In November of 2022, Jason told me that he had just been to a tattoo convention in New Jersey (the Atlantic City Tattoo Expo #18.) And then, in January 2023, he told me that he was in Pennsylvania (the Philadelphia Tattoo Arts Convention #25.) But his trip got cut short. "Unfortunately, I am in the hospital," he texted. "I was supposed to be doing the tattoo convention but got sick."

Once again, his life was sidelined by medical problems. He had tried to live in spite of his life-threatening disability, but he was tethered to a hospital, and he knew it.

It seems that Jason had adapted to his lack of arms. But his kidneys were holding him back. I kept wondering what he might have accomplished without this limitation. I asked Jason how he might have lived differently if he wasn't born with TAR syndrome. "I'm open to who I am," he said on the phone, "and I'm a strange dude naturally, whether I have a physical limitation as people see it. I'd probably still be the same me and be on tour in a band or something."

Chapter 16

Modified Marvel

"He opened his hand. On his palm was a rose, freshly cut, with drops of crystal water among the soft pink petals. I put my hand out to touch it, but it was only an illustration."
- *The Illustrated Man*, by Ray Bradbury

"A true freak cannot be made. A true freak must be born."
- *Geek Love*, by Katherine Dunn

"Gooble gobble, gooble gobble, we accept her, we accept her, one of us, one of us, one of us, one of us ..."
- *Freaks*, directed by Tod Browning

Not all sideshow freaks are natural born. Some are self-made, also known as self-inflicted.

Erik Sprague, AKA the Lizardman is not natural born, but he is a pioneer of body modification. He is tattooed green, as though scaled, with filed teeth and a forked tongue. He had his tongue sliced halfway down the middle and split like a snake's. He did this in the 1990s, before tongue bifurcation became cool.

"I could taste and smell my own burning tongue as they cut it in half with a laser," Erik told me in a phone interview in 2021. "The procedure was essentially bloodless."

Sprague, who has a Bachelor of Arts degree in philosophy from Hartwick College in Oneonta, N.Y., went to an oral surgeon in Albany who agreed to perform the tongue bifurcation with a biopsy laser.

"In 1997, I became the first surgical tongue splitting in history," he said. Which means that when he split his tongue, he didn't really know whether it would grow back, or how it would grow back, because there wasn't a precedent.

On the phone, he didn't sound like someone with a split tongue. (Or so I thought. People with split tongues can speak flawlessly once they heal up. When I interviewed Jason Brott on the phone, I didn't realize he had a split tongue until later.)

Sprague convinced the oral surgeon to perform the bifurcation with an argon biopsy laser. He considers this one of the first tongue-splittings in modern record and "almost certainly the first" with a biopsy laser. "Up until this time, modern tongue splitting was all but a myth," he wrote in his book, *Once More Through the Modified Looking Glass*. Since then, body modification has expanded exponentially, evolving into a small but fast-growing trend, with thousands of people remaking themselves through "heavy mods." He claims to have inspired anti-tongue-splitting legislation in Illinois and attempts to outlaw tongue-splitting in Michigan.

Sprague grew up in upstate New York and lives in Austin, Texas, with his wife Meghan, who is a nurse. At the time of the interview, they'd been married for 18 years. "She met me as the Lizardman," he told me. "The first time she ever saw me in person was when I ran on to the stage in a Speedo and put a skewer through my mouth."

His teeth are filed into fangs, and he has prominently pierced ears that he uses for feats of strength and endurance. With his earrings, he can swing chairs and pull cars. He has won world records with his ear lobes. He has the word FREAK tattooed across his chest in thumb-high letters in a sweeping curve like a circus banner. He has undergone more than 700 hours of tattooing and body modification, head to toe. He also has subdermal implants, in the form of Teflon ridges medically fastened to his brow. He also performs hair-raising tricks like twisting a long spiral wire known as a cranial corkscrew through his mouth and nose. He's a human blockhead and a human dartboard, a fire breather and a sword swallower who lies upon the bed of nails. He toured with the infamous Jim Rose Circus.

For the Lizardman, body modification is more than skin deep. He doesn't want to just *look* like a lizard. He wants to *be* a lizard. In his autobiography, he stated the desire to have a living alligator tail grafted onto his body. He wrote in his book, "I fully plan on living well past a century."

These days, there's a high bar to entry for being a "modified marvel," as he puts it. Everything is extreme in the wild world of sideshow. You won't get anywhere by blending in. "Normal life wasn't coming to me, whether I went freak show or not," he said. "I found a way to capitalize on my weirdness."

I asked what he thinks of the term self-inflicted versus self-made. He said that the term self-inflicted only applies when he screws up. He prefers self-made. Actually, he prefers modified marvel, and it suits him.

In my interviews with the natural borns, I would ask whether they considered sideshows, or freak shows, to be exploitative or empowering. With Sprague, I didn't ask this question. Instead, I asked if he truly was a freak, as he so proudly proclaimed in his tattoo, since he wasn't born that way. He dismissed the notion that a self-made freak is somehow less than a natural within the parameters of sideshow culture. "It's an academic distinction, an ivory tower distinction," he said. "If you're a freak, the public doesn't give a fuck, natural born or self-made, it doesn't really matter. Behind the curtain, are you a draw, or aren't you?" He said that the ability to draw a crowd or sell tickets is infinitely more important to a sideshow than its long-established hierarchy of natural born versus working acts. "It doesn't matter whether you were born this way or made yourself this way, it's whether you're a box office draw," he said.

I asked him if he felt it was appropriate to tattoo the word FREAK across his green chest in big letters. "Yeah, but nobody fucking cares, you're a freak," he said. "FREAK, to me, it's an honorific. You don't see people with FRY COOK tattooed across your chest. Being a freak, I had to achieve this."

Sprague felt that he had earned the freak title that he so confidently stamped across his chest. A few months after talking to the Lizardman, I interviewed Jason Black, AKA Black Scorpion. He lives in Austin, the same city as the Lizardman, and they have worked and played together. Black Scorpion told me in 2022, "[Sprague] is an amazing human being and one of the most intelligent people I have ever met. I really want him to do whatever he wants to do. He's a really wonderful, kind, green human being."

Aaron "Shorty" Wollin, the half-man of Hellzapoppin, also spoke highly of Sprague, who was born non-disabled but had changed himself through elective surgery and was in good standing with people who were born different. It reminded me of the scene in the movie *Freaks* when the naturals accepted a non-disabled woman as "one of us" because she married a little person.

Can a self-inflicted sideshow performer be considered a real freak? I asked Jason Black the question. "It's not really up to me to decide these things," he said. "I don't wear a referee suit. I wear a tutu with angel wings. I'm not a judge; I'm a servant. I just do what I can do for the Lord above and I try to make things better for everyone down here."

Sprague has traveled widely and met many people. He has performed for the Hellzapoppin Circus Sideshow Revue, the Coney Island Circus Sideshow and Ripley's Believe It Or Not! He has performed with Slayer and Slipknot. He is credited in the *Guinness Book of World Records* for the heaviest weight lifted and spun with pierced ears: 16 kilograms on the set of a TV show in Milan in 2014.

Erik told me that he got into sideshow after he met some clowns from Ringling Brothers and Barnum & Bailey Circus. Early in his career, he teamed up with Chayne "Space Cowboy" Hultgren, an Australian chainsaw juggler with more than fifty Guinness World Records to his name, including heaviest weight pulled by eye sockets (411.65 kg), most swords swallowed while juggling three objects (18), most chainsaw juggling catches on a unicycle (10), most swords swallowed underwater (4), etc. (Hultgren's wife, Zoe "L'Amore" Ellis, also has some interesting skills, e.g., she holds the world record for stopping electric fan blades with her tongue, 32 times in one minute.) Sprague and Hultgren started busking on the streets of London, providing a grind show for the foot traffic between the Eye and the Tower. They did that for two months.

The Lizardman is an intellectual, but he is not entirely cerebral. He is physical in his philosophy; he views mind and matter as inseparable. "Philosophy, the definition of a human being, is basically biological," he told me.

In his writings, he describes himself as Jewish and atheist. He's a believer in personal freedom. In his book, he makes a link between the right to body modification and the right to abortion. As quoted in his book, "Look at the abortion debates, the bottom line has always been one of the government deciding what women can legally do with their bodies," he wrote. "The argument of whether or not a procedure is allowed only logically follows after it is conceded that the government gets to make that choice and they get to make that choice because they are the ones that own the bodies."

His book reveals interesting tidbits, like his taste for bugs ("I will snatch up random ones and eat them if the mood strikes me") and his ability to lift empty beer kegs with his ears.

He told me that he used to be an art student. "I want to make the world more interesting by doing weird stuff in it, for people to experience it," he said. As the Lizardman, Sprague has turned himself into a live work of performance art, 24 hours a day, seven days a week. His punk rock attitude is central to his appearance. He is sophisticated and self-aware, but he shows in his book how far a shock can go: "If you want to really see how something like hair style can affect your life try wearing a mustache in the style that was chosen by Chaplin and Hitler (and was very common in its day.) I wore such a moustache for a few months in the nineties and was almost universally reviled for it, receiving harsh and negative reactions, the like of which my facial tattooing has never produced."

Fortunately, he shaved off the offending moustache and evolved into body modification. Because for the Lizardman, physical is essential. By splitting his tongue and tattooing himself green, Sprague, as the Lizardman, isn't just the way he looks, but the way he is.

"What if I stopped looking like a person?" he asked me metaphorically. "What effect does that have on humanity? Can I stop being human? Or can I be more than human? I've heard people say, 'You're not even human.'" From a carnival aspect, he is an extreme version of the sideshow classic, the illustrated man. In the famous book by Ray Bradbury, *The Illustrated Man* is covered with magical, animated tattoos. "The colors burned in three dimensions," wrote Bradbury. "They were windows looking in upon fiery reality." Each chapter in the book is a different story told by his body art. "Everyone wants to see the pictures, and yet nobody wants to see them," explained the illustrated man. He has tried to remove the pictures with sandpaper, acid and a knife. Because they are predictions for the future.

Sometimes people wonder if the scales on Lizardman's skin are real, or if the Lizardman himself is real. In his book, he cites an incident in a shopping mall where someone grabbed his arm while he was eating. Erik Sprague yelled: "Do not fucking touch me!"

A moustache can be shaved off in seconds. But a forked tongue is forever. Cutting your tongue is an irreversible decision. Once you laser your tongue in half, there is no turning back. I told the Lizardman over the phone that he didn't sound like someone who'd bifurcated his tongue. Of course, this was 24 years after it happened, and the tongue is the fastest-healing part of the body. But he said that within weeks after the procedure, he sounded completely normal. "I was on the telephone three weeks after the cut," said the

Lizardman. "My friend said, 'When are you going to get your tongue done?' and I said, 'Dude, I already did it.'"

But extreme body modification is not for the faint of heart, and there's nothing quite like the post-op hangover, when the body mod enthusiast goes home after getting sliced, stitched, pierced, inked, cauterized, impaled and/or bifurcated, and takes that first good look at the handiwork.

"I remember going to my apartment in Austin," said the Lizardman. "You look at the mirror and go, 'Fuck me!' In those moments, you might occasionally go, 'What have I done?'" But only for a moment. It's worth it, you become the Lizardman. He said that he has no regrets. "I trace all the good things in my life back to when I split my tongue," he said.

Chapter 17

Sarah the Bird Girl

"Her name is Minnie Woolsey and I want people to know that name and know that she existed."
- Sarah Houbolt

Sarah Houbolt beamed for the camera. She was wearing a black dress, her shoulders bare, her back to the bleachers of the Coney Island Circus Sideshow as she faced the stage, where she would soon perform as Sarah the Bird Girl in a tribute to the late, great Minnie Woolsey, a sideshow natural from the 20th century known as Koo Koo the Bird Girl. "Her name is Minnie Woolsey and I want people to know that name and know that she existed," said Sarah, in her enthusiastic Australian accent.

Sarah sat for an interview in August 2019 before she was scheduled to perform there. The poster for her event was eye-catching and sepia-toned, depicting Sarah in a shaggy avian outfit with a large feather spreading from her head and clunky plastic sunglasses, like a Depression-era Big Bird costume with the flare of a Las Vegas showgirl. "Koo Koo the Bird Girl," the poster read. "The Beauty of Difference. Haunting Captivating Visceral." She did, in fact, bear a resemblance to Minnie, especially when she mimicked her costume from the 1932 movie *Freaks*, but upgraded with a 21st century philosophy of feminism and disability self-awareness. Sarah described her show as a "theatrical narrative about an old freak show performer."

"I fell in love with her and I wanted to tell her story and I had an opportunity to bring it to the Coney Island stage so I'm grabbing the opportunity," she said, about two weeks before the performance, which she described as a theatrical biography of Minnie, born in 1880 in Raybun County in Georgia.

"The show is about her life," said Sarah. "Her life from living in an institution to traveling around with the circuses to being in the *Freaks* film by Tod Browning and then ending up in Coney Island to work as a freak show performer. And for me, the show is incredibly important because I share the same medical condition as Koo Koo the Bird Girl and, really, I'm the only person in the world who can tell her story authentically from that lived experience position, so it's kind of a dream come true, to be able to do this."

Sarah was born with Hallermann-Streiff syndrome, which affects her bone structure, leaving her short-statured at about 4 feet, 8 inches tall, and she is also legally blind, according to a 2016 profile by ABC Radio Sydney. This means that Sarah resembles Minnie, especially when she mimics her stage style. Both Sarah and Minnie cast themselves as large flightless birds, with shaggy feathery torsos and long legs and feather headdresses and comically large glasses, presenting themselves as avian humanoids.

The big difference is that Minnie had a reputation for being mentally disabled and didn't speak as part of her character, while Sarah is sharp as a tack and can describe her act with the eloquence of a university lecturer. Sarah explained the ableist history of disability, when people who were born different weren't allowed in public for fear of offending the non-disabled. "She grew up in a time where there were lots of laws that restricted her life," said Sarah. "So there were anti-marriage laws. She wasn't allowed to have children. She lived at the time of the ugly laws. So she had no other choice but to live in an asylum or to work in the circus. So she found herself in the circuses as a freak show performer. So she was exhibited, for want of a better word, but it was the only work she could get at the time."

"So, natural born freaks became royalty of the sideshow because, you know, without natural born freaks there would be no freak show," explained Sarah. "So she had an extraordinary life for what she could at the time, and then she found herself in the Tod Browning film and she was dancing, she was shimmying on the wedding table in the climactic scene where everyone was chanting 'gooble gabble one of us, we accept you, one of us.' And then she performed at Coney Island and lived in New York for the later part of her life, so I'm interested in honoring her story."

Sarah lit up as she emphasized certain words, like "extraordinary," and she shimmied her bare shoulders in a brief imitation, as she described Koo Koo's dance at the wedding party scene. She had chosen an extraordinary scene to focus on, because it is the part in the movie *Freaks* where the sideshow naturals ceremoniously accept the non-disabled bride of the little groom as "one of us," only to be rejected in humiliating fashion, triggering a chain of events in which the bride is, in fact, transformed into "one of us."

Sarah has traveled a parallel path to Koo Koo, following her to Coney Island more than eighty years later. She had traveled far from Down Under. She had flown from the other side of the world to perform as Minnie Woolsey in the Coney Island freak show. Her personal one-woman dedication to her predecessor clearly meant a lot to her. She knew that she was doing something historic.

But Sarah's life before she discovered Minnie was quite different. Sarah said that she grew up in Australia with Dutch parents, where she felt "isolated." She became a swimmer and competed in the 2000 Sydney Paralympic Games. Then she joined a women's circus.

"I never knew about circuses growing up and I started performing and then my mother tells me that my great grandfather was a magician who used to perform in New York at the time of the freak shows and then my friends were telling me, 'Hey Sarah, there's this Bird Girl character, you should look at her.'" She was living in New Zealand in 2013 when she started researching Minnie. "I started sideshow performance and this whole incredible journey sort of unraveled itself," she explained. "And then you know, a few years ago I put on Facebook, 'Hey, if I come to New York, who's there who would help me?' And then I found Coney Island and came here. It's been phenomenal, actually."

Sideshow is a unique medium for disabled artists because it provides a platform for them to showcase their disability in their performance, making it their own. For example, Stanislaus Berent was born with phocomelia, and his shortened arms served as the centerpiece of his 50-year career with sideshow. He demonstrated that he could shave with a straight razor and saw wood with a handsaw. He called himself Sealo, comparing his hands to flippers.

In both of their sideshow careers, Stan and Minnie created and cultivated stage personas that used and emphasized their disabilities. In this way, they created unique acts that could not be mimicked accurately except by performers who shared the same disabilities. Which is eventually what happened, with a new generation of disabled performers in the 21st century.

Mat Fraser has the same disorder as Berent, even though Stan was born a half-century before thalidomide existed because phocomelia can also occur naturally, without the influence of thalidomide. This prompted Mat to perform a series of tribute shows at the Coney Island Circus Sideshow where he dressed as Berent, talked his act like Stan did, and performed the same stunts, on the same stage where Stan used to do it, but decades after his death.

What a remarkable thing to do. Acts like this are extremely rare. Anyone fortunate enough to have seen Mat's portrayal of Stan, and Sarah's portrayal of Minnie, on the very same stage where they used to perform, is unlikely to see anything like that ever again.

Chapter 18

Jackie the Human Tripod

"This show is about what I can do. It's not a pity party. I'm proud to be a freak."

- Jackie Molen, *Los Angeles Times*, 2009

Jackie Molen, the Human Tripod, was a legend in her time, whirling across the Coney Island stage while wearing three roller skates: one on each hand, and one on her only foot. She wore athletic tube socks, pulled up to her knees and elbows, and cartwheeled across the stage like a cheerleader. She was the undisputed sideshow star.

Molen didn't even know that freak shows still existed, back in 2005, when she first stumbled across one. It was love at first sight. Jackie, who was a 20-year-old college student in Eugene, Oregon, joined the sideshow immediately, and went on the road.

She had assumed that freak shows were a thing of the past, that they had gone the way of the Elephant Man and Jo Jo the Dog-Faced Boy. She can be forgiven for assuming that freak shows had gone extinct. In truth, they were extremely rare. So it wasn't surprising that she had never encountered one until that fateful day when she finally did.

Jackie was a guitarist studying to be an audio engineer so she could record an album. She was listening to a college radio station and heard an advertisement for a show from Austin, Texas, that was coming to town called 999 Eyes Freakshow. "I was listening to the crazy, ridiculous ad they were doing about their show," she said. "They were doing a freak callout, we used to call it."

A *freak callout*. She told me what they said on the broadcast: "If you were born with an anomaly and you have an amazing talent and you want to join our show, come down and join our show."

She was surprised. She had seen the movie *Freaks* and thought of sideshows as cultural arcana that would only be found in black-and-white movies. "I didn't think that it was going on anymore," she told me.

She cogitated, weighing her talent as a musician with her unique physique and her various skills. She realized that her curriculum vitae was particularly well-suited for a sideshow job, and she was thrilled to hit the road and live a life of adventure. "I thought I would be perfect for that, because I know gymnastics and karate," she said. "They were going to Burning Man, festivals. I was into travel and also partying."

She went to see 999 Eyes Freakshow that night. "I watched them roll up and it was ridiculous," she said, describing a circus-like ensemble that included a little person and an enormous bike and various quirky characters. "I said, 'I want to join,' and they said, 'You're in.'" She made her first on-stage appearance with them that very night. "And three days later I was on tour with them."

The act of joining the circus can be spontaneous but also seem predestined. That's how it was for me when I joined Ringling Brothers at age 19. But when I was in the circus, I always felt an undercurrent of menace, like something bad was about to happen. Did she ever feel the same way about the sideshow? "At the time, it was very risky," she said. "It's not something I would advise. I went on tour with them, then went back to college, then did a thesis paper on the history of the freak show."

She was eminently qualified to write it. Back in 2005, Jackie was about to make history herself. She wasn't quitting the sideshow after just one season. She was just getting started. She was about to begin her career as a sideshow natural called Jackie the Human Tripod.

Jackie Molen was born with one leg, and it's only 15 inches long, though she can bring it up to 18 inches in a stiletto heel. She gets about on crutches. For five years she performed in sideshows as the Human Tripod. She was a star at the Coney Island Circus Sideshow, also known as Sideshows by the Seashore. A YouTube video from 2009, her final year in the sideshow business, depicts Jackie doing her signature act, skating across the stage while wearing three skates, two on her hands and one on her foot. She wore a purple dress in addition to the tube socks on her arms and foot. She has muscular arms, and her show included karate, cartwheels and handstands. She performed the one-armed handstand that's a famous trick for the so-called half-men: Aaron "Shorty" Wollin and Johnny Eck.

She would end her act by karate-chopping a flaming board. "It was kind of just me doing stuff that I liked to do when I was a kid," she told me. "That's how I used to roller skate when I was a kid."

When she was touring with 999 Eyes, she would wear a black-and-red satin skirt onstage and stand on her hands while delivering two spinning kicks, knocking a cup off a chair to her left and then another to her right, and then karate-chopping a board. She also toured state fairs with the Big Circus Sideshow, appearing alongside natural born farm animals with birth defects. Her boyfriend, a pyrotechnic juggler, accompanied her on stage.

I interviewed Jackie via Zoom in 2023; she wanted to talk face-to-face, but living 2,255 miles apart, Zoom would have to do. The window on my laptop screen showed Jackie sitting in her home in Idaho Falls, in what looked like a living room or home office. She appeared to be sitting in a chair, rather than a wheelchair.

To me, her disability was offscreen, which made it seem abstract and disembodied. Jackie said she wasn't always conscious of it. She had been born to it. There was no other way. "My condition, it's called unilateral proximal femoral focal deficiency," she said. "Everyone just calls it PFFD. It's really rare. They don't know what causes it, and I've never met or seen anyone with the same condition as me." (Actually, she had seen an online video of a woman with a similar disability, prancing about in her underwear like some sort of "weird disability fetish." She had considered contacting her but decided against it.) If Jackie's PFFD is an accident of nature, it does not feel that way to her. She's symmetrical, as if her body were deliberately molded. "I'm missing my femur, so my bones fused tougher without my femurs," she said. "I have a knee, but it's in my hip and it doesn't bend. But it happened so perfectly, I don't have any pain. I can move around like that, it's like it was meant to be like that. I don't know any different, so things don't really seem hard."

In 2009, the *Los Angeles Times* sent a reporter to cover the 137th Colorado State Fair in the city of Pueblo. There, she found Jackie, "a pretty, black-haired woman wearing a black sequined tank top and a black high-heeled sandal." She was sitting in a wheelchair and drinking a Pepsi outside her tent, next to a sign that said: "Freak animals created by God, not by the hand of man." The price of entry was $2, which seemed like a leftover from the 20th century.

At the Big Circus Sideshow, Jackie was exhibiting herself with a menagerie of animals, "living and pickled, with an array of deformities," including a duck with three legs, a sheep with five legs, a steer with six legs, a Holstein with two noses, a pig with two noses and two mouths, and a turtle with two heads. "I feel like I'm educating people about diversity and how people can be born different," she told the *LA Times*. "I'm in there doing amazing things. This show is about what I can do. It's not a pity party. I'm proud to be a freak."

A story published a few days earlier in the *Denver Post* said the exhibit also included a six-legged steer and Tyrone the Giant Rat, along with Misty the Mermaid, a fossilized monkey skull, a freeze-dried "cyclops" baby and "a devil baby with horns, fangs, pointy ears in a casket instead of a crib."

Even if you've grown accustomed to the concept of a freak show, the idea of a disabled human displaying herself alongside mutated farm animals and faux medical exhibits takes some getting used to. When I met with Kim Kelly in Philadelphia, she had viewed the jarred babies at the Mütter Museum with a mix of fascination, empathy and woe. I asked Jackie how she felt being displayed alongside animals with birth defects. "I love those animals," she beamed. "They were so cute, just to spend time with them and pet them."

She said that she loved traveling with the Big Circus Sideshow, working its grind show in the shadow of its distinctive freak show banners, and that she loved the traveling curio museum, which prompted her to get "super into collecting." The Big Circus Sideshow is where she met her future husband Josh "Flame O" Bladzik, who ran away and joined the circus at age 14, according to his bio. He's a sideshow polymath who can juggle, rope spin, unicycle and eat fire. (They were married in October 2024, a few days before Halloween.)

Josh once explained, in an undated interview with Sideshow World, that he had joined a sideshow because he heard they were dying, and he wanted to experience the scene first-hand before it was too late. "I learned the sideshow isn't dying," he said. "There are still ambitious showmen who are willing to sacrifice and take calculated risks."

He became one of those showmen. The story depicted Josh sitting on a camp chair next to a striped circus tent and eating French fries, next to the show's eccentric founder, Jimmy Zajicek. They wore fedora hats and bow ties.

Jackie said that she had nothing but respect for this mystery man who ran the Big Circus Sideshow. "Jimmy Zajicek, I would love to give him a callout because his show was so cool," she said wistfully. "He had a museum that toured the fairs, he had living animals, a six-legged cow, six-legged sheep, a two-headed turtle, a barnyard of animals, a huge tent, he moved it around, a fair circuit, he did it for a long time."

Zajicek also provided the inspiration for Strange Remains Curio Shop, the retail business she runs with Josh. Strange Remains is a Wunderkammer of phantasmagothic curiosities, from shrunken heads molded with their own hands to zombie baby head candles and miniature coffins filled with red sand. Zajicek played the midways till he died in 2014.

Jackie, like Jason Brott, has performed in many sideshows and has an insider's perspective on this niche subculture, with all its permutations and oddballs, roving across the land and working in eclectic locations. In addition to 999 Eyes Freakshow, the Coney Island Circus Sideshow and the Big Circus Sideshow, she was also in Ken Harck's Brothers Grim's Sideshow and Hellzapoppin Circus Sideshow. She performed in the Venice Beach Freakshow in its final days. She lived in a "crazy sideshow house" with Tommy Breen from World of Wonders, along with performers Satan John and Flipper Boy. She performed with the Lizardman at the Fright Dome, a haunted house that used to appear every October at the Circus Circus Hotel & Casino in Las Vegas.

Sideshows survive on sales, which means that sideshow naturals often survive on commissions. "If you do a grind show, you make tips and stuff, you're inclined to hustle, sell your pitch cards," she said. Pitch cards are holdovers from a prior century. Naturals would sell pitch cards with illustrations of themselves and brief biographies explaining their disabilities. Grady Stiles and other naturals used to sell pitch cards; I had assumed they were a thing of the past.

Coney Island is a bit special in this regard. Naturals who perform for the Coney Island Circus Sideshow are paid a modest salary for a 10-in-1 act, which goes on all day. Jackie was happy to get the gig. "Coney Island, they pay you for the show, so there's not any kind of hustling back," she said. "At the time, it was like a lot of money to me because I didn't have any."

During her years with the sideshow, she did a variety of acts, including playing guitar in a band and doing a strongwoman show where she ripped a phone book in half. She had an act where she called herself Ms. Electra and sat on a Tesla coil and became a human conductor of electricity. "You can touch stuff and it sparks and you can set stuff on fire," she said, reminding me of Jellyboy. She even walked on glass with her one foot, but she only did it a couple of times onstage.

She appeared in *This is Gonna Hurt*, a photo book by Nikki Sixx, the Mötley Crüe bassist and ex-junkie who wrote the song *Shout at the Devil*. The stylized book, published in 2011, features avant-garde photographs of crackheads, prostitutes and disabled people. Mat Fraser is in photos wearing an Elizabethan collar but no shirt. In a two-page spread, he's holding a coiled rope and posing with a Shetland pony. Jackie is in several pictures, with a circus-like spread featuring multiple poses, including a head stand where she sticks her single left foot-leg straight up in the air. In one photo, she's squeezed into a salacious black outfit and bending forward, her head adorned with a skull cap that sprouts five horns.

I asked her the question: Were you exploited as a sideshow natural? She said no. "I managed myself the five years I was performing and made all the decisions on what projects I'd take, who I worked with and what I did, so I pretty much had creative control of what was going on."

She achieved some measure of fame, appearing on National Geographic's *Taboo* and WE Network's *The Secret Lives of Women*, which were shows that profiled nonconformist behavior.

And then, she left the sideshow business. She disappeared. "I kind of left at the top of my game, abruptly, and a lot of people thought I was dead," she said. "I cut everyone off. Nobody heard from me for a very long time."

I asked her what happened. "I got sober," she said. She went straight edge, and at the time of our interview she had been that way for 12 years. "I had a problem before I started doing this," she said. "I was a rebellious teen. I was an alcoholic before I joined." She said that her alcoholism was "progressing" during her career with the sideshow. "It got worse and worse," she said. Then she abruptly retired from the sideshow and returned to Idaho Falls, where she grew up. Her mother lived there. "I came back here and I got sober."

Is the sideshow lifestyle too nihilistic? "It depends on what show you're on," she said. "Some shows were very chill. Some other places, you didn't know what was going to happen." I asked if she left the sideshow because the lifestyle was less than ideal for getting sober. "It's hard," she said. "You don't have a schedule. There's not a routine. It's just very crazy."

The website for Strange Remains Curio Shop depicts Jackie gazing with rapt attention at a rotting zombie hand displayed in a glass bell jar. Her eyes shine with excitement at beholding this sublime artifact. Josh stands beside her, peering at the hand through his spectacles, managing to look professorial and artisanal at the same time.

But it's not the hand of a zombie, Jackie informed me. It is a prop hand from *Bride of Frankenstein*, the camp classic from 1935. This is part of the traveling museum that Jackie and Josh have assembled over the years, which they transport on the road and exhibit in a tent at fairs, in true sideshow style.

She got into collecting weird things with Josh while traveling with the Big Circus Sideshow. One of her prized possessions is an ancient Egyptian cat mummy. They were offerings to the goddess Bastet, who had the head of a cat. Jackie has other mummified cats, but Strange Remains specializes in horror movie props. She said that when her fiancé proposed to her, he used the ring worn by vampire Jessica Handby on the HBO series *True Blood*.

After living in Idaho for 10 years, they moved to Las Vegas in 2019 and opened a shop downtown on Fremont Street, an old honky-tonk section north of the Strip with a cowboy-style layout and Elvis wedding chapels. They made and sold curios, including pinned butterflies, creepy dolls, crow skulls on clips, baby head candles, and so on. "We're both very crafty," she said. "We make crazy stuff and people like it."

They had the Vegas store for seven months and then COVID hit and the state of Nevada ordered the shuttering of all nonessential businesses. But Jackie and Josh still had to pay rent even though the store was closed, so they closed it down for good. "I probably wouldn't open another retail location," she said. "I don't know how people make a living like that, honestly."

They moved back to Idaho and left the store behind. Jackie and Josh moved their retail business online and on the road, like Kerouac. Their website says: "We handcraft a variety of unusual, bizarre and beautiful pieces. Influenced by nature, legends and lore, fantasy, horror, sci-fi, cryptozoology, comedy and chaos. Our one-of-a-kind art is made of a mix of recycled materials, found objects, bones, taxidermy and hand painted and sculpted items."

The Strange Remains museum travels to fairs, expos and events, with a 20 x 30 foot tent with a "full banner line for outdoor events." In her own way, Jackie was carrying on with the tradition of World of Wonders, the Big Circus Sideshow, and all the other tented sideshows that came before. She loves to travel, and her business brought them to horror cons in Las Vegas, Seattle, and Portland, Oregon.

In her day-to-day life, Jackie relies on a wheelchair. She has a bachelors degree in marketing from Western Governors University (WGU), an online nonprofit university that was founded in the 1990s by 19 governors. She recorded a mix of folk songs and electronic pieces under the name Faye Samskara, and she's co-authoring a zombie novel with her fiancé. She has a day job in e-commerce working at a music company.

When she travels to her office and other places, strangers notice her disability and offer to help her. "People will see me do normal things like walk upstairs, and they're like, 'Great job, you really go up those stairs good,'" said Jackie, imitating the voice of an enthusiastic bystander. It took her a while to get used to these unsolicited, and generally unneeded, offers of assistance. Her attitude towards them has evolved over the years. "It's weird for me," she said. "Their hearts are in the right place. It used to irritate me when I was a kid. But now I'm more compassionate."

Sometimes she'll take a break from her job and go outside the office to sit for a while in her wheelchair. People take notice. "In my wheelchair, people will offer me a ride," she said. "People are always asking me if I need help. I'm glad that people are nice enough to ask so I'm not mean about it."

"People are like, 'Do you need help going to the bathroom?' Yeah, I'm like, 'Do you want to help me wipe my ass?'" she said, laughing.

Back in 2009, when Jackie was in the Big Circus Sideshow, owner Jimmy Zajicek told the *Los Angeles Times* that he was always on the lookout for a money-making acquisition, but he only hired natural borns, drawing the line at "self-made freaks" who have altered themselves through surgery and tattoos.

"It's stupidity to deform yourself for entertainment value," he told the *LA Times*. "What Jackie's doing is she's playing the cards she's dealt. She's an inspiration."

That's a different take from the late 20th-century narrative, that freak shows are shameful spectacles of exploitation that should go extinct. But Jackie has described her sideshow career as generally positive, a fun but rigorous way to potentially make some cash, and

100% voluntary. "I think there were definitely some cases of bad things happening back in the day with freak shows and sideshows, but it just got totally demonized," she said. "Historically, I would say that it wasn't all bad."

While there were cases of exploitation and outright slavery, sideshows were also a means for some naturals to make money and take control of their lives. Some naturals were able to own property and businesses and retire with some degree of comfort and security.

In the cases where naturals were exploited, she said that a lot of those people didn't have the options that many Americans now take for granted, like Social Security. She also said that exploitation can be defined rather broadly, and it isn't limited to disabled people.

"I feel that anyone who is a performer is exploiting themselves," she said. "If you're a model, you're exploiting your beauty. I feel like if I want to exploit myself, I have every right to do that. I don't see that as exploitative. I feel like it's show business."

But she isn't so sure about her stage name. "I do wish I'd chosen a better stage name, that's for sure," she said. "I'm not a big fan of Jackie the Human Tripod." She settled on the name almost by default. She wasn't a "half-woman," so she couldn't style herself in the manner of Aaron Wollin and Johnny Eck. Better to come up with something new and different, she figured. "I came up with a tripod thing," she said, though in retrospect, she feels that the catchy moniker doesn't really convey who she is. "If I saw that in a poster I'd be like, 'What is that?'" she said. "I think it's because everybody thinks of a tripod as a little person with a giant phallus. I just don't think it's very cool."

I asked her about the label "disability," which is applied to her and millions of other people who are born different. This label can be problematic when applied to people like Jennifer Miller, aka Woman with a Beard, who does not consider her facial hair to be a disability. It also can be problematic to people who just don't like the term.

When I first reached out to Jackie by email, I asked whether it was appropriate to refer to her as disabled, and whether it was offensive to her to use the term "freak show."

"I'm fine with the term disability," she replied. "I'm not easily offended lol. Obviously we are dealing in an area with terms most of the general public is not comfortable with. That seems to be the real issue with the 'freakshow'. If we called it a disability showcase I'm sure everyone would be all for it :)."

Chapter 19

Lil Miss Firefly

"For walking on broken glass, you should get naked."
- Lil Miss Firefly

Balloon swallowing is a difficult sideshow act that involves cramming a long, tubular, inflated balloon into your mouth then appearing to force it down your throat and into your body, inch by inch, without choking, until the entire thing disappears down into your innards. The act of balloon swallowing is particularly dramatic when performed by a sideshow stripper named Lil Miss Firefly who is only three feet tall. "I'm barely 50 pounds after a Thanksgiving meal," she said.

Lil Miss Firefly, wearing a shiny little one-piece dress, must tilt her head back, like a sword swallower, to perform her most lucrative act, preparing her mouth, head, neck and body to receive a sausage-shaped balloon that is twice as long as her. She opens her mouth wide, her jaw expanding like a snake's, as she begins to feed the balloon into her mouth, her hands grabbing the tube seeming to shove it further down, fist over fist, consuming the entire thing without gagging. The latex of the balloon makes a squeaky noise as she consumes it, but it doesn't pop. She ends with a flourish, mischievously sticking out her tongue and demonstrating that the balloon is long gone. Where did it go? How does she swallow an inflated balloon?

"It's a magic trick," she said. "It's not an easy magic trick. My jaw hurts, depending on how many I swallow per night."

Lil Miss Firefly, whose real name is Crystal Lockhart, is a sideshow legend, having performed for 999 Eyes Freakshow, Coney Island Circus Sideshow, Hellzapoppin and

World of Wonders, to name a few. She performed in Dubai with Jellyboy on a five-month run. She worked the Fright Dome in Las Vegas. She toured for seven years with the Pretty Things Peepshow, a vaudevillian hoochie coochie troupe with a burlesque appetite for pasties, sword swallowing, chainsaw juggling and fire, performing in Canada, Europe (including Iceland), Australia and New Zealand.

But sideshow isn't all she does. "I'm an adult entertainer, a stripper," she said, in a phone interview in June 2023. She learned how to swallow balloons at a strip club in Colorado. She said that it's a real crowd pleaser, a veritable showstopper. In the stripper business, she said day shifts can be so slow that the strippers are literally braiding each other's hair for want of anything to do. But Crystal Lockhart says she's no house girl. She's a busker, meaning that she hustles. "I pay to work," she said, so slow shifts are unacceptable money-losers. She must spice up those sluggish shifts. Get the party started with some balloon swallowing.

"When I pull out balloons, it's like, oh shit, here it comes," she said. She said the other strippers will stop performing and surrender the stage to her. The rival strippers can't compete for the attention of the audience. "They're not looking at us when you've got that pink thing in your mouth," they told her. When Lil Miss Firefly knows she has the full attention of every patron in the place, she knows they are going to make it rain. "I pull out my balloons," she said, "and I pull out the pink ones and the black ones [depending on the audience]. It's a fucking money maker."

Crystal says she can cross between the worlds of being a sideshow natural and a stripper and also combine them. In other words, there's a sexy way to swallow balloons and there's a sexy way to dance on broken glass. There's a sexy way to do sideshow.

Swallowing balloons is her rainmaker. But her passion is dancing on broken glass.

When Crystal saw the television show *Carnivale* in 2003, she noticed that a little person, an actor named Michael J. Anderson, was playing the manager of a fictional sideshow. His character, named Samson, was calling all the shots. Ever since she saw a sideshow natural portrayed in a position of leadership, Lockhart has viewed sideshow as a career opportunity for naturals and a means of influencing the way people perceive her. "Being a natural born, I feel that I have to take control of some of that narrative," she said.

Crystal has skills. She can escape from a straitjacket while suspended upside down, and she can also breathe fire, though she has retired from incendiary entertainment. ("I was breathing fire," she said, "but I don't do it anymore because it's dangerous and I want my lungs to work.") She performs a burlesque dance on broken glass, which lends itself to little clothing. "For walking on broken glass, you should get naked," she said, "because it's more dramatic with the more flesh you have when you run around on the glass."

Sideshow performers will often put their unique spin on traditional acts, like glass walking. Her signature spin is a slip and slide on splintered glass. "The longer the stage, the better the slip and slide goes," she said. "There's a lot of little prep work to it. There's nothing on my skin to protect me from the broken glass."

She said the outcome of the act for her is not to get cut. She is usually successful at this but not always. She ended up as a "bloody little mess" at a show at the Denver Art Museum in January 2023. One of her three siblings - her sister, a physician's assistant - was in the audience that night, along with her mother. "Every time my mom's in the audience something bad happens," she said. "Mom paid for 13 years of ballet and now I'm walking across broken glass. Yay!"

She learned to breathe fire from her uncle. She learned the secrets of how to walk on broken glass from another sideshow performer. Eventually, once she got good at it, she passed the skill along to another natural. When Lil Miss Firefly was touring with Hellzapoppin in 2010, she taught Jackie the Human Tripod how to walk on broken glass. "I love Jackie," said Lockhart. "She was my road dog."

She worked onstage with multiple naturals at the Coney Island Circus Sideshow for an event in May 2019 that was called Super Freak Weekend, with Mat Fraser, Jennifer Miller, Nati Amos, Antonio J. Torres Jr. and someone she referred to as the Indian rubber boy. She said that a psychologist came and interviewed all the naturals. "They wanted to make sure that I'm there at my own free will," she said. "It was my first time working at Coney, and they wanted to make sure I was OK."

I asked about her sideshow philosophy.

"I believe in sideshow," she said. "People are going to ask you questions about your disability and how did you get it. It gets old, but if you're not going to educate people on what's going on with you, then you're part of the problem."

Crystal lives in Denver but grew up in rural Colorado. "Growing up in Podunk, Colorado, being different is not a good thing," she said. "No jobs."

She was born in 1983 with a rare genetic disability known as Morquio syndrome. She said that in families that have the hereditary condition, it is typically passed to one out of four kids. There are four kids in her family, and she's the one who got it. "It's why I am little," she said.

She is not a little person per se. She does not have dwarfism. Her short height is a result of Morquio. According to the website of the Children's Hospital of Philadelphia, the symptoms include short stature, with a "very short" torso and abnormal bone and spine development including severe scoliosis. The hospital lists other symptoms including a "bell-shaped chest with ribs flared out at the bottom," a large head and "hypermobile joints."

Another symptom is a short life span. At the time of our interview, Lockhart had just celebrated her 40th birthday. She was never expected to make it that far. "I wasn't supposed to live past two," she said. "I get very wary around my birthday." This is because on every birthday while growing up, family members kept reminding her that she wasn't supposed to live that long. The side effects and symptoms are by no means limited to small stature. They can be debilitating. "I have been in and out of wheelchairs," she said. "I have a lot of internal problems that I have to deal with on a daily basis."

She said the disease attacks her bones and organs and can result in unexpected side effects. When she took the COVID booster, she said her body was "freaking out" and she spent two months in the hospital. She said that she feels fortunate to some extent, because with Morquio it can always be worse. She has seen teenagers with Morquio confined to wheelchairs.

Crystal said she has another characteristic that would qualify her as a sideshow natural. "I can grow a beard," she said, "so that was going to be my retirement plan, but now everybody's doing it."

She started in the sideshow business in 2003 in Colorado. Three years into her career, in 2006, she joined the legendary Ward Hall's World of Wonders. He had pursued her like a classic freak finder from the old days. "Ward Hall, I don't know how he found me, but he did," she said. "It changed my life."

When she first joined the sideshow business, she admitted to being green. "I didn't know the difference between natural borns and working acts." But she quickly figured out that she wanted to be more than window dressing for other acts. "I didn't want to be the tiny peanut; I did not just want to hold the hat; I didn't just want to be the microphone stand; I wanted to prove my worth in the sideshow world," she said.

Touring with World of Wonders was a hard-working lifestyle that was akin to camping out, without the usual comforts of hearth and home. They trucked a circus-style tent around the country and staked it into the ground with sledgehammers. They ate and slept wherever. "You're sleeping in the back of semi-trucks," she said.

But World of Wonders also served as a sort of sideshow boot camp, where Lil Miss Firefly cut her teeth and learned many of the basic sideshow skills that serve her today. "If I can do World of Wonders, I can do anything," she said. "That was not an easy tour." She spoke highly of Tommy Breen, the show's sole proprietor who worked with her in the old days. I told her that I would be interviewing Tommy a few days later, as he was touring through Long Island that summer. "You tell Mr. Breen I said 'hi,'" she said.

The hardships of World of Wonders are due more to the itinerant nature of the show than the itinerant nature of its participants. Breen has been living on the road for nine months out of every year for more than 20 years. In contrast, the Coney Island Circus Sideshow stays permanently in one place. While New York is an expensive place to live, some performers make arrangements. Crystal stayed with friends, like manager Patrick David Wall. Coney performers crank out their acts all day long, day after day, but they don't have to tear down the show at the end of the day and pack it into trucks and move the entire operation somewhere else, like a small army. "Coney Island, it's a grind show, but you can go to a house and take a shower without 30 people going 'Hurry the fuck up'," she said.

Unfortunately, her sideshow career flattened during COVID, along with the rest of the job market. "Before COVID, I was set to go on a cruise ship for 10 months," she said, but the opportunity was canceled. "For me being in entertainment, I always knew my job was never secure."

But it is picking back up again, even if her most lucrative work involves taking off her clothes. "You can strip to anything that you're doing," she said. "When your wife is cooking dinner in the kitchen, she can put cake batter on her boobs. Anything can be sexual; it just depends on the costumes and the music you use."

Not every woman is willing to take off her clothes for money. I asked her why she does. "I do have fun with the job and stripping pays well," she said. "Sideshow goes so well with adult entertainment."

This reminded me of a phrase, "the pornography of disability," which I heard from Mat Fraser, who had heard it from an anti-sideshow academic. "Seen by many as crude, rude, and exploitive, the freak show is despicable, a practice on the margin, limited to a class with poor taste, representing, as one disability rights activist puts it, the 'pornography of disability,'" wrote Robert Bogdan in *Freak Show*, identifying the activist as Professor Douglas Biklen of the Center of Human Policy at Syracuse University in New York.

In addition to stripping and sideshow, Lil Miss Firefly is also a "scare actor" at haunted houses like the Fright Dome in Vegas. "I like making people happy; I like scaring the crap out of them," she said. "I'm not going to get into porn, but I like making people feel something." Her desire for the extreme is what led her to the sideshow. "I've always had the mentality [that] I don't just want to do the minimal; I want to do the maximum thing," she said.

Not everyone is amused by her exhibitionist hoochie coochie. Lockhart said that in Colorado, people often tell her that she's being exploited. "I still get that today," she said. But she doesn't see it that way. She is an entrepreneur, acting of her own volition, performing at St. Patrick's Day celebrations in Denver and screenings of the *Rocky Horror Picture Show*. She makes connections. Her Vegas gig, where she worked as a "scare actor" at the Fright Dome, led to another working stint in Hong Kong. "I signed my own contact," she said, which is what she says to people who question the way she makes a living. "I drive myself; I carry my own gear, I'm not in a cage."

Crystal said that she likes stripping, that she's not ashamed of her body. "If you don't like the way I look, then don't look at me," she said. She added that she doesn't get completely nude. At burlesque shows, she wears pasties. And she revealed the prurient core of what she's doing for her audience, that moment of singularity when a strip act crosses over into sideshow: "Some of them have never seen a little person naked before," she said.

But she also acknowledged there is a dark side to strip clubs and their patrons, including "creepy guys" who say "shitty" things to her on stage and make her wonder, "Why am I still here?" But on the upside, she also described strip clubs as protected environments. "If I have an issue with someone, it gets taken care of it," she said. She described a disturbing example from the week before, where a patron grabbed her, placed her on his crotch and started dry humping her, so the bouncers threw him out. He left a pile of cash on the table, which the strippers divided amongst themselves.

Her Instagram account is loaded with raunchy jokes and cartoons and images from her dynamic life as a tiny, tattooed stripper in black lacy underwear. There's a picture of her lying in a suitcase, and another picture of her as a blood-splattered zombie bride. In one picture she embraced a cucumber, in another she poised with a banana between her thighs. A recent posting said, "Dating me is like smoking weed in public. Sure people look at you funny but deep down they wanna hit it too." She poises with her friend and colleague Penny Poison, an angel-faced brunette with a split tongue and pointed elf ears who lives in Las Vegas. The two of them form an unforgettable Goth stripper sideshow duo. There are pictures of them traveling together, going through an airport taxi line, mugging for the camera. They are sometimes accompanied by a bodyguard. She's said she's been working with Penny since early in her career. "She grew up and bloomed into a really great performer."

When she was touring with 999 Eyes Freakshow, they ran into protestors in Minnesota. Crystal said the protestors had never seen the show but had made erroneous claims as to "what they're doing to us on the inside. They said we're in cages." She said that they invited the protesters to have a look themselves. "Come and see the show," she said. "No one's whipping anybody. We're not in cages. If anybody wants to leave, we can. If you want to protest something, protest zoos."

While some people find freak shows shocking, Crystal said she was shocked by the protesters. Sideshow people have historically blamed these "do-gooders" for the decline of the freak show in the late 20th century. Naturals who perform in sideshows say that these well-intentioned do-gooders eroded their ability to perform and make a living. "I have a genetic disability," said Lockhart. "Either you're going to sit at home and cry about it and be mad about your situation or you're going to go out and live a life."

She has traveled the world as a natural born sideshow performer. If she could have foreseen her future when she was a young girl getting taunted by bullies, she would have found it impossible. "I would not have believed you," she said, "because people called me 'midget' to make me cry."

She uttered the m-word multiple times during the interview, and she shared an anecdote about that time she was a "midget wrestler" touring with a troupe of other "midget wrestlers" and the car broke down and all the wrestlers ended up stranded on the side of the road. Some passerby called the cops thinking someone had abandoned a group of kids on the highway.

Her liberal use of the m-word surprised me because I thought that the once-acceptable term "midget" had gone out of fashion and was now considered offensive, having been replaced by "little person." But sideshow people cross the line of public sensibility and make folks uncomfortable. Some naturals use the word "freak" to take ownership of it, like Black people taking ownership of the n-word. But that's not what this was about.

She said she prefers the term "midget" over "dwarf," because she does not have dwarfism. She does not say "little person" because she said that's a term that full-sized people use for children.

In fact, her full stage title is: *Lil Miss Firefly, the Midget of Mischief*.

She told me that someone once asked her: "What's your pronoun?"

She replied, "Midget."

Chapter 20

World of Wonders

"Although I'd traveled around the Eastern seaboard states, being with the carnival made it seem completely different. I felt as though I were entering another country."
- Daniel P. Mannix, author of *Memoirs of a Sword Swallower*

"His way of life marks him as an endangered species, a relic of another era, hanging on even in normal times by a thread."
- *Harper's* profile of Tommy Breen

On Juneteenth 2023, I went to the Long Island Funfest in New York to see World of Wonders, the last traveling tented sideshow in America. The show is headquartered in Gibsonton, Florida, outside of Tampa, which has long served as a winter camp for sideshow naturals. But during the summer, it tours fairs across America. World of Wonders is the legendary freak show established by the late Ward Hall and his partner, Chris Christ, who employed such luminaries as Poobah, a fire-breathing dwarf who was with the show for half a century, Short E. Dangerously, the daredevil glass-jumping half-man who started his sideshow career there, and Stan "Sealo" Berent, a performer with phocomelia who teamed up with Ward to help overturn Florida's freak show ban back in the 1970s. This is the same Sealo who inspired Mat Fraser to emulate his work in a series of tribute performances at the Coney Island Circus Sideshow 20-plus years ago.

The Funfest entry fee was $5, sideshow included. This took pressure off the sideshow to sell tickets, so they didn't have to hustle on the bally platform. "Now we're a free act," said Tommy Breen, owner of World of Wonders. "The fair pays us to be here." World of Wonders was on the midway at the back of the fair, near a trailer masquerading as a haunted house and a flying saucer ride called Alien Invasion. World of Wonders was a great rectangular tent 95 feet wide and 60 feet deep, with bright banners announcing, "Headless Alive, Living Head Inside."

Breen, a fire eater and sword swallower who goes by Great Gozleone, knows the hard-scrabble sideshow life isn't for everyone, naturals or non-naturals. Tommy mentioned how Mannix, in his book about sideshow life, described the supposedly lazy lifestyle of the performer, who would lie in his bed (if he had one) and take hours to leisurely awaken in the morning, like a cat, watching the sunlight slowly creep in through the window. Tommy found this languid description absurd, considering that he never worked so hard as he did in a sideshow, loading and unloading trucks and pounding eight-pound sledgehammers to stake down the sprawling tent and setting up the stage and the props and the whole show, and performing throughout the day, again and again, and then tearing down and packing up the whole thing and driving across the country to seemingly random locations to eat fire, hammer things up his nose, and sleep in trucks.

The pandemic was rough for everybody, and it was particularly rough for circuses and sideshows. Live performances were shut down as COVID swept across the land in 2020. Sideshows had survived the Great Depression and all sorts of calamities over the years, but it was the pandemic that flattened them.

"The modern American carnival business is nothing if not resilient," read a *Harper's* magazine profile of World of Wonders in 2022. "It has persevered through war, depression, and ecological acts of God. Through it all, it has held its place in the cultural firmament, largely unchanged in form and function from the original carnivals that toured the country following the 1893 World's Fair. COVID-19, however, put the business on its ass."

In the 2020s, the sideshow was trying to resuscitate itself from the COVID pandemic, which had killed more than one million Americans. After a difficult hiatus, performances started to re-emerge. Mortality was finally slowing down, and the U.S. economy was picking up. Shows were back on the road.

But something was missing from World of Wonders in the summer of 2023, even with Tommy and his troupe's dangerous acts. "At the moment we don't have any natural born freaks on the roster," Tommy told me. The lack of naturals was not for lack of trying, he explained. It was just a temporary blip, Tommy assured me, in the sideshow's long history of exhibiting naturals. It happens sometimes. Sideshow naturals are rare, which is what makes them so special. "I'm always looking for people" he said. "It's hard to find people who are into this."

It's especially hard to find people like Poobah, who was the star of the show for most of World of Wonders' existence. For half a century, Poobah roamed the land with the sideshow, breathing fire before crowds of rubes, awestruck or bemused, in dusty little towns in sparsely populated sections of the country. According to a tribute written by Ward Hall, Poobah would also do an act called "iron tongue," where he hooked his tongue and lifted weights with it. Hall said his stage name was from a character in the opera called *The Mikado*.

Poobah was like a mythical character, the way Tommy described him. But the photos depict him as a nondescript little, old white man who would have looked at home sitting on a front porch, drinking coffee and listening to baseball on the radio. Poobah, King of the Pygmies, was what they called him on the bally. He would be outside the tent, luring customers inside. Tommy said that a passerby would yell, "That's terrible! He's a little person!" But Poobah would stay in character and insist to the crowd that he was a pygmy.

"We're not making fun of anybody, we're not exploiting people in any way, there's no one in a cage, there no one here against their will," said Tommy. He said that Poobah (real name Pete Terhurne) thrived in the sideshow, and it might have been the best path available to him. According to Hall's book *My Very Unusual Friends*, Poobah came home in tears on his first day of school because the other kids mocked him. His mother kept him home from then on, and he was illiterate. "I think it's important to be seen," said Tommy. "Poobah was taken out of school because people made fun of him, but he did this [World of Wonders] for 50 years and he loved it. He was a star." Poobah joined Ward's show when he was 24 years old. "He had been treated as a child until he joined the show," wrote Ward. But at the sideshow, "he was treated like a man."

In retrospect, one can see how Poobah's act might have raised eyebrows. Ward's tribute includes a photo from 1954 where Poobah and his fellow performers stand on the bally platform beneath a banner that screams: FREAKS ODDITIES CURIOSITIES. Ward described a show called "The Midget and the Monsters," where Poobah was placed in an enclosure with a large boa constrictor. In the 1960s, they developed the Pygmy act, where Poobah wore leopard skins and danced barefoot on broken glass and did the iron tongue.

I asked Tommy about sideshows being accused of exploiting naturals. "All work is exploitative," he said, repeating the common refrain of sideshow workers. "These people are playing a character and it's absolutely their right to be seen and to be on stage." He compared sideshow naturals to fashion models who are capitalizing on their beauty and their sexy figures. "If you're born with some sort of innate talent, you should share that and use it to your advantage," he said. "That's what makes pop culture great." He said that sideshow naturals can prove to the audience, through their acts, that they're capable of doing everything that you can do, and more. "The people who are do-gooders and think that they're going to help these people, they don't need your help," he said. "You should go and see what they do. Look at their art." He said the sideshow provides naturals with a way to make money. "You're creating a character that's marketable. They're buying tickets to see Poobah the Fire Breathing Dwarf." Poobah died in 2012. Tommy said that as his sideshow travels the land, people still ask about him. "Everywhere we go in the country people remember Poobah," he said.

In 2022, a natural from Indianapolis who called himself John T. Rex (birth name John Husted) made cameo performances with World of Wonders at various locations.

T. Rex has phocomelia, meaning that he was born with short arms, thus his stage name, referencing the diminutive arms of the otherwise mighty Tyrannosaurus Rex, king of the tyrant lizards. John T. Rex impresses his audience by using his small arms to do things that most people couldn't do with normal arms, like his whip act. Using his Indiana Jones-style skills, he snuffs out candles with the crack of a braided leather horsewhip. With his long hair, beard and thick glasses, he looks like a 1970s rocker. He is, in fact, a drummer, like Mat Fraser, who also has phocomelia.

T. Rex played the drums on the bally platform. Tommy said that when they played a fair in Minnesota, they weren't allowed to announce that they had a natural in the sideshow. "In Minnesota, we were not allowed to say we had freaks," he said. "We were not allowed to mention T. Rex with his little arms." In other words, they could employ disabled people, but they weren't supposed to have a freak show. So, T. Rex just kept playing the drums on the bally platform, without actually mentioning his phocomelia, and no one else at the sideshow acknowledged it. That's how they got through Minnesota.

Tommy introduced Aaron "Shorty" Wollin to the business before he joined Hellzapoppin, after a friend of Shorty's convinced him to try to join the World of Wonders. At the time, he was working as an MC at jiggle joints in Florida. "Shorty, this was his first sideshow job," said Tommy. "He was doing strip shows." Shorty's friend told Tommy about him and suggested that he hire him because he had a "crazy" attitude. Tommy contacted Shorty and asked him for a picture. Shorty sent the photo and when Tommy saw it, he exclaimed, "He's perfect!"

He said that Shorty started out by riding his skateboard back and forth across the stage but worked his way up to various acts like one-handed handstands and flipping and also throwing knives, along with daredevil stunts like breathing fire and jumping on flaming broken glass with his hands. "Shorty is amazing," said Tommy. "Everything that we did, he would say, 'I want to learn how you do that.'" They became friends. Shorty, a former race car driver, took Tommy for a ride in his car, which had hand controls. One time, Shorty snuck up on Tommy and grabbed him. "He put me in a chokehold, and I couldn't get out," he said. "He's strong from walking on his hands. Shorty is so fucking strong."

But Shorty wouldn't tour with World of Wonders forever. "He did a couple seasons with us and then he went on to become a superstar." Since then, Shorty has traveled the world. At that time, in the summer of 2023, he was touring elsewhere in the country with Hellzapoppin.

At the Long Island Funfest, the World of Wonders tent looked frayed and pin-holed, with the sunlight peeking through tiny perforations like a scattering of stars. I assumed that the tent was an old relic dating back to the murky origins of this sideshow in the 1940s. But no, the tent was purchased only in 2016, which made it authentic enough, because it was bought by none other than the late, great Ward Hall, who died in 2018 at age 88. His obituary in the *New York Times* described him as a "keeper of the flame" for sideshows.

The weather on Long Island in June was calm and warm. The tent was roomy and seemed like it would be a good place to ride out a rainstorm. But Tommy said during bad weather, the tent could be rough. "The tent is like an animal," he said.

World of Wonders was called something different when it was created, though no one seems to remember the original name. Ward Hall was not the founder of the show. Hall started in the circus business in 1946, according to World of Wonder's online history. He left home, at age 14, and became a prop hand, and eventually a performer. In the late 1940s, he joined a sideshow that had recently been formed, and he soon he bought it with first partner Harry Leonard, eventually partnering with Chris Christ in Gibsonton, Florida, and eventually renaming it World of Wonders. Tommy recited a distinguished list of naturals who had performed in the sideshow over the years, including Poobah; Short E. Dangerously; John Husted (billed as John T. Rex); Lil Miss Firefly; Jackie the Human

Tripod; Schlitzie the Pinhead (who appeared in *Freaks* way back in 1932); Emmitt and Percilla Bejano (billed as the Alligator Skinned Boy and the Monkey Girl); Stan Berent aka Sealo the Seal Boy; Bill Durks, the Two-Faced Man (who had a third eye painted in the cleft that divided his face down the middle); Bruce Snowdon, billed as a fat man named Harold Huge (607 pounds); another fat man named Tweedle Die (600-plus); Bill Cole, the Quarter Man (an ex-hobo whose legs were chopped off by a train); Emmett Blackwelder, the Turtle Man (a juggler and a mechanic missing all four limbs beneath his elbows and knees); Jennifer Miller aka Woman with a Beard; Dickie Brisbane, the Penguin Boy; Jeffrey Marshall, the Armless Guitarist (he shreds with his feet); an escape artist with dwarfism named the Mighty Huan; a giant named Eddie Carmel (the 9-foot tall "Jewish Giant" photographed by Diane Arbus); Popeye Perry, who could bulge out his eyes like eggs; Dolly Reagan aka the Doll Lady or the Bird Lady (3 feet tall, once married to a "human skeleton"); Judy Jenson, the World's Smallest Mother; a dwarf named Amazing Amy; and a giant named George Bell (7 feet, 8 inches). He said that the famous Grady Stiles III also worked there but only for one night.

Also, World of Wonders once featured a troupe of little people led by Harry Glenn Newman Sr., who moonlighted as a welder and went by the monikers "Midget Man" and "The World's Smallest Man." He was also connected to the extended Stiles family. He was the third husband of Mary Teresa Stiles and had a son with her named Harry Glenn Newman III, who was a human blockhead. Mary Teresa had married Grady Stiles both before and after her marriage to Newman Sr. Their son, Harry Glenn Newman III, was eventually convicted of hiring someone to murder Grady, to stop him from abusing his mother.

Breen, as the Great Gozleone, is a cherubic punk bassist. In a subculture of tattoos and piercings, Tommy looks disarmingly square, with his hokey 1950s Western garb and his co-star Luella Lynne in Western dress and cowboy boots. Luella danced with a lasso and they trotted out a 200-pound pig named Rosie.

When he joined World of Wonders in the early 2000s, he wanted to emulate the rough style of the new sideshow guys. But Ward and Chris told him no, to keep it old school. As the front talker, it was a deliberately square look. This is partly how Tommy, at age 42, ended up running the show after touring with them for 20 years.

"Well, this is what I've been dreaming about since I was 13 years old," said Tommy. I realized that Tommy Breen is the last living link to Ward Hall, at the helm of the last traveling tented sideshow in America. He is the cultural continuation of a relic from the past. After all this time and all that has happened, he is keeping it alive.

"I try to be true to this place," he said. "This place is like me; I've been here so long."

These days, most people have never seen a sideshow and might not even know what it is. World of Wonders is not an anachronism that arrived in the 21st century like Dr. Who's TARDIS police box. It is a thing of the past that still remains. And now, it is very much of the present. But if most people have never seen a sideshow, then it might as well be a whole new thing.

"I'm preserving it, but it's so far gone now, it's like it's new," said Tommy, perfectly at home in his barn-sized tent with its grassy floor and its outlandish marque of midway banners. "I think this is important, that this is around."

Chapter 21

Alan Silva

"Alan, I thought that was the performance of a giant."
- Sofía Vergara, judge on *America's Got Talent*

The aerialist little person, Alan Silva, is striking in appearance, an aquiline-looking acrobat with shimmering blond hair. He begins his show by stripping off his shirt to reveal his chiseled physique as if carved in marble. He has perfected every muscle of his body in function and appearance. He performs for his circus audience on aerial silks, which are beautiful fabric strands that hang from the rafters like thin curtains. Alan can climb them like ropes, hand over hand, rippling with muscle, entwining himself with his hands and feet. The silks are raised and lowered from the rafters by invisible technicians, spinning Alan around the center ring of the Big Apple Circus. Alan wraps himself in the silks and then, when no one quite expects it, drops himself suddenly, rapidly untwining from the silks and free-falling like a stone, accelerating until he abruptly catches the sheets with his legs, arresting his descent just inches from the hard floor.

"I'm free falling, from whatever height it is," said Alan, a native speaker of Portuguese who converses in English fluently. When he does the drop, his speed doubles, and triples as he plunges towards the stage. When he breaks himself suddenly, his body absorbs the high impact. The timing must be perfect because the risk is real.

"It's a very dangerous act because I finish very close to the ground," said Alan, in a phone interview. "I once fell during this act and I broke my neck and was almost paralyzed from the neck down." His sister wasn't so lucky. He comes from a circus family, and he said that his sister once fell during this same act, in 2016. She was in a coma after that though she eventually woke up. After three brain surgeries, she still uses a wheelchair to get around. This didn't stop Alan from dropping. "Yes, I'm still doing it," he said. "Crazy."

I saw Alan perform in the Big Apple Circus in the winter of 2022-2023, at Lincoln Center in Manhattan, which is a traditional wintering spot for the show. I saw the show many years after I had worked at the Big Apple Circus as a traveling vendor in 1989. Much had changed and much had remained the same. But Alan was no peddler of toys and cotton candy; he was a natural born circus ringmaster in a black top hat, jaunty red jacket, and black riding boots. He was also an aerialist, a pioneer on aerial silks, a sixth-generation circus performer and an American citizen originally from Brazil, born with dwarfism in 1982.

Alan told me that he worked for the Big Apple Circus for two seasons. At the beginning of his performance at Lincoln Center, Alan screened a video for the audience where he talked about being bullied as a youth. During his childhood in Brazil, other children laughed at him and threw stones. They told him that he would be a clown because for a man of his size, that was all he could ever do. The video also showcased his beautiful wife and two kids, a boy and a girl. The message was that he's a winner who has succeeded as an artist, a professional and a family man. He's bigger than the bullies who put him down.

I asked about how he emphasizes his ripped physique in his show. "I get a lot of reactions, yeah, especially when I'm performing. I make a point of it when I perform, I remove my shirt." He said he worked for Cirque du Soleil for 18 years in Las Vegas, starting when he was 19. This included a mature show for adult audience members, a sensual cabaret called Zumanity. "It's supposed to be like a human zoo," said Alan. "Beauty and sexuality in so many different shapes and forms."

Alan stands three feet, 10 inches tall. "I don't have a disability but I look different because I'm small," he explained. His Instagram account is loaded with selfies, sometimes on the beach wearing only sunglasses and briefs, his skin bronzed in the sun. He also holds a Guinness World Record for doing the most 360-degree spins while hanging upside down on one foot on aerial straps. (He achieved 164 spins in one minute on the Italian TV show *Lo Show Dei Record* in January 2023.)

While his social media presence is eye-catching, his Cirque du Soleil career prestigious, and his world record stunning, there's nothing quite like the magic of mainstream TV to jumpstart the careers of performers, as it did for Mat Fraser when he co-starred in the

American Horror Story: Freak Show. For Alan, the path to fame was through *America's Got Talent*.

Alan performed for the judges of *America's Got Talent* in 2020, when COVID was ravaging the land. I asked Alan if his *AGT* appearance helped ramp up his career. "TV definitely does," he said, "because you have an exposure that you didn't have before. Not everyone is going to watch a Cirque du Soleil show in Vegas."

In his appearance on *America's Got Talent*, he made an impression by stripping off his shirt and revealing his torso. He told the judges about the bullying that he endured as a boy, where his tormentors said he was doomed to be a clown. His wife and children joined him on stage and then he launched into the air on his aerial silks and performed his flying dance that culminated in his dangerous drop that ended just inches from the stage. The judges loved it, including TV star Sofía Vergara. After he landed, Sofía said, "Alan, I thought that was the performance of a giant."

I told him that his Big Apple performance and his video about being bullied as a kid had resonated with me for years. But he holds no ill will towards the bullies of his childhood. He doesn't blame them. He said that educating kids not to bully comes from the parents. "The kids that did throw rocks at me, it's not their fault," he explained. "To me, it's the parents' fault because the parents were not educating them based on respect." He said parents need to teach their kids to not disrespect people just because they're different.

His childhood experiences profoundly affected his attitude towards having kids of his own. "I did not want to have kids early in my life," he said. He was afraid that if they were natural born, like him, they might get bullied. "I didn't want children to go through what I went through. I didn't want to put them through that. I didn't want them to potentially blame me for being born different." But he was even more concerned that they might grow up to become bullies themselves, who would torment others who were born different. "I didn't want to be a horrible father and raise children who were horrible."

But Alan changed his mind when he met his wife. They had a son and a daughter who did not inherit his diminutive height. "My kids are going to be super tall," he said, laughing.

Alan said he was hired by Cirque du Soleil because of his appearance, essentially. They were hiring people who were "all types of shapes" and Alan matched the profile. "What attracted them to me was my looks," he said. "You have to look good, somewhat pretty, handsome, with a fit body."

By the time he joined Cirque du Soleil at age 19, Alan had been an acrobat most of his life. "I was always fit growing up," he said. "Basically, it just came with the job." He figured out quickly that if you're going to be on stage, you need to look good. "I make the effort to work out," he said.

Being from Brazil, he learned the styles of martial arts that are popular there, including jujitsu, one of the foundation disciplines of mixed martial arts, and also capoeira, a fighting style invented by slaves who disguised it from their overlords by making it look like dancing.

Being an aerialist is a relatively new form for sideshow, but not for the circus, according to Alan. He said it's part of circus history. "My grandma was an aerialist, my sister was an aerialist," he said. "When it comes to circus, it's not new, it's been around for hundreds and hundreds of years."

Aerial silks were introduced to Cirque du Soleil in the 1990s by French artist Gérard Fasoli and his student Isabelle Vaudelle. "I was inspired by this performance and I started to learn it myself," said Alan. "In 1998 nobody was doing it; I had to figure out a lot of these things myself. I was the third performer in Cirque du Soleil who did aerial silks, then it became popular. As of today, you can see people practicing aerial silks."

It requires a considerable amount of strength and endurance, from hands to feet, to achieve monkey-like manipulation of the climbing silks. "It does require a lot of physical strength and some people might not know it until you try it," he said. "They cannot even climb it right with their feet. You not only need to be strong, but you need to have flexibility. Also, I feel that it's important to be aware of your body. If you are in the air, you want to look pretty and effortless."

He said that it's good to have a dancing background, with strength and flexibility and be able to move and coordinate your body in the air gracefully. "Nobody wants to see a potato bag hanging in the air," he laughed.

I asked Alan about the role of aerial silks in sideshows. I told him that Alaska the Lost Boy was performing with silks and chains at the Coney Island Circus Sideshow. "It's new to sideshow, yes, because more and more people are gravitating towards it," he said.

Alan said that in the circus, its popularity evolved in phases, first as aerial silks, then as pole dancing and most recently as the combination known as "aerial pole." He said that performers also do hair suspension in the circus, where the aerialists dance while suspended by their hair. "People think that's a new thing but actually it's not," he said. "My aunt used to do that in the circus; my cousin used to do that."

I asked him about suspension, one of the edgier sideshow acts where performers put meat hooks through their skin and hang from chains. "It is freaky," said Alan. "I never have seen that in the circus."

The modern circus might seem like an extreme environment to outsiders, but it's quite normal to Alan. "I'm in the circus because I was born into it," he said. "I come from a long line of circus performers. Six generations. For me, it's just normal, it's just what we do. It's just family business."

In this way, Alan is different from natural born artists who seek out sideshows and circuses later in life because when Alan was natural born, he was already in the circus. "It's all we do, we don't know other things, this is our life. It's not a side gig that we do; it's who we are."

He believes that his short stature contributed to his appointment as ringmaster in the Big Apple Circus, based on inclusivity rather than exhibition. "It's making people more inclusive, not pointing to that person as a freak," he said. "I 100% agree with that."

But being natural isn't everything. You have to have skills. "I do look different, but I'm also at the top of the top in what I do," said Alan as he prepared to compete in the International Circus Festival of Monte-Carlo, scheduled for January 2025. "So, I'm not using my height or my looks as an advantage to achieve those things. I'm achieving those things because of the quality of my performance. But now, my look and my height go along with it."

At the time of the interview, Alan was performing a seasonal show at Broadway at the Beach, a complex of amusement parks and restaurants in Myrtle Beach, South Carolina, and he planned to return later that year for a Christmas show.

He said the circus hustle has become more difficult since the pandemic and he feels lucky to have established his career before the arrival of COVID. "I've been very fortunate along the way. I've had to turn down gigs. People have to book me a year in advance." He said, in 2024, that he was booked from the Christmas show through 2026. "It's kind of crazy because I don't even know if I'm going to be alive," he joked.

Alan started performing when he was six years old. "I did everything you could imagine in the circus," he said, including acrobatics, tumbling and even clowning. "I was actually very good at being a clown," he said, but he wanted to prove that he was bigger than that.

Little people attract a lot of unwanted attention and mockery, at least as much as other naturals. I told Alan about the other little people I had spoken to and their differing philosophies, including sideshow performer Xander Lovecraft, who wants to be the center of attention but wants the audience to focus on his shocking skills as a human blockhead rather than his size, and also Eileen Norman, president of Little People of America, who wants naturals to be considered equal to all others and not gawked at because of their size or other differences.

Alan noted that it's easy to understand the philosophy of a fellow performer like Xander, while acknowledging that Eileen is not a performer, which is partly why she doesn't want people to stare at her. But having said that, he agrees with both of them.

He said that he understands Xander because he wants to be looked at not just because he's small, but because of his skills. He said he agrees with Eileen too, because she just wants to be treated as normal, which is how he feels when he's not performing.

"If you're going to look at me, I want you to look at me because of my skills," said Alan. "But at the same time, when I'm living my life, I don't want them to stare at me. People do take pictures without consent. Growing up this way we have a sixth sense. It's almost like I have eyes in the back of my head. We know that people are coming and taking pictures, and they think they are discreet. But we can tell, we know you are taking pictures without consent, and that's not ok." He said that he expects people to look at him while he's performing, and his size is part of that, but he does not want people staring at him when's he out and about, living his life, and he does not like being laughed at. "Do I have a watermelon hanging from my neck or what?" he asked, metaphorically. He said that strangers sometimes ask to photograph him. "People wanted to take my picture just because of my size," he said. "It's not ok to do that."

Celebrities attract a lot of attention, and the interactions of natural born celebrities with the public can be complicated. One time, strangers who noticed him in public asked to take his picture, and he sensed it was because of his size so he said no, but then they said, "We saw you on *America's Got Talent*," and then he felt bad that he denied them.

Ultimately, Alan wants to be seen as an artist where he can control his narrative as a natural born and show people what he can do. "For me, performing is not just performing, it's really to send out a message to people," he said.

Chapter 22

Xander Lovecraft

"I'm going to give you a real reason to look at me other than my height. I want you to look at me because I'm hammering a nail into my nasal cavity, and you think I should be dead."

- Xander Lovecraft

On a hot afternoon in July 2023, Xander Lovecraft stood on stage and faced a scattering of spectators in the bleachers at the Coney Island Sideshow. Red curtains served as his backdrop. He was hairy, and his dark beard was angry-looking and wild, though it was hard to tell what he was really feeling under there. Xander was dressed in sideshow chic: pants with red and black stripes, and a black T-shirt that announced CULT LEADER in white block letters. He tied his long hair back in a hippy bandanna. He brandished a cane with a crooked handle.

Xander, who was born with dwarfism, had returned to the sideshow, following a pandemic hiatus. He moved to New York to perform. This meant that Coney Island USA finally had a natural born performer back on its cast.

"This is an act called the human blockhead," he announced, brandishing a shiny nail and banging it on the microphone stand for acoustic effect. "This is a solid steel nail. I'm going to be using this cane as a surrogate hammer and I'm going to ram this nail into my skull." He claimed that his real hammer had been confiscated by the Transportation Security Administration on the flight from St. Louis. (This was a little lie, he later confessed, but it was part of the act.)

The theater room for Sideshows by the Seashore was dark and cool, a place to hide from the sun and the crowds. This was just a couple of days before Independence Day, peak season for Coney Island businesses. The sideshow was located in the antique Childs building, one block inland from the boardwalk. Within the dark confines of the sideshow, it was hard to imagine that W. 12th St., a path to the beach, was just a few feet away, out one door and through the exit. A world of blazing sunshine, bikinis and beer.

Xander hammered (or rather, *caned*) the nail up his nose.

No one in the audience reacted. Sitting way up in the back of the bleachers, I made some noise to get the party going. "Someone said 'gnarly,'" observed Xander, sage-like, with the nail sticking out of his nose. "But like my godfather, Hunter S. Thompson once said, 'You bought the ticket, go for the ride.'" He kept hammering the nail and cracking jokes: "Yes, I'm an art student; how can you tell?"

He finished hammering. The nail was buried in his head. He pinched the nail between his thumb and index finger. "I'm going to remove this nail right here and right now," he said, and pulled it out and licked the snot, in a tried-and-true gross-out gag. By this point, his original audience of 11 had grown to three dozen.

Xander had meant to work at Coney Island in the summer of 2022, but was living in St. Louis with his mother and stepfather and got sidelined by dental surgery. "I was having a fucked-up pain in my tooth. My bottom two wisdom teeth were coming in sideways." By the summer of 2023, he was ready to return. Xander had been working at the Coney Island Circus Sideshow for 10 years up to that point, so it was like coming home.

Xander temporarily left the stage, which was taken over by a clown (Clawdette Smm Smm) and a mermaid (Obsidian Absurd). After a brief break, he returned. Coney Island was a 10-in-1 grind show, so he was always exiting the stage and coming back. Now he was warming up the audience for his next act. With a nod towards the nearby ocean, he joked about how he could have taken a submarine to work today, but didn't, a reference to the recent implosion of a privately owned Titan submersible in the North Atlantic, which killed five people. The tourists on board paid $250,000 apiece to view the Titanic, but instead, they joined its watery grave. Was it too soon for such a morbid joke? "It's OK, they're billionaires, they don't matter," he quipped. But if anybody was offended, they didn't show it.

His next act was called "mousetrap tongue." He hyped it up for the audience. "This is a mousetrap," he said, holding out the palm-sized wooden rectangle so they could see it. "We don't have a vermin problem in the building. I can't say that about the rest of New

York. I was mugged by a rat on the Q train the other day. I'm going to put a mousetrap on the most sensitive part of my body."

"No, not *that* part," he added, directing the comment to an unseen member in the dark audience. "No sir. That's not what we do here." He explained that he only mousetrapped his private parts for adult shows. "That's late at night and it costs money and I signed a NDA (non-disclosure agreement)."

He stuck out his tongue, which seemed disembodied against the backdrop of his shaggy beard, and placed it on the mousetrap, either lewdly or lasciviously, depending on how you looked at it. He set the mousetrap and placed his tongue over the trip pedal and had the audience count to three. Then he triggered the trap and let the hammer fall onto his little pink tongue. He flapped his arms frantically and ran around like a chicken with its head cut off. I couldn't help but laugh.

Mousetrap tongue is another sideshow trope.

When I first arrived before the show, I had rounded the corner at W. 12th St. and walked into the crowd that gathered at the entrance of the Coney Island Circus Sideshow, with its long row of gaudy billboards lining the upper walls of the old Childs building, advertising bizarre acts and human oddities. About a dozen adults and kids gathered to witness something special: possibly the only bally platform in America at that time to feature a genuine natural born. Xander stood on the bally, leaning on his cane, dressed in garish red and black while sporting wild hair and a beard and wearing wraparound sunglasses like goggles. He shared the stage with a motley crew of eccentrics: Obsidian Absurd, Clawdette Smm Smm, Niki B. the Talking Doll and Alaska the Lost Boy. Venture inside, if you dare, and watch Obsidian Absurd the mermaid climb barefoot up a ladder made of swords, watch Clawdette the Pretty Brown Clown thread a flexible rubber tube into her mouth and out through her nose then floss her nasal cavity with it and drop the free end of the tube into a glass of red Boylan's soda and drink it Jim Rose style, watch The Talking Doll put Obsidian in the blade box and slide swords through the slots while joking about "mermaid meat," watch Alaska the aerialist unfurl a mane of blue hair while dancing and twirling on a shiny loop of logging chain.

The grueling schedule of a classic 10-in-1 show requires a cycle of live acts to be played throughout the day. Coney was exhausting, but it was also Xander's dream to be doing exactly that, performing an endless parade of vaudevillian carnie acts before a paying audience at the most famous sideshow venue in the world. COVID had sidelined his sideshow career for years. But now, he had finally moved out of his mother's house in St. Louis and was back in New York, performing before live audiences. He had entertained virtually throughout the pandemic, but now the audience was in the room with him, breathing the same air in the dark theater, an artistic oasis from the blazing sun.

I watched the show from beginning to end and was working my way through a second run, when Obsidian walked onstage to announce that it was raining. She delivered the information like a news broadcast. There were no windows and no way to see the sun or rain. Sideshow people are obsessed with the weather, like sailors, hikers and tennis players. They will cancel shows over precipitation, even though it's an inside venue. Rain dampens the foot traffic.

She said they would end the show early and skip a couple of acts in this final run. But not mousetrap tongue. Xander would be doing mousetrap tongue one more time.

After the show, I ventured out to the Freak Bar with its picture windows, resplendent with sunshine after an hour cloistered in the dark sideshow watching chain dances and soda snorting. Big puddles had formed outside from the rain. Sunbeams poured through the windows, illuminating the Freak Bar's retro collection of old-timey sideshow stuff and beach bric-a-brac. The head of a great white shark sprouted from an archway in the ceiling with a sign that said, "We're going to need a bigger boat."

The Freak Bar is where I had interviewed Adam Rinn in the spring of 2022, when he told me that he recruited Xander to work at Coney but he couldn't do it because of health problems.

Xander Lovecraft has made a name for himself in sideshow, but not necessarily through his dwarfism. "He's not a little person who's going to go out and perform as a little person," explained Rinn. "He's a human blockhead."

Rinn said that he has, in the past, worked with little people who wore humiliating costumes that poked fun at their dwarfism. "I've done gigs with little people dressed in the Oompa Loompa suit," said Rinn, who is himself a human blockhead. "Why do you put yourself in the position where you're comfortable putting on the Oompa Loompa suit?" He said he once did another gig where he was dressed like a Viking, and he wheeled a small refrigerator onto the stage and out popped a little person dressed like a little Viking. It was another example of a little person taking part in an act that presented his size as a joke. Rinn said that Xander would never do that. Xander's happy to perform, said Rinn, but he's "not going to be your little puppet. That's just not his thing."

After the rain ended his show, Xander joined me for a drink at the Freak Bar, located in an open room next to the gift shop. Xander sat next to an enormous red tabby that occupied a cushioned bench near the bar. (I later learned that this cat is named Johnathan Vesuvius VonVladimir Cat Wyckenstein and has 2,094 followers on Instagram under the moniker Sideshow Cat.) I wondered how Xander's tongue felt. I wondered if the cream soda he was drinking was soothing. I asked him what it was like to catch his tongue in a mousetrap. "Any act can hurt if you don't do it right, especially mousetrap," he said. "That's designed to break the bones of mice. It's designed to kill them. You put your tongue in that situation, there's a lot of risk involved."

I reminded him about our interview from the year before, when he described how the human blockhead act can go wrong. "I've had it where I've hit the nail too hard and hit the wall, maybe the cartilage," said Xander. He described the sensation of impaling his head on a spike as "your brain shutting off, like a computer." This was from a guy who probes his nose with an ice pick.

Xander's gig with Coney was for the duration of the summer and he managed to find a place to stay with someone who lived a mile and a half away. I had been looking forward to seeing Xander swallow balloons like he did in the YouTube videos. Xander can inflate a thin balloon at least a foot long and swallow it, one inch at a time, an act that seems simple but simultaneously impossible. But he didn't do it when I was there. "I'm actually running low on balloons at the moment," he said. He refused to divulge the secrets of this arcane art. "You just kind of make it work," he said. "It is a feat of gastro-intestinal magnitude."

I told him how Lil Miss Firefly told me all about balloon swallowing, about how to sexualize the swallowing for strip shows, to make it rain, inspiring patrons to shower the performer with cash. "I've done it as a strip act," he said. "Late night." Xander sometimes alluded to this murky double life, where he would perform acts in the wee hours that were only fit for a higher-paying adult audience with avant-garde tastes. And then, presumably, he would make it rain.

I asked if naturals are being exploited by appearing in sideshows. It was a common question. "We've had this a lot," he said. "Just a couple days ago. A Facebook post, thinking people like myself don't have any choice in the matter, which is bullshit." Xander had been doing sideshow for 12 years, most of it at Coney. "I am fully in control of what I do on stage," he said. In other words, no one was forcing him to do mousetrap tongue. "People have their own beliefs," he said. "I've been performing on this stage of my own volition for 10 years now. They think that disabled people can't make decisions of their own. They're treating us like we don't know any better. If I'm going to get exploited, I'm going to exploit myself and I'm doing it for as much money as I can."

Sideshow naturals are a big draw but bring more to the stage with their plethora of dangerous and amusing acts. Xander said that he doesn't get punished if he refuses to do certain acts. "They're not going to withhold food from me or cut my pay or put me in a box," he said. "I do sideshow because I love it."

Xander had been in the sideshow business long enough to work with lots of different performers and to see the ebb and flow of different styles. Aerial acts were popular in sideshows and circuses that year. He mentioned another trend, involving Medieval-style self-torture with hooks and chains.

"I do think that sideshow has evolved," he said. "The body suspension world, a lot of people consider that modern sideshow now. Suspension has a place in sideshow. It's different from what you would see in the old days."

He was talking about piercing the body with hooks and hanging from chains in the ceiling. The hooks pierce the flesh of your thighs as you twist languidly beneath the chains, leaning backward. Two of the naturals I'd interviewed – Kim Kelly and Nati Amos – did suspension, but they did it for relaxation rather than stage work.

Xander started performing in late 2009, doing grindhouse punk shows in St. Louis. The performances were cutting-edge and cartoonishly absurd. For example, he did an Easter show where he was crucifying an actor dressed as the Easter Bunny, hammering nails into its costumed paws and spurting fake blood. The sideshow and burlesque people took notice. In 2010, he was invited to co-host a burlesque act, and he continued to get gigs after that, developing a set of cringe-worthy skills that are the bread and butter of sideshow performing.

He used to tour with burlesque performer Bella La Blanc. In 2016 in Virginia, they wowed audiences with an energetic but minimalist act involving Legos. These performances would begin with Bella and a bucket, which she poured onto the stage as if it were going to bring forth broken glass, but, instead, she dumped out a pile of Legos. The crowd seemed to get the joke immediately, that they were going to walk on the little plastic bricks instead of broken glass. Xander appeared, his hair shaved into a mohawk, wearing no shoes. He would step slowly and carefully across the Legos, and then Bella strode boldly barefoot across them, followed by a series of escalating acts in which they would try to push each other's threshold for pain. Bella did a split on the tiny spiky toys while rolling around and cavorting on them in her skimpy clothes, while Xander did pushups on the pile with his bare hands and then stripped off his shirt to reveal his chest tattoo and Buddha belly. Then he belly-flopped onto the Legos, impacting with a loud, fleshy, plastic slap. At this point, Bella also stripped off her top, popping out her breasts with tasseled pasties on her nipples. Bella then stood on Xander's back, grinding his gut into the Lego pile, as she shook her breasts for the cheering crowd. She did not stay on him long, and Xander survived the experience. He pulled himself up from the pile and picked loose Legos that had lodged in the soft flesh of his stomach. He handed them out as souvenirs to appreciative audience members.

When I first reached him by phone in June 2022, I congratulated him on finding a new way to do the classic walk on broken glass act. First Shorty, now Xander. They had each put a unique twist on it. But Xander assured me that Legos were no joke. "Legos, it definitely hurts more than glass," said Xander. "The way with glass is that if you have enough glass, it can lay flat, and you don't have many edges pointing up when you're jumping." He added, "But it still hurts, walking on broken glass." What makes his act funny, and perhaps more relatable than a broken glass act, is that everyone has stepped on Legos, and we all know what it feels like. "It takes a lot of pressure to break a Lego, so there is minimal give when you land on them," he said. "I've caused more cuts and bleeding spots on my body [with Legos] than I've done with glass at this point."

Xander explained that Bella had recruited him for a touring burlesque show and they were regular partners for three years. He said that he felt like a part of her family, dwelling in the basement of her house.

Bella and Xander are stage names. When pressed to identify his birth name, Xander finally said, "Bruce Wayne" and laughed.

At Coney in 2023, he was sporting a goatee, but hair was sprouting on his jowls, turning his chin growth into a proper beard. He told me that during the winter he let his beard grow down to the middle of his chest. "I cycle through my physical looks," he said.

We were sitting in the Freak Bar, where Rinn had told me, the year before, that Xander does not perform as a dwarf or a natural. I asked Xander to explain. "The way I deal with my performances, I don't really drum up the fact that I am a little person because, honestly, if you see me, you know that I am different," he said. "I don't need to play that up. Playing that up seems unnecessary. I don't think of myself as a dwarf performer. I think of myself as a performer who happens to be a dwarf."

Xander said that his performing streak goes back to when he was a kid. "I was the youngest of three in the family," he said. "I was always trying to be the center of attention."

He didn't have to try. It would come naturally to him. "When you have dwarfism, whether you want to be the center of attention or not, people are going to notice," he said.

But getting noticed isn't always good. Sadists and rubes inflict a special type of derision on little people, stopping them in the street, grabbing them and taking pictures, treating them as a joke, made for their amusement.

"When I was younger, the only reaction I would get from strangers was laughter," said Xander. "I was like, 'If you're really going to look at me, I'm going to give you a real reason to look at me other than my height. I want you to look at me because I'm jumping barefoot on Legos. I want you to look at me because I'm swallowing a six-foot balloon and you don't know how I'm doing it. I want you to look at me because I'm hammering a nail into my nasal cavity and you think I should be dead.'"

I told him that I had recently interviewed Crystal Lockhart, who self-identified as a "midget," even though many people consider the term offensive and old-fashioned. I asked him what he thought about the m-word. He said that he hated it. People have been yelling that slur at him since he was a kid. He said that his father also has dwarfism, and he doesn't like it either. "Having the term said to me makes my skin crawl and also makes me want to Hulk out," he said.

He noted that some people, like Lil Miss Firefly, might want to take back the m-word. "For me, personally, it's not something I want to take back," he said.

Xander once did a deeply personal work of performance art that reveals much about his experience growing up with dwarfism. He once appeared on stage with about 50 note cards scrawled with insults aimed at his disability, insults which people have said to him at various times in his life. His assistant stapled the cards to his body, one by one, turning him into a human bulletin board for insults aimed at little people and dwarves. During intermission, audience members stapled money to him as well, with $5 as the lowest denomination, adding up to $60. (He didn't let anybody staple his genitals because "I haven't found a large number for that yet.") He said that he was bedridden the next day, but it was worth it. "It was very cathartic," he said. "It was something I needed to do at that time, and to this day, I am very proud of that act."

Xander is passionate. When I mentioned details from my circus past that he found interesting, he would lightly gasp, as if he found it physically exciting. When I asked him why he does sideshow, he explained that he is trying to get that same sort of reaction from the audience. He is trying to take their breath away. "I do it because I like the shock factor that comes with some of the acts that I perform," he said. "If I can get the lady to clutch her pearls and if I hear a gasp from the crowd, I, for lack of a better term, get off on that."

He said he loved the sideshow lifestyle, and even if there are "multiple dark clouds" over its history, lots of naturals have benefited from it. "That should not disqualify the actual folks that were in it that lived very wonderful, meaningful lives and made lots of money and were known around the world for what they did," he said. I asked him how it felt, returning to the sideshow. "It feels really good," he said.

I asked him about his career aspirations. He said he was a fan of the late Anthony Bourdain. He would love to host a show modeled on *No Reservations*, where he would do a series of sit-down interviews over dinner with performers and artists and "pick their brains over this restaurant or that restaurant." He said that his number one choice for a guest would be burlesque star Miss Cherry Delight, former Miss Coney Island, which is where they met. "We became really great friends," he said. "She is, to this day, one of my very great friends."

With his taste for bizarre and carnivalesque entertainment, Xander did not sound like a man being forced to exploit himself in a freak show. "The only person who is exploiting myself is me," he said. "I choose to be a beacon in sideshow. We choose to be here. We're not being chained up. We're normal people. Well, not normal, but we walk the streets."

It was good to have left behind the family nest in St. Louis, he said, if only for a while. "I love my family dearly, but we don't all share the same views," he said.

The sideshow had ended for the day. Alaska waved while passing through the Freak Bar and headed out into the bustle of Neptune Avenue. Xander said the performers were planning a sleepover at the sideshow the night before July 4 because they wanted to be as close as possible to the original Nathan's hotdog restaurant, just a couple blocks up Neptune, where it had been for more than a century. The performers were going to be part of Nathan's Famous Hot Dog-Eating Contest, the annual extravaganza where Joey Chestnut would defend his title and win for the 16th time by devouring 62 franks in 10 minutes.

Xander said he would love to move to New York permanently someday, as a full-time performer. His dream is to be able to support himself, year after year, through his art. "You have to find a way to make it happen," he said.

When I first talked to Xander by phone in 2022, he was 35 and living far from Coney. "Sadly, St. Louis is not the hotbed for improvisational comedy that other cities are known for," said Xander at that time, spending much of the pandemic streaming *Fallout* and other story-driven games on Twitch, and doing performances by Zoom, which just wasn't the same as live because he couldn't hear the audience react.

Xander talked about his seasonal Coney experiences as the highlights of his life, an opportunity to make a living as a full-time artist, paying rent and taxes. "That time in New York is when I can prove to myself that I can be self-sufficient," he said. "I can be a bill-paying member of the society. I love the city. I love the speed."

Xander's return to Coney in 2023 was long overdue. His ultimate plan was to figure out how to extend these seasonal trips to New York to make them year-round and permanent.

"If I can do this three months out of the year, I can do this the remaining nine," he said. "I just have to figure out how. And when that day comes to me, I will be one of the happiest people in the country."

Chapter 23

John T. Rex

"I finally got a steady job with a good income, but I was bored and depressed. It wasn't what I wanted to do with my life."
- John Husted

"I'm fortunate that I've gotten to do a lot of interesting things in my life."
- John T. Rex

"I am one of the few people in this world who is immune to the lethal effects of electricity."
- Satan John

    In the sexual underworld of New Orleans, John Husted had a flair for drama. He cut his teeth on cracking a long, braided bullwhip, Indiana Jones style with his short arms, to snuff out burning matchbooks placed strategically atop a stripper's nipples, harrowingly close to her sensitive flesh. He called this his "fire act."
    John explained the "little trick" that a stripper taught him, that she would do for customers on their birthdays. "I'd fork a match over a girl's nipple, light it, and put it out by cracking my whip in front of it so the air pressure would blow it out." I asked him what he meant by "fork." He explained how he would set a matchbook over her breasts and

"fork" the individual paper matches in such a way that they would burn like candles on a cake. But they burned brightly and quickly, so he had to crack the whip fast to extinguish the flames before they burned her skin, and without flogging her by accident. As he honed his skills, he would invite volunteers from the audience and perform the whip act on them. But he eventually stopped. After Hurricane Katrina plowed through his hometown, he joined World of Wonders, then run by Ward Hall and Chris Christ, who didn't go for that hoochie coochie stuff. "I haven't done that in years," said John in 2023, referring to the whip fire act, "because I did more family-oriented shows with Ward Hall."

Before he got into sideshow, he performed whip-fire acts with strippers who specialized in BDSM. He was also a leatherworker who crafted some of his own whips. He didn't make the long bullwhips that he used in his shows. The stretching and braiding of the individual leather straps were too difficult for his short arms. He made smaller whips, with lots of titillating tails, to sell to his libertine customers. He also played drums and even served as a human conductor of live electrical currents for the amusement and entertainment of his sideshow audience.

He managed to do all of this with undersized arms. John, who was 61 at the time of this interview, was born with phocomelia. He explained that his upper limbs are missing forearms. He has shoulders, biceps and elbows, and then sprouting from his elbows are his wrists and hands. "My wrists and elbows are really close together, almost like a universal joint," he said.

Fortunately, he has four fingers and a thumb on each hand. This is a critical detail because phocomelia affects different people in different ways. For example, Mat Fraser has short arms with four-fingered hands but no thumbs. It's possible, with phocomelia, to be born with no limbs at all.

When cracking his whip, John found ways to compensate for his short arms, just as Mat found ways to compensate for his short arms in martial arts. John said that he used a snake whip, which is a long, braided whip that is flexible all the way to the ball at the end. It doesn't have a stick handle like a bullwhip. He said that cracking the snake whip is like shooting a shotgun, there's so much recoil and backlash. "I have to be more careful to not hit myself in the face because things are a lot closer to your face," said John. "I practiced a lot with them, hitting targets and what not."

That's how he ended up with the stage name John T. Rex, because Tyrannosaurus Rex had tiny arms. John was given that name by Ward Hall as World of Wonders toured state fairs. Ward put John on the bally platform, where he would play drums and, quite literally, drum up business. Ward said that he needed a new name, that his prior moniker was not fit to be blasted over the loudspeaker in God-fearing parts of America. Because his original stage name was Satan John. "They didn't want to say 'Satan John' on the mike at the fairs," he explained.

Back in the 1990s, John had a decent-paying job and was enjoying the benefits of regular paychecks and financial security as a customer service rep at a call center. But he was miserable on an existential level. "I finally got a steady job with a good income, but I was bored and depressed," he said. "It wasn't what I wanted to do with my life."

So John embarked on a quest to spice things up. He was living in New Orleans, one of the wildest cities in America. "I played drums, and I was doing sideshow, and before sideshow I did strip show," he said. That's when he started making whips and other devices for BDSM (a catchall acronym that includes bondage, discipline, dominance, submission, sadism and masochism) and sold them to kinky clients.

He made and collected vinyl and leather outfits and tools of the S&M trade. It seemed only natural that he should get on stage and exhibit his new skills. "A couple of stripper girls wanted me to join their show, especially after I did leatherwork, because I had cool equipment," he said.

John got into BDSM right as it was becoming popular in New Orleans. He had realized, while browsing a BDSM leather shop on Bourbon Street, that the adult toys were overpriced junk. "I started noticing the stuff they were selling and how crappy the quality and I thought I can make that stuff, I can make better stuff," he said. Then he started making whips, the so-called "floggers," once known as the cat-o'-nine-tails. Except that his floggers had 75 to 200 tails of soft leather rather than rough leather braided with splinters of glass in metal, like in the old days. "It's a massage tail," he said. "It's not anything that's going to hurt anybody." He would make his whips out of good leather, sacrificing half a cowhide for a flogger with a lot of tails. He also made nipple clamps out of Mardi Gras beads. He was doing well and making a name for himself. He made and sold so many whips that he opened a leather business called Satan's Workshop. "It was just a play on Santa's Workshop," he said. He ran the shop out of his house from 1998 to 2001, which was long enough to acquire a reputation. "People knew me as Satan," he said. "But other people knew me as John." One day, two of his friends, who did not know each other, bumped into each other at a bar and started discussing their mutual friend. They knew him by different names. One of them knew him as Satan, and the other knew him as John. It was only after an hour of discussion that they realized they were talking about the same person. Henceforth, they combined the names into one. "The next day, I was Satan John," said John.

He eventually stopped making whips and other toys for the BDSM crowd. "The people who were doing it were crazy and I didn't like giving them something they could hurt somebody with," he said. Via this circuitous path, he discovered sideshow and joined the Know Nothing Family Zirkus Zideshow. "They were just getting started and thought it would be cool to have a genuine biological freak," he said.

Several sideshows followed, and he didn't stay Satan John forever. The name had its limits, as he discovered at World of Wonders. Many Americans take their religion seriously, especially in the hinterland. Ward Hall's new moniker, John T. Rex, was less offensive and more mainstream, in a *Jurassic Park* kind of way.

The sideshow career of Satan John T. Rex began in the late 1990s. His friend Enigma, a veteran of the Jim Rose Circus who is covered with full-body jigsaw puzzle tattoos and has horn implants and other body modifications, suggested that he get into the business. Since then, John has worked with Know Nothing (1998); 999 Eyes Freakshow (2006 to 2008); World of Wonders (2006-2010 and 2021); and also Museum of the Weird (2011-2020), a Wunderkammer operating permanently in Austin in a neighborhood bustling with tourists and college students wandering from bar to bar.

He eventually concluded that the Know Nothings, the obscure group with whom he kicked off his sideshow career, were too edgy to get far or to make ends meet. "The Know

Nothings were gutter punks, pornographic, extreme stage persona; that's no way to be," he said. "It's like any other job: You have to be able comport yourself in a professional manner." But making a living at 999 Eyes was slim pickings. "Money was very sporadic and not that great to begin with," he said. "You had to split it with the band, 13 people."

At 999 Eyes, John started working with Black Scorpion and witnessed the transformation of his stage persona. "The tutu is pretty over the top," he said. "When I first met him, he was performing in a black business suit." He decided to partner with Black Scorpion, and the two of them performed as a duo for a while. He said that he made more money performing just with Black Scorpion.

He considers the height of his career to be working at the Museum of the Weird in Austin. Lots of street traffic and the tips were good. "We did well," he said. "It was a steady gig. It was hard work because it was a grind show. Every time a crowd comes in you do a show." He said that they worked seven-hour shifts, five nights a week, and they were hustling. It wasn't about doing a long show; it was about doing a bunch of short shows for tips.

He said the museum achieved fame when owner Steve Busti bought the Minnesota Iceman, an elaborate cryptozoological hoax that landed him a spot on the TV show *Mysteries at the Museum*. The Iceman and the TV exposure brought a lot of visitors. The Museum of the Weird was still (as of 2025) operating on Sixth Street in Austin, but John said they stopped doing live acts during COVID.

He said that he was fortunate to spend most of his career at the Museum of the Weird, from about 2011 to 2020. He did an electrical act in true P.T. Barnum fashion, a mix of reality and mystery. John claims to be a human conductor of electricity. He demonstrates this conductivity through acts too convincing to be immediately dismissed as humbug or sleight of hand. But there's no practical explanation for it either.

John heard about a man in India who could hold a bare wire and act as a human conductor, activating lightbulbs by touching them with his free hand. John said he had the same ability, which he used in an electrical act at the Museum of the Weird. He said that he would hold a live heavy gauge wire, switch on the power switch and invite a member of the audience to touch him with a light bulb, which would illuminate. Sometimes the contact of John's skin with the lightbulb would cast sparks. "People loved it," said John. "I made good tips on it." He discontinued the whip act to focus on being a human conduit for electricity.

John sent me an undated video of his electrical act, filmed in a church. In the video, he has long wavy hair and a beard. He is wearing a top hat, glasses and hoop earrings, with a ruffled purple sleeveless tuxedo shirt and white and black striped pants. He has a tattoo of the sun on his right arm. He explained his disability to his audience. "That's just the way the good Lord made me," he said. He described the economics of sideshow naturals. "Back in those days being a human oddity was a lot like being a pop star," he said. "Naturally, the pay you make today isn't a pop star salary. But it's definitely a much better way to make a living than doing customer service at a call center." Then he told the church folk why he was sitting next to a wire and fuse box with a lightning bolt painted across it. "I am one of the few people in this world who are immune to the lethal effects of electricity," he said. He grabbed a bare wire and said he was going to run 120 volts through his body and then use it to illuminate a 110-volt lightbulb. Then a boy from the audience walked into the video to serve as his volunteer assistant. John held the insulated part of the wire, just below the bare wire, as the kid flipped the switch. A humming sound pulsated as John brushed the skin of his arm with the wire, sizzling sparks in his forearm hair. John kept the wire moving, to keep the spark moving, to keep it from burning him. And then he grabbed the bare wire with his right hand and the kid passed him a light bulb which John touched with his left hand. The light bulb glowed as soon as it touched his skin and went dark when the kid pulled the bulb away. The kid also put the lightbulb in John's mouth and on his nose and it glowed each time but only when it touched John. The electric humming continued. "Don't put it in my hair or beard please because it sets it on fire," said John, who once smoldered his hair and didn't know it until he smelled the smoke.

After a couple of minutes of holding the humming wire, John ended the act with something more extreme. "I can't hold this long," he said. "It will leave me light-headed, but it does help with my depression and anxiety and so don't feel bad that I'm doing it." And then he put the bare wire on his tongue and the kid put the light bulb on his hand, which lit up while John twitched for a few seconds to the buzz of the wire and then stopped when he pulled it away.

He wasn't just natural born because of phocomelia. He claimed to have a second natural born condition that provided him with an electrical conduit superpower. "I've not found a name for the condition relating to my electrical abilities, as far as I know, it's never been studied," he said later by email. I felt that his electrical demonstration, with his explanation backed by unspecific claims of unproven science, was one of the most authentic Barnum-style deliveries I've ever seen.

The image of John zapping himself on the tongue made me wonder how much physical pain he was feeling. I asked him if he was exploited. "I never really thought of it," he said. "Any kind of job is exploiting yourself. It all comes down to how you're being treated."

He wants to build his own museum, his own cabinet of curiosities, his own Wunderkammer. Like his former employer, the owner of the Museum of the Weird. Like his former roommate Jackie the Human Tripod, who toured the West with her husband, exhibiting their mobile Strange Remains museum.

John said he started his own museum collection with a couple of elongated skulls of indigenous South Americans who practiced body modification by binding the heads of infants to flatten them out. He said his fledgling collection includes a "Peruvian skull that looks like an alien it's so thoroughly elongated." But he has a long way to go before he can build a proper cabinet of curios. "I don't have anything really good," he said. He was interested in cryptids, a phrase for legendary American monsters like Big Foot and the Jersey Devil. He didn't say whether he believes in Big Foot and I didn't ask. Maybe he wanted something like the Minnesota Iceman. Barnum made his fortune on many so-called humbugs, which were hoaxes presented in a tongue-in-cheek way, like a challenge. The humbugs were friendly stabs at entertainment, rather than fraudulent rip-offs. One of the most famous of Barnum's humbugs was the Feejee (sic) Mermaid, an overhyped and oversexed exhibit that was nothing more than the top half of a taxidermy monkey sewn to the tail of a fish. Barnum marketed this monstrosity as a voluptuous human female mermaid. He described it in his book as if the audience was in on the joke, a benign gag.

"I had a Feejee Mermaid, but I sold it," said John. "I made mine." He said that the original Feejee mermaids were made by fishermen in the Philippines as good luck charms. He said that people don't make them out of real monkeys anymore, because monkeys are "too regulated" and cost thousands of dollars. Since real monkeys are hard to come, he made his out of a baby doll and a Big Mouth Billy Bass, an animatronic fish wall mount that sings. He sent me a Facebook image of the bizarre figure, with a hideous face that combined the features of a baby and a fish, with the arms of a baby and the body of a fish, attached to a backboard with a button so it can play a song. It must have taken some skill to meld the body of a doll with a tiny robot fish in a way that the parts all moved in synchronization.

In the summer of 2023, John was not performing because of health problems, using a cane and living on disability payments in Indianapolis. He was at the age when people realize that retirement is inevitable, regardless of whether they're prepared for it. He was about the same age as Mat Fraser and other thalidomide babies, whose mothers had taken the dangerous drug without knowing what it would do to their future children. Naturals who were disabled by thalidomide can receive corporate compensation of up to about $100,000 annually, for those with the most serious disabilities. But only if they can prove it. A windfall like that isn't accessible for naturals who were born with phocomelia but who don't have the paperwork from long-lost prescriptions proving a link to the poison pill.

But was John really affected by thalidomide? He's old enough, but he's American. The height of its popularity was in Europe in the early 1960s, before its horrific effects would become widely known. Thalidomide was not legally available in the U.S. at the time that John was in the womb. There are a few thalidomiders in the U.S., but the drug wasn't approved by the Food and Drug Administration, so their parents had either brought it into the U.S. from another country or used it in another country while pregnant and then traveled to the U.S. So given the timing of his birth and his natural born phocomelia, John sometimes wonders if his mother had taken thalidomide. But now there's no way to know. The records, if there were any, are long gone.

Sideshow is fun, but it's not secure. "Getting random sideshow gigs doesn't pay enough and I don't like continuously hustling for work," said John, who's thinking of a career shift. Or rather, a career circle, back to where he started, as a tech worker. He used to build computers in the 1980s and then he became a recording engineer and maintained websites. But that was a long time ago. He figured he could return to the tech world, but much has changed in the last few decades. He would have to upgrade himself to catch up with the 21st century. He said that his nephew is a certified network administrator, and he was thinking of getting certified, too, and getting a job in cybersecurity, a field that is becoming more important as hacking and extortion become more prevalent and sophisticated.

He isn't necessarily giving up on sideshow life, with his plan to start his own oddities museum. With a decent-paying job in cybersecurity, he wouldn't have to rely on his art financially. He remembers the customer service jobs he used to do for Sears and Nestlé.

Steady jobs. But not what he wanted to do with his life. He looked back on all the things he'd done since then: the sideshows, the strip shows, the whip shows, the BDSM, the leatherwork, Satan's Workshop, the Museum of the Weird, the electrical act, the traveling.

"I'm fortunate that I've gotten to do a lot of interesting things in my life," he said.

Chapter 24

Dakota the Bearded Lady

"If there is a reason that I'm a bearded lady and also queer, so be it. I think that queer people are more willing to accept their difference and be proud of it."

- Dakota

Bearded ladies may seem like an act from yesteryear, but Dakota is a modern-day bearded lady sideshow natural. Most girls can't grow beards, and most of those who can grow beards, don't. Dakota's beard started appearing at puberty, and at the behest of her parents, she did everything to erase it during her teen years. But then she started growing it out. "I feel really pretty," she said in a TV appearance in 2021, after eight years of letting her beard grow. "I feel sexy."

She has performed in sideshows for years. She engages in popular but cringe-worthy acts like mousetrap tongue, walking on broken glass, and the human cutting board. She was also learning to crack a whip for a Western-style act but had yet to test that in front of a live audience.

But why, of all the things she could be doing, would she exhibit herself in a sideshow? "To really explain why I do sideshow, I'd have to really explain my story," she told me. Dakota chooses not to hide her beard or shave it but rather to flaunt it. But it wasn't always that way.

Dakota is Native American, of the Ute and Kiowa tribes from Utah and Oklahoma, but she grew up in Ventura County in Southern California, right next to Los Angeles. Her beard started growing at age 13. "It started out as blonde peach fuzz, and got darker and longer," she said. That's when her parents started making her shave and taking her to salons for regular waxings. Throughout her teenage years, Dakota was subjected to various hair removal techniques. "I spent 10 years trying to hide, wax it, thread it," she said. "Oh, that was the worst, threading." Threading involves taking a piece of thread, twisting it up and then cutting off the hair right at the follicle. "It's very painful," she said. Waxing is perhaps a more widespread method for ripping hair out by the roots. Despite its barbarity, Dakota said that it pales compared to threading. "Wax actually wasn't so bad for me," said Dakota. "I actually got used to it. I went to a salon in Hollywood that would smear wax on my face and rip off big chunks at a time." She said that one time when she was getting her face waxed in the salon, a young girl was watching, and the process was so intense that the girl started freaking out and Dakota tried to calm her down. "I was like, 'It's ok, it's ok,'" she said.

Not long after that, Dakota decided to grow her beard. "It just makes me feel like a better person," she said, though it wasn't easy, growing a beard and identifying as queer. Her evolution, from a girl who underwent regular waxings to a woman who let her beard grow, was a long and difficult one. Dakota said that trying to adjust to her differences during adolescence, while her parents kept getting her waxed, triggered a long-term "shame spiral," where she was ashamed of the fact that she could grow a beard.

She joined the sideshow scene quite by accident, although to her, maybe not, because Dakota doesn't believe that things happen without reason. She decided to join her first sideshow after she ran into friend Sunshine English, a veteran of World of Wonders, at a party in Los Angeles. Sunshine said she was working the Venice Beach Freakshow, where they had little people, a sword swallower and a bearded lady. Dakota realized that she could, in fact, join a sideshow and become a bearded lady. She decided to check it out. Then she decided to join, but she had anxiety. She thought about it some more and decided to go through with it. "I tried it for a week, didn't hate it, did it for another week, didn't hate it," she said.

She's still doing it.

She performed with John T. Rex. She also met Short E. Dangerously at the Venice Beach Freakshow, which she joined in 2013, the year she started growing her beard. "Shorty is one of those performers who has absolutely been empowered by sideshow," said Dakota.

She used to perform at a burlesque bar in North Hollywood, the CIA (California Institute of Abnormalarts). The underground nightclub had its box office located inside a giant skull, and exhibited sideshow memorabilia like a Feejee Mermaid, a monkey's paw and the embalmed body of a clown. But the owner, an embalmer named Carl Crew, shut it down during COVID.

She did a residency at BeetleHouse NYC, a Tim Burton-themed bar and restaurant, near Sixth Street and Second Avenue in Manhattan. She worked the Golden State Tattoo Expo in Pasadena, Calif. I asked her how many tattoos she has. She counted out thirteen over the phone, an up-to-the-minute count. Thirteen, the lucky number. She also works with Freakshow Deluxe, a sideshow collective of performers from around the country. She told me that's how she got her upcoming gig in Oklahoma City at Six Flags. And then, it will be time for a change of scenery. No more Las Vegas. "I'm moving down to New Orleans," she said. "I lived down there as a kid."

When she lived in California, Dakota frequented a gay bar in Hollywood called Gold Coast. Most of the patrons were considerably older than she, which is how it got its nickname: Old Coast. Dakota, who had a full beard at that point in her life, said it was the most welcoming environment she'd ever been in, and she became a regular. "Everybody was very loving and accepting," she said. "I never met such good people in my life as when I was going there. I remember when I was growing my beard and I was going there nobody questioned it. Everybody was just beautiful. They were some of the most beautiful people I met in my life. They just took me under their wing, and I respect them immensely for that."

The Gold Coast no longer exists. But Dakota has found a similar vibe among many of the sideshow people she's encountered. She said that being in sideshows is a way for someone who's born different to fit in. "The community welcomed me with open arms," she said. "I've never known any other community that just welcomed someone and celebrated them for their differences."

She said that sideshow people banded together, as a community, to help her mother in a time of need. Dakota told me this on Aug. 23, 2023, a few days after Hurricane Hilary plowed through Southern California, right through her mother's house. "My mother lost her home in the hurricane," she said. She told her friends, and they reacted immediately. "My performer friends know how much my mother means to me," she said. "She hates what I do, but she loves to see me perform. The human cutting board she's not a big fan of. She's not a big fan of the staples." She was referring to acts where she allowed members of the audience to staple her, and where she chopped a cucumber along the length of her forearm. She said that her boss put together a GoFundMe account for her mother, then shared it on Facebook, and then her friends started sharing it, including her sideshow friends, and they raised money. "The community really rallied," she said. "My mom said, of the people who donated, 'I don't know half these people.' I said, 'I do.' The sideshow community stepped up when she really needed it. The community is fucking fantastic."

I told her that most of the sideshow people didn't seem to have much money. "I know friends who make a very comfortable living; I know friends who don't," she said. "I know people who are some of the most incredible performers I've ever seen and they're living in poverty."

From the waxing salons of Ventura County, to a gay bar in Hollywood, to the sideshows of America, Dakota has experienced a social evolution. She has found a place where she belongs. "I've been a very lucky person in that I've been able to find my people," said Dakota. "I look for and I thrive with artists. Sideshow is just that; it is an art."

At her bartending job, patrons pepper her with questions about her hormone condition: "Is that real? Why do you have that?" She explains to them: "My adrenaline gland produces too much adrenaline, and that makes my brain produce slightly elevated levels of estrogen, and that causes the excess hair growth." I asked her the same question I asked Jennifer Miller: Is growing a beard, for a lady, considered a disability? "It's not a disability," she said. "I'm not going to get a special placard on my car because I've got fucked up hormones."

She loves performing, and bartending is more of a performance than the job she used to have, as a subcontractor for the U.S. Department of Energy at a nuclear test site in Nevada, working four 10-hour days per week, with a two-hour drive each way through the desert. "I hated it so much," she said. "I was isolated. I didn't get to be around people. It was terrible. Now I'm back to bartending, and yeah, I make way less money, but I'm way happier."

When she gets opportunities to perform, her boss lets her take time off, even for extended gigs. That's how she ended up taking the FreakShow Deluxe seasonal gig at Six Flags Frontier City in Oklahoma City. It seemed like a promising sign, that Six Flags in Middle America would hire an openly queer bearded lady sideshow performer.

I asked her about the subject of exploitation. She said that she chooses to be in sideshow. Do-gooders keep trying to save her from it, but she doesn't want to be saved. I asked if naturals have taken back the sideshow and made it their own. "I think that naturals have always had the sideshow," she said. "I think that for too long the main focus has always been, 'Oh, they're being exploited, these poor people, let's fix this for them and get them out.'"

Unsolicited saviors aren't shy about proselytizing right to her face, in public places where she's performing as the bearded lady. "I've had people come up to me and say, 'You don't have to do this.' I say, 'I know I don't.' I say, 'I know you mean well, but back the fuck off, we don't need your help.' The white savior, it's literally a thing."

Which brings us back to Dakota's shame spiral, now a thing of the past. She's proud of her beard, which celebrated its eleventh birthday in January 2025. "I've got friends, women, who say, 'I wish I could grow a beard like it,'" she said. "It's almost like a responsibility to keep the history going."

She said that the sideshow is a place for someone who's born different to fit in. But it's also a place for someone who's born different to stand out. "I realized that I have this ability to do something that not everybody can do, and not even everybody in the [sideshow] community can do," she said. "Not everyone in sideshow can grow a beard."

She met Jennifer Miller at the Venice Beach Freakshow. Jennifer introduced herself to Dakota on the boardwalk. Another bearded lady was working the freak show, too. Bearded sideshow ladies may seem like a 19th-century phenomenon, but there were three of them on the boardwalk that day.

Jennifer Miller and I had talked about how the beard seems to go well with the queer woman's look or lifestyle. I told Dakota that it seems like a coincidental combination.

"I don't really believe that anything is coincidence," she said. "I'm a big believer that everything happens for a reason. If there is a reason that I'm a bearded lady, and also queer, so be it. I think that queer people are more willing to accept their difference and be proud of it."

Chapter 25

Being Human

"Clawing, hissing, and fighting through a pandemic, against inequities in vaccine access and eugenic policies and attitudes that consider certain groups disposable, have given me the need to pause and reflect on all that I've been through. I have fought these battles for the bare minimum of existing in the same space with you all."
- Alice Wong, disability activist and author of *Year of the Tiger*

"I don't feel that anybody should have to be extraordinary, in order to be ordinary."
- Eileen Norman, president of Little People of America.

This book tells the story of sideshow naturals, in their own words. This book presents their perspectives on having reclaimed the modern sideshow and evolved it into a sophisticated and self-aware medium of self-expression. I interviewed about 20 naturals who were in sideshows, and naturally, they were pro-sideshow. But they were also taking a contrarian view against the mainstream position that sideshows are exploitative, uncivilized and offensive. The mainstream view is not without merit, however, and it's shared by many disabled people who look down on sideshows as the anathema of their existence.

In October 2023 I contacted Alice Wong, one of the leading disability activists in America. Alice, a self-described cyborg oracle, was born with muscular dystrophy and uses a wheelchair to get around and a ventilator to survive. In 2022, she published her autobiography, *Year of the Tiger: An Activist's Life*, where she described her experience surviving the COVID pandemic and also speaking with President Obama virtually, through a remote-controlled telepresence robot in the White House, as they roved about the Blue Room together. She edited *Disability Visibility*, an anthology of essays by disabled writers. She is the founder of the Disability Visibility Project, an online community for creating and amplifying disability culture.

I wanted to know what Alice thought about sideshows. But alas, she politely bowed out of doing an interview. Alice directed me to another natural who is eminently qualified to speak on the topic of sideshows: Eileen Norman, president of Little People of America.

I spoke to Eileen by Zoom in late 2023. Earlier that year, in August, she was quoted in the *Los Angeles Times* for opposing the use of taxpayer funds to host a live performance of the so-called Midget Wrestling Warriors in Sonoma County. The word "midget," she said, is a slur and she wanted it gone.

"Some of those dollars are my dollars," she told me, explaining how she was forced as a taxpayer to support a performance that exploits little people like her. "That type of event specifically is what reinforces that it's ok to treat me as an object." She blames events like "midget wrestling" for fueling some of the harassment she's dealt with because of her height, including people who pick her up in public. (This is a common complaint among little people, that strangers will manhandle them as if they were babies or Teddy bears.)

She opposes "midget wrestling" for the same reason she doesn't like sideshows: they present disabled people in a freakish way, which warps the perspective of their non-disabled audiences, who then view all disabled people as freaks. "It's how people walk away from it that matters," said Eileen. "Are they walking away with that mentality of: 'Those freaks, what weird funny people those are, and the next time I see someone who looks like them I'm going to think how hilarious was that performance?'"

I told her about Xander Lovecraft and Lil Miss Firefly, little people who performed at the Coney Island Circus Sideshow, and Alan Silva, an aerialist and ringmaster with the Big Apple Circus. They were choosing to do sideshow or circus of their own free will. I read her a quote from Xander where he talked about taking control of the perception of people who laughed at him because of his height: "If you're really going to look at me, I'm going to give you a real reason to look at me other than my height. I want you to look at me because I'm jumping barefoot on Legos. I want you to look at me because I'm swallowing a six-foot balloon and you don't know how I'm doing it. I want you to look at me because I'm hammering a nail into my nasal cavity and you think I should be dead."

His impassioned explanation did not change her mind. She said that she didn't want to pass judgment on him specifically, but she found his mentality difficult to understand. "He had to feel his self-confidence by being extraordinary," said Eileen. "But I don't feel that anybody should have to be extraordinary in order to be ordinary."

While sideshow performers are trying to stand out, Eileen feels quite the opposite about attracting the attention of strangers. She said she loves her hometown of San Francisco, "the city of outcasts," because it's easier for a natural to blend in than to stand out. "I, for one, relish in being very boring in this city," she said. "There are much more people who are more interesting to look at than me."

Instead of focusing on the issue of individual choice as a counter to exploitation, Eileen took a macro view of sideshows that questioned their very existence. "In my view of disability and advocacy and being included and equal, I focus more on systems than individuals," she said, "so individual choices are something that I support, but broken systems are what I aim to change."

In this way, Eileen was carrying forward the basic ideal that led to the Americans with Disabilities Act, that disabled people are trying to change a country that is not built to accommodate them, even though tens of millions of Americans are disabled. She is, therefore, skeptical of the sort of society that led to the creation of sideshows and their use of naturals.

"So when we're talking about these types of shows, my question that first comes to mind isn't whether the individual chose to do that, it's: Who holds the power in that structure?" she said. "Who's the one who's making money? Who's the one who's profiting off of this? Are the people being paid fairly? Are they receiving health benefits?" She recognized that disabled people might have joined sideshows in the past for lack of better options, but in 21st-century America they should have more options than that.

I told her that sideshow isn't usually that lucrative, and that some naturals just do it for art. "If the goal is meant to be a form of artistic expression that is meant to educate and bring light to diversity and the beauty of diversity, that's great," she said. But she doesn't see sideshows as a forum for diversity and inclusion. Quite the opposite, because the naturals are being set apart from the rest, as human spectacles. "I think there is this imaginary line that in society we create, this us-versus-them line," she said. "Sideshows, wrestling, what it could do is reinforce that invisible line, reinforce that these people are here to entertain me, are here to make me laugh, to do this performance on my behalf. That's the line we want to diminish, that's the line that we want to go away, if the line is based on disability."

She also said the sideshows tend to focus on one aspect of the natural born performer – their disability. "Do we get to see these characters as humans, as people, as more than one dimension, more than one feature that we're highlighting?"

She said that if sideshows were to go away, they would leave behind a void that does not need to be refilled. She sees this as the true test of necessity.

Meanwhile, Disney was having a hell of a time trying to cast the remake of its original feature-length movie from 1937, *Snow White and the Seven Dwarfs*. The film has a fundamental problem: it is universally loathed by little people for its depiction of dwarves as mythical non-human cryptids who serve as one-dimensional peripheral supporters of the main character, who towers over them.

Peter Dinklage, the actor with dwarfism who starred in *Game of Thrones*, appeared on Marc Maron's podcast in 2022 to chastise Disney for "making that backward story of seven dwarves living in the cave." Dinklage was the man on the mountain, speaking from an elevated position as a natural born professional who had succeeded in transcending ableist stereotypes.

Eileen praised *Game of Thrones* for presenting a little person as one of its main characters. Dinklage played the fictional character Tyrion Lannister, a multi-dimensional political schemer with relationships, emotions and aspirations, like a real human being. "There was this guy who had so much depth," she said, referring to Tyrion. "He was a good guy; he was a bad guy. Love interests. Family drama. There was so much to this one character. It wasn't just flat. He wasn't just there to move a story forward for someone else." In other words, the actor had succeeded in distracting his viewers from his dwarfism, to remind them that he is, in fact, human.

I asked Alice Wong if she knew disabled academics with opinions on sideshows. (In searching the writings of Professor Paul Longmore, a leading disability activist who died in 2011, I didn't find any references to sideshows.) She directed me to film critic Angelo Muredda who just a few days before had published his critique of the film *Freaks* on her Disability Visibility Project blog, after Criterion released a DVD set called *Tod Browning's Sideshow Shockers*. Muredda described the movie as "the most infamous disability film of the first half of the twentieth century and in some ways still the most progressive."

Muredda's academic review was enlightening, as a condemnation of sideshow committed to film: "Even the most generous assessment of the film's thematic and narrative machinations has to disentangle the same contradictions of representation and exploitation that power the institution of the freak show itself: it's an exploitative tradition that also employed and gave platform to a large number of disabled performers, recreated in an exploitation film that both platforms and lingers over the bodies of disabled performers." He had spotlighted the cult film's split perspective: *Freaks* humanized naturals in some scenes, making them look sympathetic, while emphasizing their differences in others, to make them look bizarre or even unsettling.

Just like a sideshow.

Chapter 26

Shorty's Last Tour

"The sideshow business is the easiest business in the world to quit. I know. I quit it a hundred times. It always pulled me back."
- *Side Show*, Howard Bone

It was early October 2023, and Halloween was in the air. The Starland Ballroom was set back from a road that wound through the scrubby woods of New Jersey. The ballroom stood apart at the far end of a gravel parking lot at the edge of a thin forest that stretched to nowhere. Starland looked like a rural roadhouse. But it's not. It's on a stretch of woods between towns in the most densely populated state in America.

Starland was across the road from a Veterans of Foreign Wars outpost with neon signs in the window, glowing with the promise of beer at reasonable prices. These buildings served as waystations on a wooded road running south from Sayreville. The city limits of New York weren't 20 miles away.

Dozens of metalheads and Goths lined up in front of Starland, a queue of black leather, tattoos, experimental hairstyles and even corpse paint. A convoy of RVs and other vehicles had tucked themselves behind the building like a gypsy camp. The night was approaching and the scraggly woods at the edge of the parking lot grew dark and foreboding as if the Jersey Devil was out there. Starland would be the perfect setting for a zombie apocalypse. An undead army could emerge from the woods and attack the ballroom while in the throes of metal. Headbanging away the last night on Earth.

But that's not what happened. On this night, the Hellzapoppin Circus Sideshow Revue was playing Starland, all the way from Florida, starring Aaron "Shorty" Wollin, AKA Short E. Dangerously, the half-man, natural born with sacral agenesis.

This was to be one of Shorty's last performances. Hellzapoppin was touring with Mushroomhead, a rock band that wore evil-looking alien monster masks, in the tradition of Gwar and Slipknot. Hellzapoppin and Shorty had toured with metal bands before, including this one, but metal was something new for the sideshow scene, historically speaking. Long gone were the old circus days, when Ringling Brothers paraded its naturals around the country by train, along with its menageries of elephants and tigers, its acrobats and clowns, entertaining the masses beneath a massive three-ring tent. In the 21st century, sideshows were driving in RVs across the country, in a convoy of metalheads in Satanic masks with a hodgepodge of opening bands, an entourage that hopscotched from one nightclub to the next. Sayreville was the tour's closest location to New York City. Hellzapoppin was the third act, behind two lesser-known bands that were along for the ride to sell T-shirts.

Bryce "The Govna" Graves appeared on stage, the human blockhead mastermind behind Hellzapoppin, wearing his trademark top hat with long brown braids that trailed below his waist, and a demon mask that he'd borrowed from Mushroomhead. It was a nice shoutout to his touring partners, and it underscored what an artistic pairing they really were. The band could belt out a demented carnival song like "Qwerty" that fit with the sideshow like hand and glove.

"Short E. Dangerously, come all the way from Daytona, Florida!" announced The Govna. "Shorty E. Dangerously, the most amazing half-man in the world!"

Shorty appeared, wearing his trademark cowboy hat and black leather vest with the patch from his favorite band, the Texas Hippy Coalition. He walked across the stage on his hands and did a handstand on the circus bucket that he always brought on tour, a beat-up relic from his extensive career. Shorty gripped the bucket and did a double handstand, suspended his legless torso in the air, lifted one of his hands away, held himself aloft on the remaining hand, and slowly revolved his body around, inch by inch, like a carousel.

After Bryce and his sword-swallower girlfriend, Willow Lauren, did their acts, Shorty returned to the stage wearing a casino slouch cap, vest and a black T-shirt with the word FREAK on it. He focused quietly on a painful-looking game that involved a metal spike hidden, pointy-side up, inside one of five cups. He invited a guest from the audience up to the stage and she shuffled the cups to conceal the one with the spike as Shorty turned his back and looked away. The idea was that Shorty would slap his hand on the cups, one at a time, and they would break apart and reveal whether the spike was hidden inside. If he slapped the cup with the spike by accident, he would crucify his hand. This act was preceded by a grisly video that showed a performer accidentally impaling his hand by playing this game. "Shorty will risk his own hand for your entertainment," explained Bryce to the audience.

Shorty slapped the cups hard, one at a time, and they broke apart, but there was no spike inside, until there was only one cup left. Shorty had guessed the cups correctly. Or maybe he had stealthily side-eyed the audience member, like a card counter. Either way, he emerged unscathed.

"I know where that spike is the whole time," he told me after the act. He was wearing rugged black gloves that served as shoes, since he walked on his hands. I asked him if he was doing a mentalist act. "I didn't want it to be like I'm trying to be a magician," said Shorty, as there already was a magician touring with Hellzapoppin. "I'm not claiming to be a magician. I'm more of a stuntman than anything." I mentioned that he was, once again, putting at risk the hands that he walks on. In this way, his hands are more important than most hands. They are his hands *and* his feet. "If I lose, I'm done," he said. "If I lose, I lose a piece of my hand, so I'm risking everything again."

But it was different this time, compared to when he was jumping on broken glass that Bryce set on fire with lighter fluid. With the cup act, he was avoiding injury completely, unlike the glass act, where he cut the hell out of himself, even if he made it look like fun. Shorty had shown me the scars, old and new, that crisscrossed his hands. He said that towards the end of a tour, his hands would look like hamburger. "I told Bryce that I wanted to take a break from the glass walking because I've been doing it so long," he told me. Fair enough.

An audience member asked Shorty about eating fire. Shorty told him that he used to do it, but it takes a toll on dentistry. "Fire eating fucks your teeth up," he explained.

Hellzapoppin had played a stripped-down show, without the flashier, more hazardous acts. The sideshow portion of the night's entertainment ended after 45 minutes.

"The star of Hellzapoppin, Mr. Short E. Dangerously!" said the Govna, who picked him up and danced with him, carrying away his old friend. Exit stage left.

After the show, members of Mushroomhead were hanging around the merch stands. The chattiest band member was the lead singer, an elfin-looking dude with a grey mask that combined the features of a devil with a Greek god. He identified himself as xstrikex and said it was awesome touring with a sideshow. It created a "different atmosphere stagewise" because it helped to break up the show, since it was inserted between musical acts. He compared Hellzapoppin to Jim Rose, and said they were a good fit with Mushroomhead's music and masks. "It's all art," he said emphatically, still unseen beneath his mask, and practically shaking with a post-performance rush.

I asked him to compare the 21st-century sideshow style of touring with a metal band, to the olden days, when P.T. Barnum transported his circus with its sideshow naturals by rail. xstrikex said that things would have been extra crazy during the Barnum days, and he relished the thought of it. "There were some real freaks back then," said xstrikex. "I wish I lived back then. That was some fun shit!"

Shorty told me that Nik Sin was joining Hellzapoppin for the fall tour. Nik was a little person who had worked at Coney. I asked him about the Lizardman. I knew that the Lizardman had toured with Hellzapoppin earlier that year. "Awesome, he's one of my best friends, I love that guy," said Shorty. "That's the best part of being in the business. People who I saw on TV, people I grew up watching, people who I was a fan of, these people are now my friends." I told him about my phone conversation with the Lizardman, and how

I had read his book with its insightful and eccentric philosophies. I thought it was crazy that the Lizardman cut his tongue into a fork. "You got to be a little off to do something like that," said Shorty. This was coming from a guy who used to drive race cars and jump on broken glass. I asked him: What are your goals with sideshow? What's your long-range plan? What's your end game? "It's funny you should ask," he said, "because after I do the fall tour, I'm taking a hiatus. The grind is starting to wear on me. I have sacrificed my personal life to chase this dream. I've got it now. I've accomplished more than I ever thought I would. When I started this, I never thought I would get this far."

Shorty was an MC at a strip club when he joined World of Wonders in 2012 and eventually worked for multiple sideshows, performed in dozens of countries, and immortalized himself in Ripley's Believe It or Not! His goal was to surpass *Freaks* star Johnny Eck as a legendary half-man.

He said that he wasn't going to stop performing completely. He would still do one-off shows and big events and overseas gigs. But after the fall tour was over, he was going to take a year off from touring, get a job to pay the bills, and get his mental health back in order. "I'm going to take better care of myself, which is hard to do when you're on tour," he said. "I'm 45 years old. I don't have a girlfriend. I lost my dog six years ago. I'm going to live a normal life for a while. I've done all this amazing stuff, and I've had no one to share it with. It's hard to have a relationship when you're gone six or nine months a year."

He had peaked. It was time to do something else.

"I don't want to hate what I'm doing," said Shorty. "Because I love it so much, I got nothing. I don't want to be one of these: 'I've accomplished so much professionally, but personally, I don't have anyone close to me to share it with.'"

Later, I mentioned this to Tommy Breen, who introduced Shorty to the sideshow business when he joined World of Wonders back in 2012. "He went pretty hard for quite a few years," said Tommy. "I'm glad he's taking a break to heal a bit." I pictured Shorty at home in Daytona, lounging with a girlfriend, like the picture that was taken of him by *National Geographic* a few years before. I asked him what kind of job he plans to get. "I'm going to work in a dispensary," said Shorty, "or a hot rod shop."

Chapter 27

Nik Sin

"I think the key is making people forget you're at a freak show. Which is important, because a lot of people have this negative aspect of sideshow and freak show. They think it's exploitation."
- Nik Sin

Though he planned to retire, Shorty took part in Hellzapoppin's Christmas 2023 tour, as one of two naturals on the billing, a rare event in 21st-century sideshows. Shorty shared the stage with one of his favorite co-performers: Nik Sin.

Nik Sin is a little person who is well-known in the sideshow scene. He has performed for years with Hellzapoppin, 999 Eyes Freakshow and the Coney Island Circus Sideshow. He has also performed in non-sideshow venues. He has had many stage personas including his Mini Manson character, as a member of the tribute band Mini Kiss, and even as an elf, every now and then, like when he joined Hellzapoppin for its holiday 2023 tour.

"They needed an elf for the Christmas spectacular, so I was the elf," he told me, in his no-nonsense Yankee accent. "They kind of switched up the show to make it like a Christmas thing which was weird, but it worked. We kidnapped Shorty, and Shorty was Santa. We sawed him in half and separated his legs from his body." The sawed-in-half act made use of Shorty's sacral agenesis and was similar to an act performed in the 1930s by his "half-man" predecessor, Johnny Eck. He didn't mind playing a Christmas elf, within the cognizant environment of 21st-century sideshow. "When you have the control, it makes things like that not so degrading," he said. "You're going to use what you have either way."

Nik said it was his first time in five years performing with Hellzapoppin. He said the show has taken more of a theatrical turn. He said they have more of a story to tell "rather than just go out there and put a screwdriver up your nose."

I spoke to Nik via Zoom in February 2024. At that time, he was 37 years old. It was deep winter, and he was speaking from the basement of his mother's house in Pittsfield, Massachusetts, in the heart of the Berkshires, where he lived at the time. (He cracked a self-deprecating joke about living where the snow is "balls deep.") I could tell he was a performer by how he chose to present himself, in the way he set up the Zoom shot: He was long-haired and bearded, wearing black, poised in front of a spiral staircase of black metal. He sat beneath a framed drawing of a skeleton on the wall. He said it was by Paul Booth, a tattoo artist who'd inked members of Slayer and Pantera. "I actually bought this for my mom, but she didn't like it," he said, gesturing at the picture behind him with his black fingerless skeleton gloves. He told me that in the picture, if you look closely, you can see that the skeleton is breastfeeding a baby. "I've always been a metalhead," he said. "I've always been into Paul Booth."

He had been an introverted child who emerged from the quiescent shell of high school like a rock n' Goth chrysalis. He started growing his hair long after high school, then dyed it black and stole and used his mother's eyeliner. He started performing at age 21, and for a while, he was a member of Mini Kiss. He assumed the role of guitarist Ace Frehley for eight months. He said that a lot of guys who perform as Mini Kiss didn't know anything about the band, unlike Nik, who's a fan, and a soldier of the Kiss Army. He gestured with one of his skeleton hands down the hall towards his off-camera bedroom. It was the room he grew up in, and it hadn't changed a bit. He lived in a time capsule from his younger life. "There's wall-to-wall Kiss stuff in my room," he said. "It's kind of embarrassing, but that's what it is: Kiss and wrestling." (Both Mini Kiss and Ace Frehley were still touring in 2024.) Around the time he joined Mini Kiss, he adopted another persona: Marilyn Manson. He loved shock rock and the Halloween style of performers like Alice Cooper and John "Ozzy" Osbourne. "It sounded cool, looked cool, I had the Goth clothes and already had the Goth look," said Nik, who was photographed with Marilyn Manson in 2011, poising pensively with his chin resting in his hand. (At several points during our interview, he would habitually hold his chin in his skeleton glove.) "You're not going to hire me to be a clown at your kid's party," he said. "I look like Marilyn Manson; you don't want me as an Oompa-Loompa at your kid's birthday party. I've seen guys get paydays off gigs that I thought were awful: leprechaun, elf, Oompa-Loompa. I felt that I was better, that I could do more. I just felt that there was more to it than dressing up as a stereotypical character." Nik spoke from experience because he's played some of these controversial characters himself. "I've done the leprechaun stuff, I've done the elf stuff, you've got to be more than that," he said.

When he played a Christmas elf during the Hellzapoppin's holiday tour, he put his own spin on it, to make it his own. "I came out as an elf, but I also came out as a drunk elf telling people to go fuck themselves," said Nik. "I was still me. It's like that movie *Bad Santa*. It's like an X-rated Christmas show." After the Christmas skit was over, he shed the elf costume and went back to being Nik Sin.

He commented on how young he looked in some of his earlier Nik Sin photos, including the one with Marilyn Manson. He used to be clean-shaven, but he had since grown an impressive beard. He had patterned his image after Manson, but he had grown more seasoned over the years, and now, as a grizzled rocker from a snowy mill town in Massachusetts, he reminded me of Rob Zombie.

Nik cut his teeth at the Coney Island Circus Sideshow, where Dick Zigun hired him on the spot. "Dick originally had me just as a natural born," said Nik, meaning that he didn't have stage skills like fire breathing and sword swallowing. He was assigned to the bally platform, outside the sideshow as an outside talker, to try to lure customers in. But Nik didn't like being a public "spectacle," as he put it, for the seething crowds of Brooklyn. "I never wanted to be on the bally stage because I was terrified of talking," said Nik. "This idea, that I was going to be a talker, I didn't want to be a talker. I didn't want to be out there and have people poke at me. Coney Island's a rough place."

In the sideshow business, Nik worked with some of the most fascinating individuals he ever encountered, including Erik Sprague, the Lizardman. "It's refreshing that someone can look the way he does and knock it out of the park," said Nik, noting that the Lizardman incorporates comedy into his stunt acts. Like other people who have worked with Sprague, Nik described him as charismatic, intelligent, well-read and down-to-earth. "When I met him, he had a six-pack of Miller Lite and a book of philosophy on him," said Nik.

Nik was also inspired by Black Scorpion. He described him as "super shy" backstage but an amazing comic performer when onstage. "I loved his act when he had the gloves on and he had fake fingers and he was smashing them," he said. "I loved that act. It was definitely more comedy than, 'Look at me, I'm weird.'"

Nik concluded, early in his sideshow career, that being natural born wasn't enough. "I saw so many natural borns, no offense to any of them, but they were just being natural borns and that was their gig," he said. He needed an act. But which one? Selecting which stunt seemed an exercise in masochism. Being a human blockhead was out of the question. "I could barely put a Q-Tip in my nose and these guys are putting power drills up there," said Nik, who had just completed a tour with Hellzapoppin.

"I wanted to do the big spectacle acts like sword swallower and fire breather," said Nik. He experimented with various stunts, including razor blade swallowing, an act honed to bloody perfection by his Hellzapoppin colleague, Willow Lauren. During one of their 2023 shows in New Jersey, I watched her swallow a string of razor blades and then retrieve them, like she was hand-fishing for the blades, one by bloody one. It looked real. Nik assured me that it *is* real.

Nik learned how to swallow razor blades from a fellow performer, which wasn't easy, especially while in motion at high elevation. "We were on a tour bus, going over the French Alps," said Nik. "He's like: 'Here's a razor blade, put it in your mouth.' So you try not to panic. I've messed up a couple times, and it's not fun. It's not something you want to mess up, or you cut yourself really bad." Nik gestured in front of his mouth as he told this story, miming the act of feeding himself razor blades. I tried to imagine that moment when he put a shard of edged steel in his mouth while sitting on a bus while winding its way among the highest peaks in Europe. He said that it's important, when you have a razor blade in your mouth, not to panic. "It's like being stuck in a trap, except that it's inside your mouth," he explained. Mind over matter is equally important for other dangerous tasks, like sword swallowing. "You mess that up, you're in trouble," he said.

He finally settled on a professional specialty. A couple of weeks after he mounted the bally platform at Coney, Nik decided to become an escape artist. "I realized that nobody else was doing it, especially at my stature," he said. Donny Vomit, a well-known sideshow veteran with a penchant for Jim Rose-style gross-out stunts, bought him a straitjacket. But it isn't easy being Houdini. Slipping out of a buckled canvas coat designed to restrain people in mental institutions is something that isn't supposed to happen, but Nik figured it out. His advice from other performers was to pretend like he was getting bullied as he struggled furiously to escape.

This was an act that Nik learned and improved, to make it more dramatic, more risky, and more exciting. His colleagues would fasten him into a straitjacket and suspend him from the rafters of the Coney Island sideshow. In this way, Nik would achieve a metamorphosis, hanging by his ankles in a straitjacket, only three feet tall, but suspended 30 feet above the stage. And then, while he had their rapt attention, he would escape. It was a different perspective for him, and it was a different perspective for them on the ground.

"I could just be that insecure kid in high school for the rest of my life," said Nik, "or I could be 30 feet up in the air at Coney Island being a badass." They were looking up at him, instead of down at him. "You've got to control your narrative," he said.

A sideshow is a spectacle, made for your entertainment, and perhaps for your education, too. Nik is focused on the total concept of the freak show, which has evolved over the years into something quite different from what it was before. Most importantly, he is autonomous. "Nobody's forced me to go onstage," he said. "I can get a job doing whatever I want, but I love what I do. To make people forget that you're three feet tall because you're putting on a badass show."

He knows who he is and he wants to project his self-confidence onto the audience. They must see him the way he sees himself. This is the reality that he wants them to understand. Their perception of sideshow is paramount. "I think the key is making people forget you're at a freak show," said Nik. "Which is important, because a lot of people have this negative aspect of sideshow and freak show. They think it's exploitation."

He said that when he worked with Shorty and Black Scorpion, they tried to relate with people and get them to enjoy the show, to take away negative expectations. Nik said it's good to let the audience feel like they're in on the joke. "We're all in this fucking weird thing together," he said.

Nik knows naturals who don't like attention and wish they could avoid it. But he resigned himself long ago to the fact that people will always stare at him. He sounded like Shorty, when he described the inevitability of being human. "I'm going to get looked at anywhere I go," said Nik. "I'm not going to be able to walk into a grocery store with a suit and tie on and expect people to forget that I'm three feet tall." Nik said that you can be empowered by your self-image. He said this is the world we live in and you can make it your own.

Naturals have always been confronted by a world that is not built for them except for the controversial institution of sideshow which was built *especially* for them. Naturals like Nik are the unassailable kings of this irresistible subculture. Sideshow is theirs for the taking, their exclusive platform for the world. "I've always known that I'm going to be in the spotlight," said Nik. "To take that spotlight and make it brighter and make it a positive instead of a negative is what we've been trying to do."

Nik didn't live in his mother's basement for long. He was back on the road in March 2024. He had joined a wrestling group of little people called Micro Mania.

Chapter 28

Nati Returns to Coney

"Hello world! It feels good to be onstage."
- The Patchwork Girl

"Sideshow, there's no tricks. No illusions. It's all real."
- Alaska the Lost Boy

A savage rainstorm swept through New York City after April Fool's Day 2024, flooding the streets as lightning hit the Statue of Liberty. Her green copper skin served as an excellent conductor, and she survived. After the storm broke, the clouds parted, and sunlight bathed the city, which was then (April 5) rocked by an earthquake centered in nearby New Jersey, measuring 4.8 on the Richter scale, followed by an afternoon eclipse (April 8) where the moon obscured the sun. These were all rare events, and they all happened within one week.

But that wasn't all. That same week, beginning on the day of the earthquake, Coney Island USA hosted the Sideshow Hootenanny, an annual extravaganza of human blockheads, sword swallowers, contortionists, fire breathers, fire eaters, stomach pumpers, erotic dancers, glass eaters, geeks and freaks. They descended on Brooklyn and converged on Coney Island USA and the House of Yes for a festival of vaudevillian and burlesque performances by masochists and daredevils. Shows were sold out and it went on for days. I went to the Coney Island Circus Sideshow for a packed Saturday night of weird, stomach-churning, death-defying acts, some comical and all crazy.

This was the culmination of everything. Full circle, from beginning to end. I got the idea for my book from Southern Sideshow Hootenanny. That was the original name for Sideshow Hootenanny, which took place in New Orleans in 2023, but they shortened the name to be more regionally inclusive. While promoting my first book *Circus Jerks* in May 2021, I noticed on the Sideshow Hootenanny website that they offered membership discounts to "natural born." This struck me as politically provocative because I only knew the term from the U.S. Constitution, which says that only a "natural born" American can be president. But the sideshow meaning of "natural born" was completely different and once I found out what it meant, I was amazed to learn that there were still disabled people performing in sideshows, and there were enough of them to warrant a discount from Sideshow Hootenanny. *Natural Born!* became the title of my new book and my book was an excuse to talk to the most interesting people in the world.

Adam Realman, sword swallower and artistic director of Coney Island USA, wore a black sequined jacket as he hosted the Hootenanny, introducing one stunning act after another.

But none of those performers were natural born. Patrick Wall, general manager of Coney Island USA, told me that over the last 15 years, it's been getting hard to get naturals. He said there are fewer naturals doing sideshow than there were before.

But the Hootenanny did have a natural, after all: Nati, the Patchwork Girl. She was an attraction, and they saved her until almost the end. Adam Realman introduced her as "literally the smartest person in the sideshow scene" and said that she's going for her doctorate.

Nati the Patchwork Girl made her appearance. She wore clown face paint, mostly white with a little red, and a dress of diamond patterns with a feather headdress and black buckled boots. She was the smallest person on stage that night and she radiated with energy that seemed amplified by the white face paint and the colored diamonds.

"Hello world!" she beamed. "It feels good to be onstage."

Nati Amos, the lab technician born with amniotic band syndrome, explained to her audience that the sideshow was a special place for her. "Being born weird and using it to my advantage for once in the world," she said.

She said that years ago, she had performed as a sideshow fire twirler. She joked that in her first audition she set her hair on fire but "he still hired me," referring to Dick Zigun, freak show founder and ex-artistic director for Coney Island USA.

Nati's act did not include an educational discourse about her disability. Many of the people in the audience at Coney already knew who she was, while the others just took her at face value.

Nati was a trickster. "Quick, quick, how many fingers am I holding up?" she yelled, flashing her hands up and down enthusiastically. "The answer is, of course, all of them! It's a quantum leap."

She had bigger things in store for her act. Offstage, at the edge of the bleachers, I asked Adam what to expect from Nati, but he didn't know what she was going to do.

Nati played romantic music, as she typically does, and performed a short but sensual dance with Alaska the Lost Boy, who was dressed in a black jacket and tight pants, letting slip the jacket to bare his shoulders. (After the show, Alaska informed me that his pronouns are he-him.) They had rolled out the bed of nails, wooden boards with hundreds of evenly-spaced sharp thick spikes driven through them.

Someone placed a cinder block on Nati's torso as she lay on the board, and then Alaska brought down an eight-pound sledgehammer and smashed the block to bits. Nati survived and emerged from the bed of nails to applause from the crowd, no worse for wear.

Alaska, in an interview following the show, told me that he doesn't get nervous doing stuff to his own body, because he knows his body, as a sword swallower and as an aerialist. But doing something physical to someone else is another story. He does the act with Nati because Nati trusts him to do it. "It's a really emotional, bonding moment," said Alaska, explaining that it's important to have been hammered yourself, before you hammer someone else. "I think it's really important to do both."

I asked Alaska what he would say to naysayers who believe the act is faked. "Why can't you let yourself feel the joy and excitement of knowing that it's real?" he said.

After the show, Nati donned a studded vest, a brightly colored shirt and a plaid cap, looking like a hip-hop star, and wandered out to the Freak Bar, still wearing her white and red face paint. When I interviewed her back in 2022, she was between jobs. But now, she said she was back at work as a clinical research associate. She was also a PhD candidate to study immunology, with a focus on microbiology.

She told me that she was a veteran of the bed of nails. She's been doing it for years. It was one of her signature acts. She used to lie on the nails and have people stand on her. The bigger the better. "Because I'm tiny," she said. She figured it was more dramatic to have big people stand on a tiny person like herself, while she was impaling herself on a bed of nails. She said that she once had a 360-pound man stand on her. But her performance at Sideshow Hootenanny that night was the first time she let someone hit her with a sledgehammer live on stage. She said there's no easy way to do it, no trick, no short cut. "It's physics, right?" she said. "You have to essentially brace yourself. There's no magic to it."

Chapter 29

Rik Daniels and the Omnium Circus

"I think that people with disability have as much right as anybody else to objectify themselves."
- Rik Daniels

Rik Daniels, a member of the Omnium Circus, appeared on stage in a wheelchair at Queens Theatre amid a circus of acrobats and dancers. He was an acrobat and a dancer himself. He emerged from the wheelchair on his hands instead of his feet. His upper torso rippled with muscle while his legs and feet were small like a child's. He stood on his hands, pointing his diminutive legs up towards the ceiling, and placed his bare hands into a pair of glittery dancing shoes at the end of the stage. Then he tap danced on his hands, keeping in time with the other dancers on stage.

In a separate act, Rik danced in his wheelchair to Mozart's *Marriage of Figaro* and then did another handstand, raising his small legs to the heavens as the muscles of his arms bulged. Then he danced acrobatically on his hands, swinging his legs and torso around and under his arms, spinning with athletic control and grace. He combined leg circles and breakdancing with the pommel horse moves, he told me, of his acrobatic youth. Over the years, he said he had designed and refined this unique act.

Every act in the Omnium Circus was different, and the cast was diverse. Omnium also featured Jen Bricker-Bauer, an aerialist born with no legs. She performed a roll-up in the silks, using her arms to pull herself up while reeling herself into the fabric, then unspooling herself to drop back down. Her husband Dominik Bauer played trombone while she flew above the stage, suspended from the silks. Then she performed a romantic aerial silks dance with her husband, lifting him into the air. At the end of the show, when the cast members gathered for the grand finale, they brought their toddler on stage with them.

Lisa B. Lewis, founder and executive director of the Omnium Circus, offered Rik Daniels the job in 2022 as an acrobatic dancer. But he didn't want it at first. "Initially, I was like, 'I don't want to be part of a disability circus,'" explained Rik, in an interview a couple of years later. She told him it wasn't just a disability circus, that there are people who are not disabled. But it is about accessibility. Omnium Circus features a mix of performers who are disabled and non-disabled. Their website said that it includes "the beautiful mosaic of humans who make up our world." Rik doesn't like the term "disabled" and is hesitant to identify with it, though he realizes it is the common label that people use for individuals like him. "I will refer to myself as disabled because, colloquially, that's how we're categorized," he explained. "That's how we organize the chaos that is life." He told me that Omnium lives by the code of EIA, which stands for equity inclusion accessibility. He decided to join.

Omnium is Rik's third circus, having already performed in Circus Culture, a circus school in Ithica, N.Y., and CirqOvation, a provider of corporate entertainment with a "cirque vaudeville flair," according to its website. "Performing was almost inevitable, when the whole world looks at you constantly, and you're a spectacle," he said.

In Rik's earlier life as a competitive acrobat and student, his teachers and his mother were interested in "mainstreaming" Rik by embedding him in the general population rather than keeping him separate, in the traditional way that schools have handled disabled students.

Rik was 56 years old at the time of this interview, in October 2024. He grew up in the Throgs Neck section of the Bronx and now lives in Ithica, working full-time for the Tompkins County Department of Social Services. He uses a wheelchair, drives a car and rides a horse side-saddle to compensate for his legs. He is gay and has a husband. He takes care of his ailing mother-in-law to postpone her entry into a nursing home. His own mother died in 2016. He credits her for saving him from an institution and making him the man he is today.

Rik has the muscular upper body and torso of an athlete, though his body tapers into small legs with limited mobility that he has had to learn. As a result of that training, he sometimes stands on his legs and even spins on them. But his wheelchair is always part of his act. He dances in a wheelchair with his partners. He performs with it in the *Nutcracker Suite* and does handstands on the armrests.

"I was born the way I am," said Rik, meaning that he was natural born in 1968 with a condition that his doctors diagnosed as arthrogryposis. (According to the Cleveland Clinic, the full name is arthrogryposis multiplex congenita, or AMC, and it refers to multiple contractures that are congenital anomalies that cause permanent "crooking" of a baby's limbs.) He said that when he was in his mother's womb, the umbilical cord was wrapped around his legs and neck, which could have killed him, but didn't, though it did prevent his legs from developing. "I was folded in half, with my legs in front of me," he said, and then he joked, "I was born to be gay."

He said his hips, knees and ankles were deformed, lacking the usual ball and socket. His legs were small, with clubbed feet that his doctor deliberately broke and fused with pins. He said he has full feeling in his legs, which he's grateful for, but he cannot move his extremities from the knees down. He said he has trouble making lateral moves outward, but he has always moved his legs however he needed to, and he can kick.

This was not the future that his doctors envisioned for him at birth. He said that when he was born, his doctors told his mother, "His arms and legs will never develop. He'll never sit up by himself. He'll never run and play with other kids. We strongly suggest you institutionalize and try to forget about him."

But Rik said that his mother insisted on bringing him home, telling the doctors, "He will not only survive, he will live." He eventually came home from the hospital and underwent multiple surgeries. His mother trained him to sit up by coaxing him with a lollipop.

"It was never a question of *if* I would do anything, but *how*," said Daniels. His mother taught him to swim in a pool in their yard, and his grandparents taught him to use a skateboard. He started breakdancing as a teenager, during its wave of popularity in New York in the late 1970s and early 1980s, then moved into acrobatics when he attended Harry S. Truman High School in Co-op City.

He engaged in the usual teenage shenanigans with his friends, who would greet him with familiarity by saying, "Here comes the crip," and he would reply, "What's up, bitch?" It was all part of social mainstreaming. "We'd smoke weed and drink beer," he said. "Nobody was overly sensitive."

He soon learned that he was different in other ways. "At this point, I started to realize that I was gay," he said. He also liked girls and was friends with them, but when he asked them out, they weren't interested, because "You don't date the wounded gazelle." He discovered that gay boys were more amendable. "I had some sexual experiences with boys and I thought this is great because I don't have to be someone I'm not, with them," he said. "That's why I gravitated towards being gay." One day, he wheeled past the gym and took a good look at the male gymnasts. "All the guys in there were really cute," he said. "They were specimens."

For years, Rik had been doing handstands and messing around on the monkey bars and developed an interest in gymnastics. He told one of his teachers, who knew him from his neighborhood, that he wanted to join a gymnastics class. He said, "I wheeled up to her and said, 'I'd like to try that,'" and she replied, "'Ok, that's a good idea, Rik.' The other teacher looked at her like, 'What the fuck, lady?' But she was like, 'I know what this kid can do.'"

His mother wanted him mainstreamed in all classes to get a diploma. Thus began a Kafkaesque journey to get him approved for gymnastics, which he said that some administrators supported, including the coach who taught the gym class, and some did not, including the principal. He encountered bureaucratic barriers along the way, but a friend who observed him doing handstands on desks encouraged him to keep trying. He jumped that last hurdle when the coach, in an argument with another administrator, brandished a signed note from Rik's mother and said, "This is why I'm doing this, because his mother signed the same release as every one of your other students, and he has the same right as any other student to have this opportunity."

Rik was good enough to compete as an NCAA All-American seven-time champion, placing on pommel horse, parallel bars and still rings. But when the principal announced his successes over the intercom, he was not thrilled. "The very principal who didn't want me to take the class, now wanted to celebrate my achievement," said Rik. "I was like, fuck you."

When Rik was still a kid, his mother remarried and his new stepfather adopted him, which is how he got the last name Daniels. (His original name was Henning.) His stepfather did the necessary paperwork to make him eligible for benefits as a "disabled adult child," which means that he continued to receive disability payments after his stepfather died.

Rik went to college, where he continued to compete in gymnastics, but he failed because he said he was more interested in smoking weed than going to class. "I would get up at 10 in the morning and do bong hits and watch Rosie O' Donnell," he said. He had a boyfriend at that time and the relationship went on for more than 10 years, but it ended when Rik got a job and got off disability at age 29.

At that time, Rik was into skiing and he was doing snowboard jumps with a monoski. One day, he said, the executive director of Rise, an organization that provides services to families and children, rode the ski lift with him and asked why he wasn't working. She offered him a job that paid $20,000 a year with benefits and he accepted. "I thought, this is what changing your life looks like," he said.

He said it wasn't an easy decision, giving up his disability benefits "to put yourself at the mercy of corporate America," but he's still working nearly 30 years later. He has had different jobs since then, including being a bank teller and working at a Wegmans grocery store and at the time of the interview he was the receptionist for the Tompkins

County Department of Social Services. He described himself as the "ringleader of the lobby circus."

He continued to adapt. He started with sitting up when he was a baby, which evolved into gymnastics, and then into the working world, where he figured out how to move gracefully, whether it was behind the bank teller window or while loading and unloading himself into and out of his car, which required manhandling his wheelchair as well as himself. He considered these actions mundane, but strangers noticed the unusual grace with which he performed these ordinary tasks.

"Sometimes when I get out of my car, people come up to me and say, 'I saw you get out of your car, it's amazing,'" he said. He didn't like this attention at first. "It's fucking ridiculous," he said, "I just got out of my car." He said a friend noticed his dismissive attitude towards these strangers and told him, "You're potentially robbing them of the inspiration you're giving them. You drive and you work and you engage in all of this shit. It might not be that amazing because you expect yourself to do it, but it is amazing to people."

His friend referred to his movements behind the teller line as being like a dance, and his gracefulness in getting into and out of his car with his wheelchair was also like a performance, and that's why non-disabled people were responding to it. "It made me realize that we all take things for granted," he said. "Disabled people can take our lives for granted, too."

He realized that his public life had become a performance, whether he intended it to or not. "As a performance, you are not only the performer, you are the art," he said. "I know that God created me unique for a purpose."

He decided to become an acrobat once again and a dancer. He joined a succession of circuses, including Circus Culture, CirqOvation and Omnium Circus. The circus had appealed to him since he was a kid. He would watch old black-and-white movies on TV about circuses and sideshows, featuring disabled people like himself.

"There were sometimes the freak shows," he said. "I was very much aware that those were the only opportunities for people. I saw circus not as an exploitation but as a harbor or community for people with disabilities. Even though I didn't see myself as disabled, I knew the world saw me as such, and I saw myself as one of those people. If I lived in those days, I'd rather be in the circus than live in the attic. I always thought, that could be me. I could do that. That could've been me, but maybe in a different time or place."

He doesn't identify with the more masochistic acts in sideshow, like Shorty the Half-man throwing himself onto broken glass. "I would never choose to pierce my nose and swing a bowling ball from it or whatever the fuck these other people are doing," he explained. But he started performing in burlesque, which he compared to sideshow because it's frowned upon by some people as exploitative. But the objectification doesn't bother him. "I think that people with disability have as much right as anybody else to objectify themselves," he said. When asked about exploitation, he echoed the comments of sideshow naturals who refer to the traditional job market as exploitation. "We all exploit ourselves," he said. "Any talent is an exploit."

He said his religious faith also factors into his philosophy as a performer and a human being. He began to cry as he explained that his late mother, Pastor Donna M. Daniels, told him that God created him as unique and beautiful for a purpose and "loves him just the way he is." "I often think of my deformity as a blessing," said Rik. "I wouldn't be performing with Omnium Circus if I wasn't in a wheelchair. I've been blessed to have a lot of opportunities because I'm so unique. I have a unique physique."

Chapter 30

Cottonmouth Clown

"Bite Size"
- Lizz Porter's tattoo

TV actress and Canadian clown Lizz Porter, who has appeared in shows like *Star Trek: Discovery* and *What We Do in the Shadows*, was taking her career to the next level. At age 33, the mother of four decided to become a sideshow performer.

"I want something daring and crazy: blockhead!" said Lizz, who wears a nose ring, earrings and glasses. Porter, who's from the Toronto area, is natural born with dwarfism, standing at three feet and nine inches. "I'm height limited, or bite size, I like to say," said Lizz, who has the words "bite size" tattooed on her knuckles, one letter per knuckle.

But she knew that being natural born wasn't enough to be a sideshow performer on its own. She had to have skills. She decided to become a human blockhead. She was psyching herself to shove a nail up her nose. "I haven't really tried yet," said Lizz in a Zoom interview in March 2025. "I'm really nervous about shoving a foreign object up my nose. But when I've got the human blockhead down pat, I'm going to jazz that up so much, it's going to be amazing." After she learns how to hammer nails up her nasal cavity, she wants to train with fire, and then she wants to do a "painless princess" act where customers staple money to her body.

She has years of theatrical experience, much of it as a recurring actor on *Star Trek: Discovery*, where she played different roles including aliens called Ckaptir, which have tentacles sprouting from their heads. Lizz traveling widely for this role, visiting spaceships and different planets across several seasons. "That was one of my various joys," she said.

"The people I worked with were great. It was a real great experience." But eventually, the show went off the air. She also appeared in a comic horror show called *Chucky*, about the infamous killer doll.

Lizz said she was married with two step-kids and two biological children, though she was going through a separation. She said that both of her biological children were little people, like herself, even though their father was not. Her teenage son would accompany her to the *Chucky* set, and they hired him to be an actor for the show.

All the while, she felt a gravitational pull away from the mainstream media, and towards the bizarre world of sideshow. "I'm a freaky person to begin with and I like the freaky dark stuff," she explained. "It's my personality. To be involved with [sideshow,] it's a neat feeling and an accomplishment for myself. It's showing people what I have to offer to entertain them and also to have fun."

Lizz explained how she saw a performance by Ringling Brothers and Barnum & Bailey Circus within the last three years and was enthralled by the acrobatics. "I had my butt on the edge of the seat the whole time," she said, puffing on a cigarette. Then, she ran into a colleague who cast her in the Something Strange Sideshow Festival in Toronto in January 2025. She loved the variety and the change. "I'm open to doing anything and everything that I can get my hands on to. I'm very optimistic to try new things and I'm pretty brave," she said.

Why sideshow? "It's not just for the pay; I do it for the exposure," she said. It's hard to get noticed in show business. She immediately realized that being a sideshow natural provides her with something every actress craves: "automatic attention." She said that she also gets exposure to different people in the business, who have further projects in the future, so the contacts she meets from the sideshow business set her up for additional gigs. She has established a reputation as a "rambunctious crazy little thing that can do more than they think and beyond."

Not everyone sees sideshow in such a positive light. She said that most little people don't like it. "That's what I don't understand with the majority of little people; they think it's exploiting people," she said, "but it's showing others what you're good at."

I mentioned that one of the naturals I interviewed, Lil Miss Firefly, is a stripper as well as a sideshow performer. Lizz said she respects Lil Miss Firefly and other little people who want to be strippers, so long as they're enjoying it and making money.

Lizz, who has played various types of elves including a Christmas elf, a "sweet" elf and a "punky freak" elf, said that she's caught flak from other little people for her career choices.

"A majority of them don't agree with half of the stuff I do for a living," she said. "They think I'm exploiting myself, that I shouldn't be doing that kind of job, that I should be sitting down at a computer." She said she's been criticized for presenting little people as a "laughing icon." But she doesn't agree with this negative perception.

"Do it, if you enjoy it," she said, adding that her status as a natural born brings a certain edge to her act. She said that being short can be advantageous on stage. "It adds more tension to my act."

Lizz had previously gone by the stage name Cotterly Fairy, an apparent nod to a mischievous series of hoax photos from the early 1900s known as the Cottingley Fairies, which fooled even the likes of Sir Arthur Conan Doyle into believing they were real.

But Lizz shrugged off the name, having redubbed herself with a new one more befitting of her Insane Clown Posse lifestyle. Lizz referred to herself as a "juggalette," a female juggalo. She said that she had been performing as a cannabis Christmas clown over the holidays, wearing a Santa hat and face paint, when her new name occurred to her.

"Cottonmouth Clown," she said, "because I like to smoke a lot of marijuana and I love clowns."

Chapter 31

Florida Man

"Al and Jeanie had heard from their friend, 'The Crocodile Man,' that the place to go during the off-season was Gibsonton, a town on the Gulf of Mexico, twenty miles south of Tampa."
- *Lobster Boy*, by Fred Rosen

"We never used the word freak. We used the word *attraction*."
- Chris Christ, ex-owner of World of Wonders

Gibsonton is an inconspicuous Florida town carved from the swamps along the Alafia River and Hillsborough Bay, with a two-lane highway running through it. It used to be known as the town where all the sideshow freaks lived, but now it's the town where they *used* to live.

Gibsonton, colloquially known as Gibtown, is just south of Tampa, past the smokestacks and the phosphate mines. If you're driving through Gibsonton on Highway 41 and you blink or glance at your phone, you might miss it. I was surprised to learn that thousands of people live in this town, because it doesn't look like much from the main road. There's the Showtown bar where Grady Stiles Jr., the Lobster Boy, used to drink, a nearby museum about the town's sideshow past, and a monument of sideshow giant Al Tomaini's boot. While all this is very interesting, it is a mere shadow of the town's carnival and sideshow past, as a winter home for sideshow lifers, most especially the naturals.

NATURAL BORN!

Anybody who's been to Gibtown says there's nothing there. This refrain is repeated by people who've just driven through it and by people who've lived there much of their lives, like Chris Christ. But what they're really saying is that its glory days as a sideshow town, where performers breathed fire outside their trailers and grazed circus animals on their front yards, have receded into the past.

"We live in a different society now," said Chris Christ, as we sat down to lunch at the Apollo Beach Diner, a few miles south of Gibtown. "We live in a different world."

Chris had once owned World of Wonders, but now, even World of Wonders had skipped town. The current owner of the sideshow, Tommy Breen, moved to South Carolina just that winter. (Tommy assured me, a few days later, that World of Wonders had not actually moved. "It's been nice here," he said in an email from his new home in South Carolina, "but I'm looking forward to getting back to Gibtown.")

Chris, who was 76 at the time of this interview in April 2024, is one of the last remaining vestiges of sideshow life in the legendary town of Gibsonton, a man who had survived and thrived as a vernacular artist, roving across North America with a vagabond business that lived off the land, recruiting naturals in whatever corner of the country he could find them. He retired from the sideshow business a few years ago; he couldn't remember exactly when. He was an institution in the sideshow scene, as one of the previous owners of World of Wonders, an ex-partner of the deceased Ward Hall, the King of the Sideshows. A *New York Times* profile of Hall in 2006 described Chris as his "disheveled, mutton-chopped, chain-smoking business partner." Chris is a mentor to Tommy Breen, to whom he sold the show years ago, and a recruiter and employer of dozens of naturals, from Aaron "Short E. Dangerously" Wollin, the half-man, to the late Pete Terhurne, a little person better known as Poobah, the fire-eating dwarf. But times had changed. Chris told me, in his gravelly phone voice the night before our meeting, that kids these days don't see much point in going to a sideshow because they can Google "Chinese two-headed girl" on their phone and instantly conjure images.

When we met in person the next day, I named several of the newer naturals in the current sideshow scene, but Chris had never heard of them. The 21st-century freak show world had passed him by. "I would say, in general, I miss it every day, but I miss what it was, not what it is," he said through his grey beard. "We can't operate like we used to. Now everything is electronic. It changes the demographics of your clientele."

For much of his career, he toured the country in a multi-truck circus or sideshow convoy with all the infrastructure of a traveling show, including the World of Wonders tent, which is smaller than a circus big top but still sprawling at 60 feet by 95 feet. "In the tent business, we call that a handkerchief," he explained. He would sell tickets for cash. The business of a 20th-century sideshow ran on crumpled dollar bills. But he said that a modern sideshow like Hellzapoppin can tour nightclubs and other venues, without as much infrastructure, and sell tickets online. The modern sideshow is streamlined and the finances are electronic.

Chris didn't say whether cash or nightclubs were better than Ticketmaster or tents. He just said that sideshow is different now and will continue to evolve. "I think it will always exist in some altered form," he said, adding that Breen, the new owner, had adapted to the demands of running a sideshow in 21st-century America. As an example, when I saw World of Wonders on Long Island, N.Y., in the summer of 2023, Breen was paid by the fair to be there, and my $5 admission to the fair included free access to his sideshow. This is different from the old days, when locals visiting the fair paid admission specifically to see World of Wonders. The tiny sideshow industry had become less of a cash-in-hand hustle and more of a consolidated institution. "There's probably five major carnivals that cover the top fifty fairs in the continent," said Chris Christ. "We're in the big box business. They're getting like Walmart."

Gibtown is beat-up old Florida, which means it's authentic and not too touristy. Showtown Bar & Grill is still there, but it's more of a biker bar (with 75-cent wings on Wednesday) than a watering hole for sideshow naturals like the notorious Grady Stiles Jr. There's a paddleboard rental place on Bull Frog Creek, which runs through the middle of the town. Bait shops, ubiquitous in this watery part of the world, appear along the road. The Showmen's Museum is in Riverview, a town on the north side of the Alafia River, showcasing the area's sideshow history.

Gibtown served for many years as a winter off-season bedroom community for multiple sideshow naturals, developing a reputation as a town inhabited by carnie freaks living in trailer parks with elephants grazing on their lawns. These naturals included Al and Jeanie Tomaini, the giant (8-foot-4) and the half-girl (2-foot-6) who once inhabited the south side of the river, the Gibtown side, where they built the Giant's Fish Camp back in the 1940s. The camp was a complex of buildings including a diner and cabins for paying guests. Other sideshow naturals poured into Gibtown, too, making the place famous as a sideshow wintering spot. But the Giant's Fish Camp is gone now from the banks of the Alafia.

I was born in St. Petersburg, less than 20 miles away across Tampa Bay, and I grew up north of Clearwater Beach, along the Gulf of Mexico. In coming to Gibsonton to meet with Chris Christ, I felt once again that I had gone full circle, that my sideshow adventure had taken me, quite literally, back to where I came from. I was the prodigal Florida man.

St. Pete is a tourist mecca, but Gibtown represented the old Florida, chopped out of the jungle along the riverbank by people who then blazed a road and built a bridge and then a town. But famous residents like the Tomainis were eventually overshadowed by the infamous Grady Stiles Jr., an abusive alcoholic born with ectrodactyly – so-called lobster claws for hands and feet - who was shot to death by a hit man hired by his wife.

Chris is a regular at the Apollo Beach Diner. I lured him out of his lair with an offer to buy him lunch. Chris confirmed that Tommy Breen had been living in a trailer on his property for years, but he finally pulled stakes and drove off in the fall of 2023. He said that Tommy Breen's dad had died and he inherited his house in South Carolina. He moved there with his pet pig and he took World of Wonders with him. The sideshow had been headquartered in Gibtown for much of its 70-plus years in existence.

He said that he spent his career bringing something exotic to rural towns, and, in this way, he saw many corners of America. But it was a fleeting view. "I saw half the world through the windshield," he said. "It all looks alike, too, when you're driving one of those big trucks."

I told him that the sideshow was like an artistic economic organism, living off the land as it traveled from town to town. It was a transient lifestyle, he said, never staying in any location long enough to establish anything. "It was an avocation, not a location," he said.

I told Chris that I had been in contact with Grady Stiles Jr.'s son, Grady Stiles III, who had moved to Tampa at some point after the death of his father in the 1990s. I bought a signed photo from him, where Grady peered at the camera through his splayed claws, but my attempts to interview him fell apart.

"I've known him since he was a little boy," said Chris. He said that Grady III did a cameo show for World of Wonders a few years back, and it had to do with the short-lived AMC series, *Freakshow*.

His father Grady Stiles Jr. had four kids (according to the Showmen's Museum), including two with ectrodactyly like himself: Grady III and his sister Cathy. Chris remembered her as a newborn infant coming home from the hospital. Fred Rosen's true crime book *Lobster Boy* says that Cathy and Grady III did the sideshow circuit with their father. They sold pitch cards depicting the three of them as the lobster family. But Chris said the only time she did the show was when her father was too drunk to do it.

"Her father was a terribly abusive guy," said Chris over his chopped steak. "I could get along with him great, but I knew when to get away from him. He was a guy, if you wanted trouble, you added alcohol. If he wasn't drinking, he was ok."

Chris estimated that he's worked with 35 to 40 naturals in his career, including the legendary Pete "Poobah" Terhurne, the little person who toured with World of Wonders for 50 years. Chris built a "mother-in-law"-style efficiency apartment as an addition to his house so Poobah could live there; eventually Pete moved into a long-term-care facility, where he spent his final days.

Chris said his favorite natural was Emmett Blackwelder, the Turtle Man, a Black man from North Carolina whose limbs ended as stubs at the knees and elbows. "I would say he was the best," said Chris. "You can be their friend, but you also have to be their boss. He was my friend. He drove in my truck." In the circus, riding shotgun with the boss was considered a privilege. This anecdote reminded me of traveling in the Big Apple Circus truck convoy. It mattered who you rolled with. You didn't want to ride shotgun with an asshole.

He said the naturals shared a theatrical philosophy about their sideshow personas. "They had the attitude that they were actors in a play. I never had anyone who was bitter." But that was a long time ago. "Most of them are dead," said Chris.

The only sideshow people who still remained in Gibtown, as far as I could tell, were the reclusive Cathy, the daughter of Grady Stiles Jr. and possibly the only natural left in town, and also Chris Christ himself.

Chris joined the sideshow business in 1964, and was also in the circus for many years, retiring at a forgotten date in the gray past. He was writing a book about his adventures, which included an earthquake, a hurricane and many tornados. He used to do a knife-throwing act, he was a sword swallower, and he toured with trained chimpanzees. He was brimming with stories from his long years on the road with eccentrics and absurdities. I was there to talk to him about naturals, specifically.

Chris wasn't a natural, but he had recruited dozens of them during his long career and trained them to perform, including some of the people I'd met. I asked him what it was like to be a freak finder. "We never used the word freak," said Chris. "We used the word attraction." He said they didn't call them naturals. "I've heard the word 'naturals' used, but usually from the academic types," he said.

World of Wonders used to tour fairs, just as it does today. But he said that things were completely different back in the old days, when bookers for sideshows would sometimes require, in writing, that naturals *must* appear in the sideshow. For example, Chris said that a booker in Dallas once provided him with a written contract to sign, requiring a set minimum number of naturals. "The contract said you had to have four freaks," said Chris. He was presented with another contract in Columbus, Ohio, that required him to have three naturals on the billing. But times have changed, and the situation has reversed. "And now, if you would book one today, the first question out of their mouth is: 'You don't have any freaks, do you?'"

I asked him about the mainstream reputation of sideshows, that they allegedly exploit disabled people. He dismissed the controversy as inaccurate and misguided because it vilifies a voluntary profession for people with fewer options. "People made this a livelihood for years," he said, referring to sideshow naturals. "They bought their own houses. They weren't supported by the government. They were doing what they wanted to do. Nobody forced them to be there."

He said that he used his in-house naturals as recruiters for new naturals. He used a little person performer as a "qualifier" to approach disabled audience members. When the sideshow came to town and they spotted a natural in the audience, the qualifier would pull the local aside to ask if they wanted to join the sideshow. "You would tell right away if they were interested," said Chris, "but they wouldn't be offended that way."

Chris had many stories about the naturals of his sideshow past. His former partner, Ward Hall, had written a book about them called *My Very Unusual Friends*. The book was hard to find, but Chris said he would send me one. The diner was closing and the people were cleaning up. Chris said there wasn't much else to see. The Showmen's Museum was only open on weekends, and it was a Thursday.

As we were leaving the diner and heading back to the parking lot, I asked what he thought sideshows would be like in the future, since he didn't seem to think they would go extinct. "It'll never be like it was in my prime," he said. "It will just be different, and I'm not exactly sure what that will be."

I told him I would go and visit the giant's boot, since that was all that was left. Chris told me where it was. I had driven right past it on my way into town, near the sign that says, "Welcome to Gibsonton." But he didn't talk it up. He implied that the monument would be underwhelming. In fact, he said I would be "totally disappointed."

That was the last thing he told me. And the first thing he told me, over the phone the night before, was that if I was coming to Gibtown to write about a book about sideshow attractions, I was "30 to 40 years too late."

I drove north, back through Gibsonton, past the gas stations, the paddleboard rental shop, the taco stand, the smoke shops, the car dealerships, the Showtown Bar & Grill, and past the monument of the giant's boot and back over the bridge over the Alafia River and out of town, in order to execute a U-turn in Riverview and cruise back south past the "Welcome to Gibsonton" sign and past the boot again to pull over at a collection of bungalows called the East Bay Motel. Giant's Fish Camp was in the fenced area between the motel and the bridge.

Tommy Breen had told me there used to be a cabin, behind the fence, behind the sculpture of the boot, but it was burned down by meth heads in November 2022. The monument of the boot was still there, mounted on a stone pedestal etched with the words: Al & Jeanie Tomaini Gibsonton Civic Leaders. Back in 2022 the *Tampa Bay Times* published a dramatic photo, courtesy of Hillsborough County Fire Rescue, of firefighters responding to the blaze, which engulfed the cottage that stood behind a black metal fence, which stood behind the stone pedestal with the sculpture of a black boot, wreathed by the inferno as the giant's cabin burned.

The truth is, Gibtown had become emptier without its sideshow naturals, and now even the last shack of the Giant's Fish Camp was gone to ashes. But the boot sculpture was still there.

I walked a few feet back up the highway and there it was, a giant-sized boot, an enlarged replica of the already enormous boot of American Giant Al Tomaini, mounted on a stone pedestal the height of a man, an opaque black form against the blazing sun.

Additional Photos

Scan the QR code to view additional images of the performers profiled in this book.

Photo Credits

Chapter 1: Shorty the Half-Man

Shorty Photo: Aaron "Shorty" Wollin the Half-man doing his signature one-armed handstand while touring with Hellzapoppin in Clifton, N.J., 2021 (© Aaron Smith).

Chapter 2: The Lobster Girl

Kim Kelly Photo: Kim Kelly, Greta the Lobster Girl, in Rittenhouse Square in her hometown of Philadelphia, 2021 (© Aaron Smith).

Mütter Photo 1: Sign for Mütter Museum, a medical mausoleum in Philadelphia, 2021 (© Aaron Smith).

Mütter Photo 2: Mütter Museum sign during COVID pandemic, Philadelphia, 2021 (© Aaron Smith).

Chapter 3: The Seal Boy

Mat Fraser Photo 1: Mat Fraser, the Seal Boy, with drum set at Coney Island Circus Sideshow (© Laure Leber).

Mat Fraser Photo 2: Mat Fraser (center, sitting) in Coney Island, with cast at Sideshows by the Seashore (The other people are Nasty Canasta with the snake, Donny Vomit and Heather Holliday.) (© Laure Leber).

Chapter 6: Black Scorpion

Nik Sin Black Scorpion Photo: Nik Sin, little person second from left, and Black Scorpion, right with ectrodactyly, with cast at Coney Island USA (FYI: The other people in the photo are Serpentina, Insectavora, Heather Holliday, Donny Vomit and outside talker Scott Baker.) (© Laure Leber).

Black Scorpion Photo: Black Scorpion's ectrodactyly "claws," pictured at Coney Island USA (© Laure Leber).

Chapter 7: The Bendable Girl

Camille Zamboni Photo: Camille Zamboni, contortionist foot archer touring with Hellzapoppin in Atlantic City, N.J., 2022 (© Aaron Smith).

Chapter 9: Tyler West

Tyler West Photo: Tyler West performing (© Jim R Moore).

Chapter 10: Coney Island

Wonder Wheel Photo: Wonder Wheel, an icon of Coney Island, NY, looms over the sideshow (© Aaron Smith).

Adam Rinn Coney Photo: From left, Adam Rinn with Coney Island cast members Alaska the Lost Boy, La Reine the Thrill, Niki B. the Talking Doll, Obsidian Absurd, Kita St Cyr, and Cyclone Jack Sullivan (© Laure Leber).

Chapter 11: Freak Finder

Jellyboy Photo: Jellyboy at Coney Island USA ~ Sideshows by the Seashore (© Jim R Moore).

Chapter 12: The Patchwork Girl

Nati Amos Photo 1: Nati Amos, fire dancer, at Union Square subway station, NYC. 2022 (© Aaron Smith).

Chapter 13: The Mayor of Coney Island

Zigun Photo: Dick Zigun, co-founder and former artistic director of Coney Island USA (© Laure Leber).

Chapter 14: Woman with a Beard

Miller Zigun Photo: Prof. Jennifer Miller of Pratt Insitute, AKA Woman with a Beard, with her former boss Dick Zigun, co-founder of Coney Island USA (© Jim Moore).

Chapter 17: Sarah the Bird Girl

Sarah Jellyboy Photo: Sarah Houbolt the Bird Girl with Jellyboy at the Freak Bar, Coney Island USA, 2019 (© Jim Moore).

Chapter 18: Jackie the Human Tripod

Jackie Molen Photo: Jackie Molen, the Human Tripod, at Coney Island Circus Sideshow (© Laure Leber).

Chapter 19: Lil Miss Firefly

Lil Miss Firefly Photo: Crystal Lockhart, AKA Lil Miss Firefly, on stairs leading to Coney Island Museum (© Laure Leber).

Chapter 20: World of Wonders

World of Wonders Photo: World of Wonders, the last traveling tented sideshow in America, at Long Island Fun Fest, New York, 2023 (© Aaron Smith).

Tommy Breen Photo: Tommy Breen, sword swallower and sole proprietor of World of Wonders, eating fire at Long Island Fun Fest, New York, 2023 (© Aaron Smith).

Chapter 22: Xander Lovecraft

Xander Photo 1: Xander Lovecraft on the bally platform with his Coney Island crew outside Sideshows by the Seashore, 2023 (© Aaron Smith).

Xander Cat Photo: Xander Lovecraft with Sideshow Cat at Freak Bar, Coney Island Circus Sideshow, 2023 (© Aaron Smith).

Chapter 23: John T. Rex

John T. Rex Photo: John Husted, AKA John T. Rex and Satan John, selfie, 2025 (© John Husted).

Chapter 26: Shorty's Last Tour

Shorty Photo 2: Aaron "Shorty" Wollin performing a handstand during his last tour with Hellzapoppin at Starland Ballroom in Sayreville, N.J. 2023 (© Aaron Smith).

Chapter 27: Nik Sin

Nik Sin Photo: Nik Sin, little person escape artist, wrestler and soldier of the Kiss Army, at Coney Island USA (© Laure Leber).

Chapter 28: Nati Returns to Coney

Nati Amos Photo 2: Nati Amos after surviving her bed of nails sledge hammer act at Sideshow Hootenanny, Coney Island Circus Sideshow, 2024 (© Aaron Smith).

Chapter 29: Rik Daniels and the Omnium Circus

Rik Daniels Photo: Acrobat and dancer Rik Daniels onstage at Omnium Circus, Queens Theatre, NY. 2024 (© Jim Moore).

Chapter 31: Florida Man

Aaron Showtown Photo: Author Aaron Smith in Gibsonton, Florida, selfie outside Showtown Bar & Grill, 2024 (© Aaron Smith).

Giant Boot Photo: Gibsonton boot sculpture at site of Giant's Camp, dedicated to Al & Jeanie Tomaini, 2024. The last bungalow of Tomainis' camp stood behind this sculpture until 2022 when it burned down (© Aaron Smith).

Bibliography

999 Eyes Freakshow website, https://www.999eyes.com/

Alaska the Lost Boy. Instagram account, https://www.instagram.com/alaskathelostboy/

American Horror Story: Freak Show, Season 4, broadcast on FX from 2024 to 2025, produced by 20th Century Fox Television, https://www.fxnetworks.com/shows/american-horror-story/ahs-freak-show

American Horror Story: Freak Show, Season 4, Internet Movie Data Base, https://www.imdb.com/title/tt1844624/episodes/?season=4&ref_=tt_eps_sn_4

America's Got Talent YouTube video of Alan Silva,
   https://www.youtube.com/watch?v=d7hMP0i0BdU

Amos, Nati. TEDx speaker in Jersey City in 2014, https://www.ted.com/tedx/events/12937

Arndt, Tobias, Johnson, Martin, and Stokes, Raymond. *The Thalidomide Catastrophe: How it happened, who was responsible and why the search for justice continues after more than six decades*, Onwards and Upwards, 2018.

Aptowicz, Cristin O'Keefe. *Dr. Mütter's Marvels*, Penguin Random House, 2015.

Barnum, Phineas Taylor. *The Life of P.T. Barnum*, Nabu public domain reprint, Redfield, 1855.

Barnum, Phineas Taylor. *The Art of Money-Getting*, Ixia Press, 2019.

Blacha, Tommy and Small, Brendon. creators of Metalocalypse, aired on Adult Swim, 2006 to 2012, https://www.adultswim.com/videos/metalocalypse

Black Sabbath. "The Wizard," from the 1970 album *Black Sabbath*.

Blackwelder, Emmet. Sideshow World profile, https://www.sideshow-world.com/73-Art-G1/SS-B-Gallery/Turtle/Man.html

Bogdan, Robert. *Freak Show*, The University of Chicago Press, 1988.

Bone, Howard. *Side Show: My Life with Geeks, Freaks and Vagabonds in the Carny Trade*, Sun Dog Press, 2001.

Booth, Paul. Art website, https://www.paulboothart.com/fine-art

Bradbury, Ray. *The Illustrated Man*, Doubleday & Co., 1951.

Brantley, Ben. "A Beauty and a Beast, but This One's for Adults," *New York Times*, 17 March 2014, https://www.nytimes.com/2014/03/18/theater/julie-atlas-muz-and-mat-fraser-reinvent-a-fabled-couple.html

Bricker, Jen. *Everything is Possible: Finding the Faith and Courage to Follow Your Dreams*, Baker Books, 2016.

Brooklyn Museum, cat mummy, https://www.brooklynmuseum.org/opencollection/objects/4197

Broomfield, Eric. *Memoirs of a Coney Island Clown ~ Jellyboy's Sideshow Saga*, Outside Talker Press, 2024, https://outsidetalkerpress.bigcartel.com/product/memoirs-of-a-coney-island-clown-jellyboy-s-sideshow-saga

Brott, Jason. Lower Case J sizzle roll, https://www.youtube.com/watch?v=VN3ddQ-YPJc

Browning, Tod, director of *Freaks*, 1932, https://www.imdb.com/title/tt0022913/

Bunker, Chang & Eng. Mütter Museum, Death-Cast, https://muttermuseum.org/stories/featured_objects/death-cast-chang-eng-bunker

Calder, Rich. "Coney Island 'Mayor' Dick Zigun Ousted, succeeded by sword swallower," 1 Jan. 2022, *New York Post,* https://nypost.com/2022/01/01/coney-island-mayor-dick-zigun-ousted-succeeded-by-sword-swallower/

Carson, Annette. *Richard III: The Maligned King*, first published in 2008 by the History Press, republished in 2013 following Richard III's exhumation.

Children's Hospital of Philadelphia, "What is Morquio syndrome?" https://www.chop.edu/conditions-diseases/morquio-syndrome

Chinese Kung-Fu, Wu-Su Association website, https://kungfuwusu.com/

Clark, Laura. "The 61 Tattoos of Ötzi, the 5,300-Year-Old 'Iceman,'" *Smithsonian Magazine*, 27 Jan. 2015, https://www.smithsonianmag.com/smart-news/61-tattoos-otzi-5300-year-old-iceman-180954035/

Cleveland Clinic on arthrogryposis, https://my.clevelandclinic.org/health/diseases/23190-arthrogryposis

Coney Island Circus Sideshow website, https://www.coneyisland.com/coneyislandcircussideshow

Coney Island USA press release, "Announcing Adam Rinn, aka Adam Realman as Coney Island USA's new Artistic Director!" 28 Dec. 2021, https://www.coneyisland.com/news/blog-post-title-three-5jakb

Correll, DeeDee. "She's at home in the circus sideshow," *Los Angeles Times*, 7 Sept. 2009, https://www.latimes.com/archives/la-xpm-2009-sep-07-na-freak-show7-story.html

Dakota the Bearded Lady, "My Beard Makes Me Feel Pretty," iWonder TV interview in Los Angeles, 2021, https://www.youtube.com/watch?v=BUorcOPLU5U

Dakota the Bearded Lady. Instagram account, https://www.instagram.com/dakota_t2he_bearded_lady/p/CTR_S3qlpYn/

Dangerously, Short E. Website, https://www.shortedangerously.com/

Daniels, Rik. Website, rikdanielsperformer.com

de Freytas-Tamura, Kimiko, "Reign of Coney Island's 'Mayor' Ends in a Sideshow by the Sea," *New York Times*, 5 Jan. 2022, https://www.nytimes.com/2022/01/05/nyregion/dick-zigun-coney-island-boardwalk.html

Delight, Miss Cherry. Website, https://www.misscherrydelight.com/

Denson, Charles. *Coney Island Lost and Found*, Ten Speed Press, 2002.

Drimmer, Frederick. *Very Special People: The Struggles, Loves and Triumphs of Human Oddities*, Citadel Press Book published by Carol Publishing Group, 1976 and 1991.

Dunn, Katherine. *Geek Love*, Warner Books, 1990.

Ehrlich, Brenna. "Sideshow Performer Who Was Never Supposed to Live Still Defies All Odds," Vice Media, 3 April 2016, https://www.vice.com/en/article/sideshow-performer-who-was-never-supposed-to-live-still-defies-all-odds/

Fraser, Mat, presenter of Cripfest, produced by the British Council, hosted by Brooklyn Academy of Music Fisher 25 July 2015, https://cripfest.splashthat.com/

Fraser, Mat. *Happy Birthday Thalidomide*, Channel 4 documentary, 2004, https://www.youtube.com/watch?v=Uv39wavt-ME

Freakshow, AMC, 2013-2014, https://www.amcplus.com/shows/freakshow/episodes--1060070

Fuller, Lucian. Website, https://www.lucianfullershow.com/

Geetanjali, Jindal, co-author, *Indian Journal of Human Genetics*. NIH National Library of Medicine paper on ectrodactyly/split hand feet malformation, 2009, https://www.ncbi.nlm.nih.gov/pmc/articles/PMC2922631/

Genova, Alexandra. "Meet the Remarkable Man with Half a Body," *National Geographic*, 14 Sept. 2017, https://www.nationalgeographic.com/photography/article/meet-short-e-the-incredible-halfman

Genzlinger, Neil. "Ward Hall, Who Kept the Sideshow Going, Is Dead at 88," *New York Times*, 6 Sept. 2018, https://www.nytimes.com/2018/09/06/obituaries/ward-hall-dead.html

Gofundme page for Jason Brott, Bionic Kidney & Medical Expense Fundraise, https://www.gofundme.com/f/kidney-transplant-amp-major-medical-expenses

Graves, Bryce. Hellzapoppin website profile of The Govna, https://hellzapoppin.com/bryce-%22the-govna%22-graves

Grünenthal press release, "60 Years after the market withdrawal: Dr. Michael Wirtz apologizes to those affected on behalf of his family," 27 Sept. 2021, https://www.grunenthal.com/en/press-room/statements/wirtz-apologises-on-behalf-of-his-family

Guinness World Records description of first modern tongue bifurcation,
    https://www.guinnessworldrecords.com/world-records/652670-first-modern-tongue-bifurcation

Guinness World Records description of heaviest weight lifted and spun with pierced ears, https://www.guinnessworldrecords.com/world-records/116045-heaviest-weight-lifted-and-spun-with-pierced-ears

Guinness World Records profile of Space Cowboy Chayne Hultgren, https://www.guinnessworldrecords.com/news/2012/9/the-space-cowboy-chayne-hultgren-record-holder-profile-video-44570

Guinness World Records profile of "Zion Clark: The fastest man on two hands," https://www.guinnessworldrecords.com/records/hall-of-fame/zion-clark-the-fastest-man-on-two-hands

Guzzo, Paul. "Fire destroys cottage built by Al Tomaini, known as the Gibsonton Giant," 7 Nov. 2022, https://www.tampabay.com/life-culture/history/2022/11/07/fire-destroys-cottage-built-by-al-tomaini-known-gibsonton-giant/

Hall, David. "Down the Hatch: On the road with the last American carnival sideshow," *Harper's*, May 2022, https://harpers.org/archive/2022/05/down-the-hatch-on-the-road-with-the-last-american-carnival-sideshow/

Hartwick College of Oneonta, N.Y., website: https://www.hartwick.edu/

Hartzman, Marc. *American Sideshow: An Encyclopedia of History's Most Wondrous and Curiously Strange Performers,* Penguin Group, 2005.

Hickling, Alfred. "Richard III review – Mat Fraser proves a brilliant villain for Northern Broadsides," *The Guardian*, 11 May 2017, https://www.theguardian.com/stage/2017/may/11/richard-iii-hull-truck-theatre-review-mat-fraser-northern-broadsides

Hill, Walter. Director, *The Warriors*, 1979, Internet Movie Data Base, https://www.imdb.com/title/tt0080120/?ref_%3Dnv_sr_1

Hoh, Amanda. "Sarah Houbolt brings her circus act and advocacy for disabled arts to the Festival of Dangerous Ideas," ABC News of Sydney, Australia interview with Sarah Houbolt, 1 Sept. 2016, https://www.abc.net.au/news/2016-09-01/sarah-houbolt-proud-natural-born-freak-festival-dangerous-ideas/7804774

Houbolt, Sarah. Instagram account, https://www.instagram.com/sarahbirdgirl/

International Independent Showmen's Museum website, https://showmensmuseum.org/

John, Emma. "Finally, I'm going to stick the knife in," *The Guardian*, 7 Nov. 2005, https://www.theguardian.com/stage/2005/nov/07/theatre

Johns Hopkins Medicine medical explainer, "What is amniotic band syndrome?" https://www.hopkinsmedicine.org/health/conditions-and-diseases/amniotic-band-syndrome

Jordan, Otis, the Frog Boy. Sideshow World profile. https://www.sideshowworld.com/76-Blow/Otis/Jordan.html

Kelly, Kim. "Charlottesville: Witnessing the 'monstrous' attack," *Aljazeera*, 14 Aug. 2017, https://www.aljazeera.com/features/2017/8/14/charlottesville-witnessing-the-monstrous-attack

Kelly, Kim. "The Coney Island 'Freaks' and Me: The true tale of a bona fide, one-of-a-kind 'Lobster Girl,'" *Vox*, 30 Sept. 2019, https://www.vox.com/the-highlight/2019/9/23/20870620/carnival-disability-coney-island-sideshow-ectrodactyly

Kelly, Kim. "What *AHS: Freak Show* Got Right (And Wrong) About Ectrodactyly," *Jezebel*, 27 Jan. 2015, https://www.jezebel.com/what-ahs-freak-show-got-right-and-wrong-about-ectrod-1682114817

Kelly, Kim. "What Mat Fraser's Cripfest Taught Me About 'Crip Pride,'" *Jezebel*, 29 July 2015, https://www.jezebel.com/what-mat-fraser-s-cripfest-taught-me-about-crip-pride-1720630398

La Blanc, Bella and Lovecraft, Xander. Great Southern Exposure 2016, YouTube video, https://www.youtube.com/watch?v=gak0kuGSMNc

LeDuff, Charlie. "Step Right Up, Ladies and Gents, to See the End of an Oddity," *New York Times*, 13 Nov. 2006, https://www.nytimes.com/2006/11/13/us/13album.html

Leret, Xavier. Director, *Kung Fu Flid: Unarmed but Dangerous*, 2005, https://www.imdb.com/title/tt1289414/

Lil Miss Firefly. Instagram account, https://www.instagram.com/lilmissfirefly/

Longmore, Prof. Paul K. *Why I Burned My Book and Other Essays on Disability*, Temple University Press, 2003.

Mannix, Daniel P. *Memoirs of a Sword Swallower*, Re/Search Publications, 1996.

Maron, Marc. Podcast Peter Dinklage on WTF, episode 1299, 24 Jan. 2022, https://podcasts.apple.com/us/podcast/episode-1299-peter-dinklage/id329875043?i=1000548790352

Mayo Clinic staff description of Ehlers-Danlos syndrome, https://www.mayoclinic.org/diseases-conditions/ehlers-danlos-syndrome/symptoms-causes/syc-20362125

Micro Mania Midget Wrestling Tour website, https://www.micromaniatour.com/

Miike, Takashi. Director of *Ichi the Killer*, 2001 film, Internet Movie Data Base, https://www.imdb.com/title/tt0296042/

Mini Kiss, The Hottest Littlest Band in the World. Website, https://www.minikisses.com/

Mitchell, David. "Exploitations of Embodiment: *Born Freak* and the Academic Bally Plank," *Disability Studies Quarterly*, University of Illinois at Chicago, summer 2005, vol. 25, no. 3, https://dsq-sds.org/index.php/dsq/article/view/575/752&lang=en

Mitchell, Kirk. "Sideshow in spotlight at Colorado State Fair," *Denver Post*, 28 Aug. 2009, https://www.denverpost.com/2009/08/28/sideshow-in-spotlight-at-colorado-state-fair/

Molen, Jackie. Jackie the Human Tripod YouTube video, performance at Coney Island Circus Sideshow, 2009,
   https://www.youtube.com/watch?v=HKvVB9Se7AQ&t=11s

Molen, Jackie. Sideshow World interview, 2007, https://www.sideshowworld.com/9-ms-pi/interview-JackieF.html

Moore, Jim R. Vaudevisuals interview with Sarah the Bird Girl at Coney Island USA, 5 Aug. 2019, https://vaudevisuals.com/vaudevisuals-interview-with-sarah-the-bird-girl-at-coney-island-usa/

Murphy, Ryan. *American Horror Story* director YouTube channel interview with Mat Fraser, 2015, https://shorturl.at/YVshx

Muredda, Angelo. "One of Us: Tod Browning's *Freaks*, Disability Culture, and the Criterion for Inclusion," 8 Oct. 8, 2023,
   https://disabilityvisibilityproject.com/2023/10/08/one-of-us-tod-brownings-freaks-disability-culture-and-the-criterion-for-inclusion/

Museum of the Weird, Austin, Texas, website, https://www.museumoftheweird.com/

National Geographic video interview with the Lizardman, https://www.youtube.com/watch?v=toAzd1Fps2c

National Library of Medicine definition of ectrodactyly, https://www.ncbi.nlm.nih.gov/medgen/78566

National Library of Medicine description of Thrombocytopenia Absent Radius Syndrome, 2009, https://www.ncbi.nlm.nih.gov/sites/books/NBK23758/

Ohler, Norman. *Blitzed: Drugs in the Third Reich*, republished by Mariner Books, 2018.

Omnium Circus. Website, https://omniumcircus.org/

Pitts, Mike. *Digging for Richard III: The Search for the Lost King*, published by Thames & Hudson, 2014.

Plath, Sylvia. *The Collected Poems*, edited by Ted Hughes, HarperCollins, 1981.

Pretty Things Burlesque: Little Miss Firefly – Balloon Swallowing, https://www.youtube.com/watch?v=P41p3HnkiFk

Richard III Society homepage, https://richardiii.net/

Ripley's Believe it or Not! Presents Sideshow and Other Carnival Curiosities, Ripley Publishing, 2020.

RTÉ-IRELAND, Irish broadcaster. "The Lizardman puts a corkscrew through his face!" YouTube video from 2012, https://www.youtube.com/watch?v=4aee1eWOZcE

Rosen, Fred. *Lobster Boy: The Bizarre Life and Brutal Death of Grady Stiles Jr.*, Pinnacle, 1995.

Sapin, Paul. Director and Producer of *Born Freak*, presented by Mat Fraser, Channel 4 UK, 2001, https://www.sapinxray.com/portfolio/born-freak

Schillace, Brandy. *Clockwork Futures: The Science of Steampunk and the Reinvention of the Modern World*, Pegasus Books, 2017.

Shakespeare, William. *Richard III*. T*he Oxford Shakespeare: Richard III*. Oxford University Press, 2000.

Showtown Bar & Grill menu special, https://www.showtownusa.com/specials/

Sideshow Cat. Instagram account, https://www.instagram.com/sideshow_cat/

Sideshow Hootenanny website, https://www.sideshowhootenanny.com/

Sideshow World, The Big Circus Sideshow, Austin, Texas, Jimmy Z and Josh Bladzik, August 2008, https://www.sideshowworld.com/10-SP1/RW-BCS-08/SSP-RW-BCS-Austin-3-2008.html

Silva, Alan. Instagram account, https://www.instagram.com/alanjonessilva/

Silva, Alan. Website, http://www.alanjsilva.com/

Sixx, Nikki. *This is Gonna Hurt: Music, Photography and Life Through the Distorted Lens of Nikki Sixx*, 12 Feb. 2013, William Morrow Paperbacks

Smith, Aaron. *Circus Jerks*, October 2019, https://coney-island-usa.myshopify.com/products/book-circus-jerks-a-memoir

Smith, Aaron. "Shorty: Weed-Smoking Sideshow 'Half-Man' Lives on Bong Hits and Broken Glass," *High Times*, 20 June, 2021.

Smith, Aaron. "When I ran away and joined the Ringling Brothers circus," *CN-*

NMoney, 6 March 2015, https://money.cnn.com/2015/03/06/news/ringling-brothers-elephants/index.html

Smith, Dinitia. "Step Right Up, See the Bearded Person!" *New York Times* profile of Jennifer Miller, 9 June 1995,
   https://www.nytimes.com/1995/06/09/arts/step-right-up-see-the-bearded-person.html

Spiegelworld website, https://spiegelworld.com/shows/atomic-saloon-show/

Sprague, Erik, the Lizardman. *Once More Through the Modified Looking Glass*, a collection of essays from Body Modification Ezine, www.bmezine.com, 2011.

Squidling Brothers website, https://squidlingbrothers.com/

Strange Remains Curio Shop website, https://www.strangeremainscurioshop.com/

Sulcas, Roslyn. "A Fairy Tale Stripped to the Bones of Beastliness." *New York Times*, 21 April 2020, https://www.nytimes.com/2010/04/21/arts/dance/21beauty.html

Swatman, Rachel. "Daredevil female entertainer breaks record stopping fans with her tongue," Guinness World Records Italian Show,
   https://www.guinnessworldrecords.com/news/2017/3/daredevil-female-entertainer-breaks-record-stopping-fans-with-her-tongue-guinne-467200/

Taylor, James, interview with Jim Rose, *Shocked and Amazed! On & Off the Midway*, Vol. 5, 1998, https://www.shockedandamazed.com/volume-5/

Taylor, James, interviews with Dick Zigun and John Bradshaw, *Shocked and Amazed! On & Off the Midway*, Vol. 7, 2003, https://www.shockedandamazed.com/volume-7/

Terhurne, Pete. Sideshow World profile of Pete Terhurne, AKA Poobah, excerpt from Ward Hall's *My Very Unusual Friends,* https://www.sideshowworld.com/56-Tribute/Little-Pete/Poohba.html

Thalidomide Trust financial statements, https://www.thalidomidetrust.org/annual-accounts/

Vertical Wise, https://www.verticalwise.com/exploring-the-history-behind-aerial-silks/

Vincentelli, Elisabeth. "*Dick Rivington & the Cat* Review: A Civic-Minded Holiday Treat," *New York Times,* 15 Dec. 2022, https://www.nytimes.com/2022/12/08/theater/dick-rivington-the-cat-review.html

Wakefield, Nathan. *The Rise and Fall of the Sideshow Geek*, Outside Talker Press with Shocked and Amazed! Imprints, 2023, https://outsidetalkerpress.bigcartel.com/product/the-rise-and-fall-of-the-sideshow-geek

West, Tyler. Website, https://theoriginaltylerwest.com/

Wollin, Aaron. Hellzapoppin website profile, https://hellzapoppin.com/short-e-dangerously

Wong, Alice, ed. *Disability Visibility: First-Person Stories from The Twenty-First Century*, Vintage Books, June 2020.

Wong, Alice. *Year of the Tiger: An Activist's Life*, Vintage, Sept. 2022.

Woolf, John. *The Wonders: The Extraordinary Performers Who Transformed the Victorian Age*, Pegasus Books, 2019.

Worden, Gretchen. *Mütter Museum of the College of Physicians of Philadelphia*, Blast Books, 2002.

World of Wonders tent specs from website, https://theworldofwonders.com/specs

Youngs, Ian, "Mat Fraser on playing Richard III and TV's 'pathetic' disabled casting," BBC, 4 May 2017, https://www.bbc.com/news/entertainment-arts-39749041

Zamboni, Camille. Hellzapoppin website profile, https://hellzapoppin.com/camille-zamboni

Zamboni, Camille. Instagram account, https://www.instagram.com/zazathustra/

Zamboni, Camille. YouTube channel, https://www.youtube.com/user/firefirecz11

About the Author

Aaron Smith is a Florida native who thru-hiked the Appalachian Trail from Georgia to Maine as a teenager. He then joined the Ringling Brothers and Barnum & Bailey Circus and the Big Apple Circus as a cotton candy vendor and a roustabout. He lived on the train and set up the big top, encountering clowns, alligators, Zulu dancers, dancing girls, elephants, Russian bears and a flaming train. He wrote about those adventures in his first book, *Circus Jerks*. Aaron has a Bachelor's degree in Creative Writing from Northern Vermont University and has been a journalist for 30 years, writing for CNN, Forbes, *Financial Times*, *People* magazine, *New York Sun*, *Staten Island Advance*, *Bangor Daily News*, *Boston Globe*, and *High Times*. He has covered the gun industry, the cannabis industry and white-collar crime. He interviewed Bernie Madoff and Mr. T. Now he's ready to take on a controversial subject: disabled performers in 21st-century sideshows. Aaron believes that circuses and sideshows represent the ultimate way of life and the pinnacle of American culture. He interviewed 20 sideshow naturals to write his magnum opus, *Natural Born!* Aaron lives in Brooklyn near Coney Island, with his wife and two children.

About the Foreword Author

Lisa B. Lewis began her career as a graduate of Ringling Bros. and Barnum & Bailey Clown College. She has a BA from Brandeis University and earned a Master's Degree in Clown/Circus History from NYU, co-founded the Super Scientific Circus, and spent many years working with the Big Apple Circus in multiple capacities. She is the founder and Executive Director of Omnium: A Bold New Circus, whose mission it is to include and welcome the beautiful mosaic of humans who make up our world, creating joy and entertainment for all no matter the body you inhabit and the skin you are in. She is a recognized leader in the area of DEAIB (Diversity, Equity, Accessibility, Inclusion and Belonging) and a passionate advocate for making the magic of the performing arts available to all.

STEP RIGHT UP, FOLKS!

Gaze upon these remarkable WONDERS OF THE MIDWAY!

Dearest friends, feast your eyes to these **ASTOUNDING BOOKS** of carnival lore! Never before assembled in one collection!

Prepare to be AMAZED by EXTRAORDINARY BOOKS

DARE TO DISCOVER!

These unique and wondrous books are not for the faint of heart. They're full of thrills, marvels, and mysteries!

YOUR ADVENTURE AWAITS!

SHOCKING BIZARRE ODDITIES

OUTSIDE TALKER *Press*.com

IMPRINTS

For 30 years, Dolphin-Moon Press has been publishing the world's first journal devoted to circus & carnival sideshows, novelty & variety exhibition: ***James Taylor's Shocked and Amazed! – On & Off the Midway***.

In every volume you'll find first (and often last) interviews with performers from the "good old days," from the Golden Age of the sideshows between the World Wars, and the stunning, more recent talent born of those eras, born of those inspirations and knowledge. And with the launch of the Shocked and Amazed! Imprints series, you can now own the best of first-time and reissued classics of the weird, the wild, the strange, the bizarre and the unusual!

ShockedAndAmazed.com

www.ingramcontent.com/pod-product-compliance
Lightning Source LLC
Chambersburg PA
CBHW052128030426
42337CB00028B/5066